# ONE

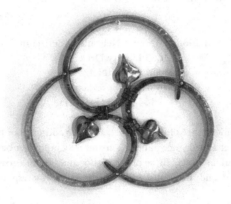

*God is Love.*
*This is the Sentence of Existence and Life*

## A BIBLICAL STUDY
## OF EXISTENCE AND LOVE

Gary W. Parnell

WESTBOW
PRESS®
A DIVISION OF THOMAS NELSON
& ZONDERVAN

WestBow Press books may be ordered through booksellers or by contacting:

WestBow Press
A Division of Thomas Nelson & Zondervan
1663 Liberty Drive
Bloomington, IN 47403
www.westbowpress.com
844-714-3454

Because of the dynamic nature of the Internet, any web addresses or links contained in this book may have changed since publication and may no longer be valid. The views expressed in this work are solely those of the author and do not necessarily reflect the views of the publisher, and the publisher hereby disclaims any responsibility for them.

Any people depicted in stock imagery provided by Getty Images are models, and such images are being used for illustrative purposes only. Certain stock imagery © Getty Images.

Scripture quotations are taken from the King James Version, public domain.

Credits for the cover (and interior artwork too) Karidy Shawn Walker as the designer, and Paul Thorne's metal sculpture as used for the cover art.

Interior Graphics/Art Credit: Larry Elliot photographer/ Paul Thorne metal artist

ISBN: 979-8-3850-4273-9 (sc)
ISBN: 979-8-3850-4274-6 (e)

Library of Congress Control Number: 2025901140

Print information available on the last page.

WestBow Press rev. date: 02/06/2025

This book is dedicated to my perfect wife
Karen Elizabeth Peterson Parnell

Her love, support and assistance
are inspirations for all that has been written.

## PURPOSE AND INTENT

The purpose of this writing is to encourage the enjoyment of life, the state of human existence. In the same way that the Bible has been written for us, this book has been written for the one who will choose to read what has been written. This a basic simple truth, for Jesus also said, "He that has ears to hear, let him hear." (Mark 4:9) Jesus also rejoiced in spirit that the good news of eternal life had been revealed. (Luke 10:21)

God is Love. This is the sentence of life. This is the sentence that explains the existence of life.

## EDITORIAL COMMENTS

The writers of the New Testament often used the words "we who are" to refer to the disciples of Jesus; however, unless otherwise stated, personal pronouns are used to refer to all of us who are in a state of being – one.

The primary reference for this composition is the King James translation of the original Hebrew and Greek text. For this reason, a Bible will be required for a complete reading of this book.

To accurately evaluate words, phrases, or statements of scripture, passages are often considered independently or out of context. As well, the words of scripture may have been revised for grammatical reasons or for clarity of understanding. For this reason, the revisions of scripture used in this book should not be quoted as scripture.

Permission to use passages of scripture would require written permission from the authors of scripture, therefore credit for all comments or teachings about the nature and character of Deity must be given to the authors of scripture. A standard reference notation of book, chapter, and verse in standard print, has been used to identify the location of the words of scripture, and to give credit for the use of the passages of scripture.

Quotation marks have been used for notation of words that are comments or statements by the authors, or for direct quotes of scripture.

This writing is not a book of scriptural proof, word analysis, language comparison, or a research paper with correct scriptural exegesis. Scriptural references have not been given for every statement. Although credit should be offered to professors at Southwestern Baptist Theological Seminary for an understanding of Greek and Hebrew, and credit and appreciation should be expressed to many writers and authors for thoughts or comments, and although no original thoughts of wisdom or theological information has been included, I have not directly relied upon any specific writing from other authors or individuals. All statements concerning scripture are offered as a personal understanding; therefore, I accept full credit for any error of interpretation.

A simple process of gathering information was used. I began reading the book of Genesis, noting each scripture that applied to any specific topic or characteristic of YHWH. I searched for an understanding of his nature and attempted to answer questions concerning the existence of Deity. What has been written is based upon the words of Scripture. Therefore, unless the actual account that is the Word of God is read, the teachings will be incomplete. This book is a black and white presentation of information that has been obtained from a simple reading of scripture. The beauty and wonder of the fact that God is Love will only be understood by reading the actual words of scripture.

The primary source for definitions is from the spelling or thesaurus search on Word Document processing. As well, personal pronouns have been used to emphasize the personal aspects of scripture.

Except for the subject of love, the character statements of Yahweh are listed alphabetically, as topical subjects and not according to preference or importance. Each characteristic is defined and explained. A brief theological lesson for each topic has also been included. The lessons are not offered as direct theological teachings. The thoughts are included because the nature and character of God is often expressed in that which mankind has been told to do or to believe.

I considered using simple statements such as God is Love for the introduction of specific topics or characteristics; however, because statements that are similes or metaphors are not specifically correct, I have chosen to use a single noun, adjective, or simple phrases for each topic, although all are as well incomplete without explanation. Although the characteristics have been separated as topic discussions, the oneness of the nature of Yahweh should not be separated, for every aspect of his existence or nature are together as Love.

Surely, there would be joy and excitement when attempting to explain the existence of a radiant rainbow, or the brilliant wonder of a sunrise or sunset. There is joy and excitement when describing the birth of a child or the wonder when a child learns to read or to multiply numbers. In the same way, enjoyment of life has been offered to those who discover the simple and complex nature of the One of existence.

When I decided to write about the One known as I Am that I Am, I had a common academic attitude. I had a task to accomplish, study and work to be accomplished. As I read scripture and searched for understanding, I began to wonder how I would ever be able to adequately explain the presence of love, and honor, faith, majesty, purity, beauty, and the mysterious wonder of God, all wrapped up into the oneness of existence. As I continued to read scripture, my thankfulness for life and love for God was strengthened with joy. My prayer and wish for you is that you will also read the Bible and discover the wonder and beauty of Deity.

## SPECIAL RECOGNITION AND CREDIT

The photographs used for each chapter are from Larry Elliot, Anacortes, Washington. *larrydowntown01@yahoo.com*

The Celtic Metal Art for the book cover was crafted by Paul Thorne, a full time talented Architectural Smith and Instructor. Thorne Metals Studio, Anacortes, Washington.

The stone wall in the photo was crafted by Mike Harris, master stone-works artist. Michael Harris Stone and Wood Creations, Anacortes, Washington.

Larry and Paul and Michael are Christian friends. Their love for God is expressed in their gift for this book. I wish to express my deepest appreciation.

A special expression of love is offered to my precious daughter. The beautiful design of the cover of this book is by Karidy Shawn Walker.

# CONTENTS

## INTRODUCTION

# EXISTENCE IS A STATE OF BEING ONE

This writing is a study of the miracle of existence, love, and eternal life, as recorded in the inspired words of the Bible.

According to the teachings of scripture, an understanding of the existence of Deity provides an understanding of the meaning and purpose of our own human existence, for understanding the purpose and meaning of life can only be obtained by understanding of one profound statement - God is love.

To understand the truth of this statement, the existence and being of God must be identified. The state of being one must be explained or understood, and the significance of the relationship of love to God must be discovered.

The Word of God is a book of wisdom, order, records of history, and a description of Deity that includes the account of the life of Jesus Christ. The Word of God tells the story of the creation of the kingdom of Heaven, a new existence, that is like a hidden treasure waiting to be discovered. (Matthew 13:44-46)

Because the sacred writings are declared to be inspired or approved by God, the accounts are accepted as accurate and truthful records of the existence of Deity and of the origin and purpose of the earth and universe. To state that these writings are words of scripture is to believe that the teachings are not independent thoughts of the writers or authors but are words of prophecy and instruction that are inspired by God. (2 Peter 1:20-21) (2 Timothy 3:15-17)

The accounts of the Bible include the story of God's creation and interaction in this world. The scriptures contain accounts of miracles and tragedies and celebrations and teachings of wisdom, and stories of Yahweh's involvement with mankind.

Wisdom is a gift from God, for the essence of wisdom is to understand that God is love. The purpose of wisdom is to offer an understanding of the truths of existence. This truth is found in the words of the Bible. The Bible is the word of God and the word of life. The purpose of life for human beings has been expressed in a simple yet complex prayer that was taught by Jesus. (Matthew 6:9-13) An understanding of the nature and character of God is also revealed in the records of miracles and words of prophets that offer insight concerning the miracle of salvation. (1 Corinthians 1:18-31)

The collection of writings of the Old Testament includes historical accounts and chronicles, covenant agreements, rules of law, psalms and poetry, and words of wisdom and prophecy that have been collected by the scribes and scholars of the tribes of Israel. The writings of the New Testament are letters and accounts of first century Hebrews who believed that Jesus of Nazareth is the Messiah, the promised prophet who is to bring peace and liberty to the children of Abraham. The narrative accounts include an account of the life and works of Jesus, which is in essence the purpose of all of scripture.

Every account in the Bible provides information concerning the character of the one and only Deity. A description of Yahweh's person and nature may be found in brief statements, or even in the use of a single word. For example, the word "one" has been used to describe the complex Lord God Almighty, the amazing One who is known as I AM, the Father of Abraham and Isaac and Jacob, the Father of Israel, and the Lord of Hosts.

The use of a simple sentence or a brief description would obviously not reveal everything about the God of Israel. Correct interpretation, for each sentence, phrase, or description, is required. The words of scripture must be clearly defined and explained.

As an example, the statement, I Am, without a stated object, is a description of Deity. The statement also includes a definite reason or purpose of existence. (Exodus 3:13-14)

A study of every name or description of Deity will not provide a complete understanding of the Lord God of Israel. As well, a comprehensive study of passages of scripture in which the word one is used will not provide an adequate explanation of the oneness of Yahweh. The oneness of Elohim, the Almighty One, is unique. In essence, everything about YHWH, the I Am that I Am, is unique. Yahweh is not one of a kind; he is one, period. He is not the first one; he is the only one. He is not the best or first of the order; he is the only order. In scripture, Deity is not always described as a tri-unity, nor as a unity of one. Therefore, this writing is not intended to be a theological defense of the plurality of God, or the teachings of monotheism.

The theological questions concerning monotheism, and the tri-unity nature of Yahweh are important; however more essentially, the primary theological question that every individual must understand concerns the deity of Jesus Christ. The unity of God and Jesus has been clearly stated in scripture. (Philippians 2:6-11)

Every writer begins a composition with a purpose, a thesis, a plot, a goal, a reason, or several reasons for writing or telling a story. Although the primary purpose of this book is to encourage the enjoyment of life, my prayer is that those who read this book will be encouraged to read the words of scripture, to understand the joy and peace and fulfillment of knowing that God is Love. A blessing of freedom and joy has been offered for those who choose to open their heart and allow God to share his love.

Absolute proof that the words of scripture have been truthfully and accurately recorded is not available. Nevertheless, a gift of joy has been offered to those who believe that the words of scripture are inherent words of truth.

# CHAPTER ONE

# THE ALMIGHTY YAHWEH
# IS I AM THAT I AM

Any teaching of theology that makes Jesus less than the same Deity as the Father is a denial that God is I Am.

*A theological note of biblical interpretation should be made concerning the use, or misuse, of any verb used to identify existence, or a state of being. God did not say to Moses, "I am One." God said, "I Am that I Am." (Exodus 3:14) Jesus said to his disciples, "I and my Father are one." (John 10:30) This statement may be interpreted as, "My Father is deity; and I am also deity." The statement of being may also be interpreted as, "The Father and I are one deity."*

*Although in this writing Yahweh may be identified as "the One" or simply as "One" it is necessary to note that the name of Yahweh is not One. According to the words of scripture, God is love; however, his name is not Love. The name of Yahweh is YHWH or I AM that I AM.*

On an ordinary day in a certain place, when Jesus had finished a prayer, one of his disciples asked Jesus to teach the disciples how to pray. As a response, Jesus offered a simple yet profound prayer. (Luke 11:1-4)

This prayer was included among instructions that were offered by Jesus concerning wisdom and spiritual truths. The prayer, modestly recorded and placed among several lessons, is introduced with a statement that the Father knows what we need, before we ask him. (Matthew 6:7-13) The prayer is an example of the interrelated aspects of simplicity and complexity. The words and phrases are simple, the meaning is complex. Every phrase of the prayer teaches a simple truth about God; but the use of the statement "Our Father which art in heaven..." is extremely complex.

This prayer is an amazing prayer, with words and phrases that reveal theological truths. However, unless the father is identified, the words of the prayer are of limited value. If we are to be taught how to pray, we must know the Father to whom our words are offered. A primary truth about this father is that he is Love. To understand the meaning of the simple sentence or statement, God is love, we must search through the holy scriptures, the inspired word of God, to find the knowledge that is required. The task is to read and study, and to question the validity and worthiness of the words and accounts that have been recorded. The mission is to search for understanding of the truths of existence. Our task is to ask questions and to find simple truths. We must learn everything possible about this incredible Deity who is the Father in Heaven. We must consider how this almighty Deity can be defined in terms of logic and existence.

An understand of the father who is I Am that I Am is of extreme importance.

## Yahweh is One of Existence.

A state of oneness may be defined as a state of existence. (John 1:1)

To understand or to know the Deity that has been identified and proclaimed to be the single one deity of existence, one must first believe that Yahweh truly does exist. Existence implies reality and identity. According to the words of scripture, although the existence of Deity is invisible or undefined, the existence of Deity is undeniable. (Romans 1:20)

The statement, "I am that I am," is a statement of existence. Because God is in a state of existence, he is also in a state of being or of being "one." As well, because Yahweh does exist, he is identifiable. Yahweh is not one in a state of undefined existence. As a simple, yet profound testimony of existence, Yahweh has declared that he is the only deity that is a reality. (Exodus 3:14) He is the unique one, not a unique one. (Deuteronomy 4:39)

The possibility of the existence of a false deity does not exist; however, any assumed deity is a zero, not a one. (Isaiah 44:8-17) As well, because a numerical zero may be the beginning or ending of the numerical number one, all false deities are less than zeroes. False gods are nonexistent, without reality or identity, and without possibility of becoming a one. Yahweh is One; he is the only deity of existence. He is the beginning and end for existence.

A logical explanation for our present state of order has been clearly stated in scripture. The physical evidence of life on earth is evident or visible; however, the actual or true evidence of existence is invisible. (Romans 1:20) For example, the presence of love, although invisible, is clearly seen. Love is understood by the things that exist in our amazingly beautiful world and universe. The invisible eternal power of creation is evident in the presence of the unity and preservation of our natural biological existence. The eternal power of the unity and oneness of Deity is also revealed in the preservation of our existence and that of the universe.

In several separate occasions the Jewish leaders of Israel asked Jesus to identify his authority to teach lessons about God. (Matthew 16:1-4) The religious leaders were unprepared to accept the teachings of an uneducated citizen, from the rural community of Nazareth. Apparently, these scholars also had a limited understanding of the prophecies of the promised Messiah. (Matthew 22:43-45)

Instead of performing a miracle or presenting scientific proof, Jesus offered a simple answer. Jesus said, "Before Abraham existed, I Am." (John 8:58) His answer created a theological problem, for Jesus was clearly making himself equal to God, or declaring a status of Deity. These religious leaders, who reverenced a strong faith in monotheism, received his simple statement of existence as an insult to their theological teachings. The scholars of Old Testament scripture clearly understood that Jesus was referring directly to the Old Testament passage where God answered the question of existence offered by Moses. (Exodus 3:14) In Jewish writings this statement is recorded as YHWH or YWHH without the vowels, as a tribute to the holiness of YaHWeH, the translation with vowels. This is a statement that God has eternal life, and the words "that I am" means that there is no other deity, and that deity is unchangeable in nature.

In defense of the tri-unity of Deity, Christian theologians often quote the words of the New Testament concerning the existence of the word of God. (John 1:1) Before an assumption that the tri-unity of deity is described, the complex nature of the statement should be considered. Obviously, in defense of monotheism, an honest theological attempt to explain how Jesus can truly be One with Yahweh should be made.

The Heavenly Father, the Father of Abraham, Isaac, and Jacob, and the Messiah Yehoshua, the word of God, and the Holy Spirit have authority to say, "I Am." As One, they can say, "Let Us make man." (Genesis 1:26) The wonderful fact about this complicated Father is that he does not require an understanding of his existence. Yahweh simply requires faith, even without scientific or physical proof, in what he has said and in what he has done.

This requirement is a blessing to mankind, because faith is the only acceptable gift that may be offered to an Almighty Deity.

We, as a complicated one human being, and the existence of the earth and universe are evidence that has been presented to prove that Yahweh does exist. However, the fact remains that truth can be misunderstood or rejected. Alternative explanations for existence have been convincingly presented; however, without definite proof or without complete scientific knowledge, every ontological or scientific explanation concerning our present state of existence will require faith for acceptance.

The presence of Yahweh can be clearly seen in what has been created. Faith or acceptance of the existence of deity is supported by the presence of Truth. Any theory of spontaneous evolution of life is discredited by the presence of design and order in our physical existence. The miracle of life, as well as the unexplained presence of love and evil, is a declaration of the existence of Yahweh. The presence of biological order and the need for reproduction is sufficient evidence of the existence of Deity. As well, because the evidence is obvious, rejection of the truth of the evidence is inexcusable.

Although a comprehensive explanation or an apologetic defense may be offered, the existence and presence of Deity must be accepted by a personal choice of faith. Scientific proof, a miracle, or an appearance could easily be rejected. (Luke 16:31) "Without faith, it is impossible to please God, for the one that comes to God must believe that he exists and that he is able or willing to reward the one that diligently seeks him." (Hebrews 11:6)

Simply stated, although the existence of Deity is evident, this truth must be accepted as an act of faith.

## Yahweh is the Irreplaceable One

A state of oneness can be identified as a state of singularity or uniqueness.

To be unique means that there is no other one like, this one. (Isaiah 46:9)

Although Yahweh is identified as I Am that I Am, additional names and descriptions are used to describe and to explain the existence and character of this one supreme deity.

The children of Israel recite a daily prayer taken from the instructions of Moses. The words are given as part of the commandments, the statutes, and the judgments which God gave to the children of Israel. The words were to be held within their hearts and diligently taught to their children. This passage of scripture clearly states that God is One, that God is love, and that he deserves to be loved, with deep appreciation for the love that he has offered to Israel. (Deuteronomy 6:4-7)

The words of the prayer "Hear, O Israel: The Lord our God is one Lord" does not acknowledge the complexity or uniqueness of Deity. Yahweh is a complex one, not an undefined one.

Belief and faith in either monotheism or the tri-unity of Deity can easily be defended by use of selected passages of scripture or by defining specific words of Greek or Hebrew; however, for a true understanding of Deity, acknowledgment of the tri-nature of Yahweh is required. This nature is described or explained in New Testament scripture. (1 Corinthians 8:5-6) This passage of scripture describes the oneness of the existence of deity and the fact that this Deity is the creator of our existence.

Jesus would be described as the only one son, or as the one with no exceptions. Jesus is an only begotten son, just as the Father is an only father. As well, Jesus and the Father are One, and together with the Holy Spirit are the One, and only Deity. (James 2:19) (John 10:30)

New Testament passages are basically used to support the unity nature of God; however, in a passage in the book of Isaiah, the Lord of Host speaks to Jacob and Israel to tell them, "I am he. I am the first, I also am the last." Then, as a change of voice, one who is sent speaks. The one who is sent states that he has not spoken in secret, for he has existed from the beginning, from the time that was. And now Yahweh and the Holy Spirit has sent the one who is speaking. (Isaiah 48:10-16)

In several passages of scripture, at different times and places, Jesus offered statements and descriptions of the unity of Deity. (John 14:1-11, 15:23, 16:15 & 17:3-5)

Jesus also used Old Testament scripture to explain both the resurrection and the unity of the Father and the Son. Several Sadducees, religious leaders who did not teach that there is a resurrection, came to Jesus to question him. (Mark 12:18-19) After these noted theologians presented their argument, Jesus replied with a teaching that God is not the God of the dead, but of the living. As a theological response, one of the scribes asked another debated question. He wanted Jesus to identify the most important commandment in the Laws of Moses. Interestingly, Jesus answered with a passage of scripture that acknowledged his unity with the Father. (Mark 12:24-34)

Jesus was teaching a valuable lesson about existence and love. When we recognize and accept the fact that there is an Almighty Deity that loves us, who has chosen to offer eternal life to us, we are not far from the kingdom of Heaven.

As previously stated, Yahweh exists because he has said that he exists; and he is I Am that I Am because he has said that he is the only one. (Isaiah 46:9) (Deuteronomy 4:39) Therefore, Yahweh is irreplaceable because there is no other God, nothing else, to put in his place. There isn't even a zero to put in his place.

Yehoshua, who is One with the Father, is a unique one, the first born of God.

His existence as Emanuel, God with us, seems to separate him from the Father; however, because Elohim is One, separation is not possible. The angel Gabriel, who stands in the presence of God, was sent from God to tell Mary that she would have a son that would be called the Son of the Highest. (Luke 1:32-33) (Isaiah 9:6-7) Mary wanted to know how this would be possible. The angel Gabriel gave a simple answer, "This will be an act of the Holy Spirit; for all things are possible with God." (Luke 1:35)

Jesus admonished the religious leaders of Israel for failure to correctly interpret passages of Old Testament prophecy. (John 5:46-47) A complete description of the relationship of the Son of God who is the Messiah, and God the Father has been offered by Jesus. (John 5:19 - 6:71) This passage of scripture should be read and carefully studied. Jesus clearly stated that the words of the Old Testament scripture testify of his existence. (John 5:39) As well, Jesus clearly stated that he is one with Yahweh. (John 6:46 & 10:30) Jesus did not simply make a statement about his relationship to the Father, his statement is supported by the prophecies of scripture. Jesus also, with words of truth, clearly explained how the gift of eternal life may be accepted from the I Am who is Love. (John 17:3-8)

Although a complete understanding of how Yahweh, the one true Deity, can be both the Father and the Son and the Holy Spirit is not possible, this must be accepted by faith because Jesus said, "I Am" making himself equal with his Father. The fact that Yahweh shares power and existence and divine nature with his son, Yehoshua the Christ, does not eliminate the fact that Deity is One. (2 Peter 1:2-3) There is only one God and one mediator between God and man. (1 Timothy 2:5) There is one Lord, one faith, one baptism, and one God and Father of all who is over all and through all and in all. In whatever manner we describe the oneness of Deity, God and Christ are non-spreadable and irreplaceable.

Yahweh is the King eternal, immortal, invisible, the One and only Deity. He deserves honor and glory, forever and ever. (1 Timothy 1:17)

## Yahweh is an Identifiable Personal One

Oneness may be defined as a state of identifiable properties or substance.

Yahweh is identified and defined as deity. (Isaiah 46:9)

The prophet Jeremiah offered praise for the existence of the true God, the living and everlasting king. (Jeremiah 10:10)

God is not just one who creates, or one who loves, he is Love and he is the Creator. He is the Almighty. Amazingly, he is also personal. However, because he is more than a unique one alone, he loves through and by his son who is with him. As well, Jesus, the Holy Spirit, and the Father as One, love together as a personal identifiable One of love.

The One, who is Deity, is never described as a presence of identifiable universal properties or substance. As well, although Yahweh is never identified in universal terms, as a deity for everyone, he is a personal existence. He is I Am, that you and I or anyone can expect to be able to know through the gift of the Holy Spirit. Of course, this relationship is not an earthly or human relationship. Relationship with God is to be able to know him in a unique spiritual way.

There are numerous historical accounts concerning those who would testify that the Lord of Abraham, Isaac, and Jacob is an identifiable personal God. Adam and Eve, Noah, Abraham, Isaac and Jacob, Moses and Joshua, king David and king Solomon, the twelve Apostles and the apostle Paul had personal encounters with the almighty deity who is One. In various ways, others have also been made aware of his presence.

As well, we can have a personal relationship with the living Father of heaven and earth. The New Testament clearly states that God has made himself available to anyone who will hear his voice. (Matthew 7:7-8, 10:32, 11:28-30)

Yahweh is as identifiable as our own existence. Being personal and approachable is an amazing characteristic of an almighty deity. We are allowed to pray, "Our Father, in heaven, hallowed be your name."

Being personal means that God has a name and that his character can be describe or defined. Being personal means that other personal entities can be like him, created in his image. Almighty YHWH, through the children of Abraham, has revealed his true nature and character to the world. The fact that many individuals have created gods in their own image has brought a great deal of pain and frustration to Yahweh. He has in fact, because of lack of faith or hardness of heart, almost chosen to eliminate mankind. However, because of his great love and patience, he has chosen to intervene, almost as against his own will. His choice of compassion and grace is called the gospel, the good news, brought to us by his precious Son, as a personal gift of love. For our personal God so loved the world he gave his son, as a gift of love, to every individual in the whole world. (John 3:16)

## Yahweh is a Complete Unity of One

A state of oneness can be described either as complete and consistent or non-complete or inconsistent.

The Lord of heaven and earth must be described as a complete and consistent unity of oneness. There is only one God. There is only one mediator between God and mankind. (1 Timothy 2:5-6) Jesus Christ is the one who gave his life as a random of sin for all of mankind. Yahweh's desire is for everyone to know this truth. (1 Timothy 2:4)

No one has seen the Father of Heaven, except the one who is from heaven. Jesus is the one who has seen the Father. He is the one who knows the Father. (John 6:46)

The angel Gabriel stated that Jesus would be called the Son of God. (Luke 1:34-35) Jesus is also called "the son of man." (Luke 19:10) Jesus is the king of Israel, the one who will reign over the house of Jacob forever. (Luke 1:30-33) The angel Gabriel also said, "Nothing will be impossible with Yahweh." (Luke 1:37, 24:1-8)

To describe God as a tri-unity would be an inaccurate description of Deity. Because there is no other divine being, the son must be deity with Yahweh. In the same way that a part of the number one cannot be separated by a zero, the One of deity cannot be separated. The number one should not be identified or described as three parts in one. As well, as living beings we should not be identified as three parts in one, or as mind, body, and soul.

An adequate explanation of the complete and consistent unity of Deity has not been provided in scripture. The understanding for this state of existence lies within the area of unknowable knowledge. Although a logical explanation of the oneness of God or the relationship of the Father and the Son and the Holy Spirit has not been provided, belief or faith in the existence of God is essential for a proper relationship to the Father; and as well, an acceptance of the fact that Jesus and God are one, as Father and Son, is essential for receiving the gift of salvation.

Our present state of order is a state of existence that has been established within the creation of our world and universe. Jesus, the son of God, has been given the authority over mankind; however, all things originate from God. (Romans 11:36))

The Messiah is the one who was prophesied of in the Hebrew writings by the prophets of Israel. The prophecies stated that there would be a prophet who was sent with the message of the prophet Elijah, to identify the Messiah. John, the apostle called "the baptizer" was identified as that prophet; and Jesus is the one who was recognized by John.

Jesus, speaking to the religious leaders in Jerusalem, attempted to explain his relationship with the Father. Jesus was aware that the Sadducees and Pharisees, filled with pride, loved to be called Rabbi, most worthy teacher. As an admonishment for their pride, Jesus offered a lesson of equality and unity among mankind. The reason for equality is because we have the same Master and the same Father; therefore, we are all brethren and children of God. (Matthew 23:7-12) Before this statement is discounted, what Matthew has to say about faith in Christ should be considered. (Matthew 7:13-23) Jesus did not say that he and the Father are both deity; he said that he and the Father are One, or the I Am.

The complete unity of Yahweh, of person and purpose, is clearly illustrated in scripture, both by descriptions and actions.

For example, in a passage in Proverbs one who is with God, is speaking as wisdom or truth to explain his personal involvement in the actions of One. The existence of this one was from the beginning, the earliest times of the earth. This one clearly says, "Then I was by him, as one brought up with him; and I was his daily delight." (Proverbs 8: 30) Of course any theologian can argue that, in this passage of scripture, only wisdom is speaking. The choice between believing that Yahweh is One, with Jesus, or a choice to not believe is available. Yahweh offers free will, to everyone.

Consider the prophesy of Isaiah to king Ahaz. Isaiah told the king that God himself would give the king a sign or miracle. A virgin would bear a son, and his name would be Immanuel, God with us. (Isaiah 7:14) The child would be called Wonderful Counselor, Mighty God, Eternal Father, and Prince of Peace. This would be accomplished by the zeal of the Lord of Hosts. (Isaiah 9:2-7)

Jesus is the King of Israel, for Yahweh was the original King of kings, and will always be the true King of Israel.

There are several passages in Isaiah that testify to the unity of One, but none are more definite than the following passage offered by the King of Israel and his Redeemer, the Lord of Hosts. (Isaiah 44:6-8, 45:22-25)

For the scribes and religious theologians of Israel the state of eternal existence was a debatable question. The Sadducees, who did not openly accept the theology of eternal life were in direct conflict with the Pharisees who professed faith in the resurrection. (Mark 12:18) (Acts 23:6) Nevertheless, all the scribes and religious theologians of Israel believed that eternal life, if possible, would be obtained through faith in the word of the God of Abraham, the Laws of Moses, and by keeping the commandments as a way of life. The theological teaching of the Pharisees offers hope of eternal life only to the descendants of Abraham who are the children of the living God, YHWH.

The religious leaders of Israel, who were angry with Jesus, complained, because he was healing on the Sabbath day. They wanted to know by what authority was Jesus performing miracles. They wanted to know why he was saying that God was his Father or making himself equal with God. Jesus offered an extended explanation. (John 5:17-30) Finally Jesus stated that the proof that he and the Father are One is the work, the miracles and the gift of love, that he had done. (John 5:36)

To accept Jesus as the Messiah, is to accept God's gift of love. (John 12:44-50)

Before he was crucified Jesus testified to the disciples concerning his relationship to Yahweh and clearly explained his relationship to the Father. (John 14:1 & 6-21)

The apostle Paul gave a complete explanation of faith in the deity of Jesus. (I Corinthians 8:4-6) The apostle said that Jesus is "the radiance of God's glory and the exact representation of his nature." (Hebrews 1:1-14) All power and authority has been given to him. (Hebrews 2:8-10) All the fullness of the One of Deity resides within him. (Colossians 2:8-9)

Therefore, we have the liberty to say, "In Christ, I am." As well, we can agree with the humble statement of the apostle Paul, "For us to live is Christ, and to die is gain." (Philippians 1:21) (1 Timothy 6:13-16)

Jesus has said that he and the Father share thoughts and the right to judge, and the power to give life, and therefore the right to be honored together. (Luke 10:22) If Jesus, the Messiah, the King of Israel, who came in the flesh is not divine deity, all that he has said and all that he has done would not give him the power to give eternal life to anyone.

Eternal life, offered by Jesus the Christ, is a gift of love that has been freely offered, to be accepted by a simple child-like act of trust. There is no other person or being that has offered eternal life, in the past, present, or future without a requirement of moral or religious performance. No other has offered an unearned gift of grace and love. Therefore, we must agree with the apostle Paul that if eternal existence is not a reality, we would be false witnesses of our state of truth, wisdom, logic, or reality. If Christ has not been raised, our faith is worthless. Existence would be a state of undefined lack of hope. Of all men, we would be most to be pitied. (1 Corinthians 15:11-19)

If Jesus is not the I Am, all of existence would be vanity or worthless.

We will not be able to understand or explain the oneness of deity. We are only required to accept the words of scripture. (Isaiah 44:6) We must believe and accept the words of Jesus. (Mark 14:62)

If Yahweh is not the One Deity and if Christ Jesus is not exactly the divine One that he has testified to be, then all religion, philosophy, science, knowledge and everything in this world and the entire universe is completely worthless. If eternal life is not possible, the universe would continue to spin around without purpose. All would be vanity; all of existence would be useless and less than zero.

As well, there is one, called the Antichrist, that will attempt to convince the world to believe that God does not exist and that the Father and Son are not One. This evil one came to Jesus and tempted him; but Jesus admonished him by declaring his own divinity. (Luke 4:8 &12)

The apostle who wrote the book of 1 John has basically explained this situation. The apostle said that when we see the Antichrist, we will know that we are in the last days before the return of the victorious Christ. We should trust the anointing of the Holy Spirit, and we will recognize the liar and the untruth. The one who denies that Jesus is the Christ is the same that denies that the Father is One. We must understand and accept the fact that the YHWH is One. If we accept what was taught by Jesus, we will abide in the Son and in the Father. This is the promise that Jesus himself made to us. His promise is the gift of eternal life. (1 John 2:18-25)

An additional warning concerning false theology is offered by John. The false teaching that Jesus was only a mighty deity will be offered. The teachers of another gospel will state that if he were flesh, he could never be a holy divine being. This concept is an absolute rejection of belief in monotheism and as well, that Jesus and the Father are One Deity. (1 John 2:23) The teaching is also a dismissal of the statement that anything is possible with God. (Mark 10:27) (2 John 1:7-9)

The words of king Solomon are worthy of being offered as a valuable teaching of wisdom and of vanity. (Proverbs 9:7-10) "The fear of the Lord is the beginning of wisdom, and the knowledge of the Holy One is understanding." (Proverbs 9:10)

## Yahweh is One of the Only Order of One

A state of oneness may be described as existence within an order, or as a unique state of oneness.

Yahweh is not number one within an order; he is the only One.

The existence of the one and only Deity was declared by Moses. There is no other Deity, no one else. (Deuteronomy 4:39)

Adonai is our heavenly Father. He is not one of many fathers. He is the Father of every family in Heaven and earth. (Ephesians 3:14-15) He is the only One that exist. He is the only One that has ever existed. He is the only One that will ever exist at any time in the future. The one who is learned may doubt the existence of deity, but the wise would never say, "There is more than one god." (Psalm 10:4, 14:1)

The fact that Yahweh is the only Deity is a truth that is worthy of being restated. There is only one Deity. His name is I am that I am or YHWH. He is the only God that has ever existed. He is the only deity that presently exists. He is the only deity that will ever be in existence. Anyone that teaches that another God has existed in the past, or that another deity will be in existence at any time in the future, or that any other god or form of deity will be created or will come into existence is an anti-Christ. Anyone that teaches that Yahweh has or will create another deity is an anti-Christ. Anyone who teaches that another son or deity will be born or will exist is an anti-Christ. Yahweh is One and he is the only One who is deity. No other deity has ever existed. No other deity, not even a lesser form of deity will ever be created. No other deity will ever be able to say, "I Am."

Yahweh is the One God and Father of heaven and earth. (Ephesians 4:7) He is the God of every man, and all of creation. Regardless of what one may believe, he is the God of everyone. He is our Father, of heaven and earth. Regardless of what name is given or what is known about what he has done, he is our Heavenly Father. (Joel 2:27)

As well, within this order of unity, there is one God and one mediator. (1 Timothy 2:5) There is one Lord, one faith, one baptism, one God and Father. In other words, God shares divine nature with Christ Jesus, the one who has been sent. (John 17:21) Although this unity cannot be completely understood, the union of deity must be recognized, and accepted.

The Apostle Paul explains that the oneness of the Father and the Son and the Holy Spirit is more than a simple spiritual oneness. "For in him dwelleth all the fullness of the Godhead bodily." (Colossians 2:9-11) Although truth may not be accepted, truth exists, whether recognized and accepted, or denied and rejected. (James 2:19)

There is one Deity that is transcendent and is the source of all order. We are in the order of beings, earthly creations, living beings. There are heavenly beings, but only one divine being or Deity in Heaven. This structure of existence is evident, and we are not independent from the divine order of Almighty YHWH; for the unity of God is Spirit.

Yahweh is one in Spirit and One in being. God has revealed himself to the world by his Son; and the son has been revealed by his Spirit. (1 Corinthians 2:10-12)

Yahweh is an amazing "I Am that I Am"

# CHAPTER TWO

# YAHWEH IS OUR FATHER

Jesus identified Yahweh as our Father, who is in heaven. (Matthew 6:9-10)

There is only one Almighty Deity. He is known as YHWH. He is also identified by names or phrases that are descriptive expressions of his character. Throughout centuries of study, theologians have attempted to explain the character of this divine being. The task is sometimes as difficult as describing a mystery, a miracle, or the essence of love. As well, the task is often simple, for the nature of Deity can easily be explained with simple descriptions or explanations.

A proper way to describe this Father of Israel has not been established; however, an acceptable way to learn about the character and nature of God is to read the words of the scribes and prophets and the accounts of the apostles of Jesus Christ. Although the Almighty One has not revealed everything about himself, a treasure of information has been recorded in the scriptures. When studying scripture, one should ask for wisdom and assistance from the Holy Spirit; for Yahweh has stated that when we seek to know him, we will find him.

The scriptures, written by scholars and scribes of Israel or by the apostles and disciples of Jesus Christ, are accounts or descriptions of what men and women encountered in specific events or personal encounters with YHWH, or by hearing God speak directly to them. The thoughts, reactions or responses of the poets, prophets, or chronicle scribes are recorded. As well, the thoughts and comments of the characters of the story are often also included; however, the accounts are specifically written to describe or explain the nature or character of God or the Holy Spirit or Jesus the Christ. (John 5:39)

Therefore, when reading scripture, we should be aware of the presence of God. We should consider Yahweh's response to every event, and search for evidence of his purpose and intent. We must be aware that all that has happened in the world has been according to his plan, and for his purpose. For example, when reading the accounts about Daniel and the kings of Babylonia, we should consider how Yahweh used the characters of the story to defend the children of Abraham, and for demonstrating his sovereign power of authority over heaven and earth. The Bible is Yahweh's story. The Bible is not the story of mankind or of the nation of Israel. In essence, the Bible is Yahweh's story about himself, the One who is Love. And specifically stated, this is the amazing story of his son Jesus the King of king.

The Bible Is the story about the one called I am that I am. The subject, intent, and purpose are introduced in the first sentence of the book of Genesis. The first sentence is a statement of existence. (Genesis 1:1) This bold statement of the existence of deity and of the origin of life is the theme of the collection of writings.

As a matter of identity, according to the words of the Old Testament, Yahweh is the Father of Israel. He is the Lord of lords and King of kings. He is identified as the Almighty Father of the Nation of Israel and as the Father of many nations, of those who are called children of God. He is the One, the Lord of Hosts, in whom every family in Heaven and earth derives its name. (Ephesians 3:15) Yahweh is identified as the one and only creator. (Genesis 1:1) He is the creator of earthly biological life. The possibility of biological life was introduced by the presence of the light of life. The earth was formless and lifeless, and the earth was in darkness. "The word of life" spoke, and light and life together were present. (Genesis 1:2-3)

For personal introductions, individuals identify themselves by name and then share personal information, both past and present. Several names or phrases are required for the One that is simply known as God, the English word for deity. As well, names or phrases are also used to identify his character and purpose and existence.

Within scripture, the names or descriptions of Deity have not been recorded in any order or preference, except for the name I Am that I Am, that was offered by God himself. The name Immanuel, I will be with you, expresses his willingness to allow his son to reveal his love to a lost world. YHWH, the Hebrew letters without vowel points, used in the statement, I am who I am, is his memorial name that is given forever. This statement may be properly interpreted as Yahweh or Jehovah. In this writing, for purpose of clarity and not of preference, the translation of Yahweh has been chosen as the primary name for Deity.

Nevertheless, Jehovah is identified as the God of Abraham, Isaac, and Jacob, and he is called the Almighty or El Shaddai, for the children of Abraham are to be like him. He is called Abba, Father, and is described as the One, by the Holy Spirit, to make a family of God, in Christ Jesus.

The prophet Isaiah refers to God as the Holy One of Israel, the Lord of Hosts, and the mighty one of Israel. (Luke 24:1-53) (Isaiah 1:24) The names given in scripture for the One true God are offered as expressions of his character. YHWH is the ultimate expression of godliness or holiness. His goodness is expressed in brotherly kindness and Christian love, and he deserves gratitude, recognition, and honor. (2 Peter 1:7) (Hebrews 12:28)

The difference between knowing a person's name, of having a personal relationship, and of truly knowing a particular individual is obvious. To discover what can be known about this Almighty Deity, a comprehensive study of scripture must be accomplished.

We can assume that part of Elohim's character is revealed in that fact that man is made in his image. This does not imply imperfection, for man was not created as an imperfect being. According to the account of creation, in the Word of God, Adam and Eve gave away this right of righteousness and life. Obviously, love is a major part of the character and being of Yahweh. His love for his children is expressed in redemption or restoration to a position of righteousness, and specific descriptive names have been given to express this gift of love.

Reading scripture has been described as discovering a treasure or a precious stone of great value. Discovering the mysteries of God will be like finding the answer to a scientific unknown of great value. Considering the beauty of God will be like experiencing the meaning of love and peace and eternity. Understanding the love of God will be like experiencing the joy of the birth of a precious human being, or the joy of a smile or of hearing someone say, "I love you." To attempt to know Yahweh will be awesome and amazing, for an understanding of God offers the gift of eternal life.

The ability to understand a mystery is a mystery. The mystery of understanding Yahweh lies within the understanding of the mystery of Christ Jesus. The spiritual understanding of this mystery is a gift from God and the understanding of this mystery reveals the joy of eternal life. (Ephesians 2:4 & 3:8)

The true treasures of life are not found in having wisdom or strength, glory or wealth, but are found in understanding and knowing God. The blessing of joy and peace and eternal life has been offered to anyone who chooses to believe that God is love. (Jeremiah 9:23-24) The true meaning of wisdom is to understand that Yahweh is our Father and that he is Love.

As stated, the Lord's Prayer is simple and complex. The prayer is plainly stated; however, when each phrase is evaluated, we find that every characteristic and purpose of our Heavenly Father is expressed. He is the one and only father in heaven, who is worthy and holy. His desire for the world is the presence of the kingdom of heaven, where justice and love will reign. He provides our daily care and spiritual welfare through faith in Jesus; and honors us as we honor others. He has promised to protect us from evil and to share his love.

When we understand, the prayer is more than a prayer. The prayer is a joyful shout of praise.

"Our Father, who art in Heaven..." Yahweh is the Father of Israel, the Father of unity, the Creator of Heaven and earth who is infinite, transcendent, present in light, and full of wisdom and authority. He is a personal Father. He is our spiritual Father of faith and hope and love.

"Hallowed be thy name..." Yahweh is an awesome God of love and honor. He is worthy of blessings and praise, for he is perfect in righteousness, purity, and love.

"Thy kingdom come…" Yahweh is the King of a renewed kingdom, an everlasting kingdom, a world of faith and truth, hope and love, peace, and liberty.

"Thy will be done on earth as it is in Heaven…" The existence and life that God has established for mankind is perfect and true; for He is a God of commitment, goodness, purpose, and knowledge.

"Give us this day our daily bread…" Yahweh is a God of awareness, empathy, mercy, kindness, charity, comfort, and compassion; and is willing to give the blessing of eternal life to all who have faith in Jesus Christ, the bread of life.

"Forgive us our debt as we forgive those who trespass against us…" Yahweh is a God of forgiveness, understanding, mercy, judgment, and justice; and he is also a God of humility and meekness who is willing to forgive those who are merciful and forgiving. He is the one who is willing to say, "Father, forgive them …" (Luke 23:34)

"Lead us not into temptation…" Yahweh is a God of assurance, freedom, friendship, grace, and protection.

"But deliver us from evil…" Yahweh is capable of anger and wrath, judgment, and justice; but he is also a defender of those who are worthy of protection and forgiveness. He is our God of love and salvation.

"For thine is the kingdom and the power and the glory…" Yahweh is the almighty sovereign King of kings, full of glory and majesty, holy, unchangeable, and faithful. He is our redeemer and savior who offers joy, hope, peace, and love.

"Forever and ever, Amen." Yahweh is our victorious eternal Father who is also able to say, "It is finished!" (John 19:30)

In other words, when we know the Father, we can understand that this prayer is a prayer of faith and love and thankfulness for our amazing state of existence, of being one that is loved by God, because God is love.

When we understand, when we know the truth, when we know God, the prayer is no longer a simple prayer. The Lord's Prayer becomes a jewel or treasure of great value. The prayer becomes a shout of joyful praise. However, the Lord's Prayer is only one prayer in a chronicle collection of words and phrases and sentences and accounts that that have been recorded to reveal the true nature of Yahweh. A treasure of knowledge, understanding, joy, and peace is available to all who wish to read the words of Scripture.

## CHAPTER THREE

# YAHWEH IS LOVE

Love is not merely a primary characteristic of Yahweh; Yahweh is love.

Love is the essence of the being of Yahweh. Love would not exist without the existence of Deity. Yahweh would not be the I Am if love did not exist. Yahweh cannot be presented or described unless the truth that God is love is understood; for every characteristic of the Almighty is influenced by love.

When evaluating the character or actions of YHWH, we must constantly be aware that the brilliance and beauty, value and holiness of his character is fully expressed by the presence of love. We must remember that every thought, word, or action is touched or blessed by the presence of love.

In the same way that light influences every aspect of the value of a gemstone, the light of love enhances the actions of Deity. In the same way that purity determines the value of gold, the brilliance and purity of love reveals the amazing brilliance and value of the one almighty Deity. Everything that Yahweh has done or said, or will accomplish, is influenced by love.

Unless we understand that love is always present with God, we would fail to understand how honor or judgment are influenced by this oneness of his being. As well, unless we understand that deity love is without measure, or that his love is pure and perfect, we would fail to understand simple statements or descriptions that adequately express Yahweh's loving kindness. For God so loved the world, without measure, with unlimited comparison, with mercy, and grace and understanding, that he gave an amazing gift of love to the entire world and to all of creation. (John 3:16)

The beauty of the love of God is like the light of dawn when the sun is rising, enlightening the morning sky, stretching high into the heavens, and chasing away the darkness of night. Love rises above the mountains and places silver shimmering traces along the highest ridges. Love spreads across the landscape, tumbles down the mountainside, spreads shimmering light in rippling streams and bright colors in fields of flowers. Love brings the brilliant light of day to an awaiting world. Love is beautiful. Love is amazing. Love is joy and peace. Love is light. Love is life. In the account of creation, Yahweh said, "Let there be light!" The light revealed the existence of the earth. (Genesis 1:4) In the same way, Yahweh has said, "Let there be love! Let there be life!"

Nothing about Yahweh, or about what he has done or will do, can be adequately explained without understanding the amazing, magnificent, and beautiful aspects of love, or the mystery of love. The mystery of love is that Yahweh gave his only son as a gift of love and that all of mankind has been offered his gift of love.

Yahweh may be referred to as an ultimate being or existence; however, his state of perfection is fulfilled or completed by the presence of love. Love gives meaning and purpose to his existence. The fact that love influences and fulfills every aspect of Yahweh's being cannot be over emphasized. He is perfect in mind and will, in spirit and in love. As a supreme being God should not be influenced by emotions or stress or pain; however, as love he expresses human-like, or God given responses. As well, wherever love is, God is present; and wherever God is, love is present.

One amazing aspect of love, that is amazingly simple but extremely difficult to explain, is that the presence of love is the evidence of the presence of Deity. Love was present when I AM that I AM created the world, and when he formed mankind. Love is present in every aspect of creation and in his actions in heaven and on earth.

Love resides within the being of Jehovah; for he is Love.

A simple definition or a simple description of Deity love may be offered; however, the definition or description would be incomplete. A complete description of love must be presented or identified as several different aspects or actions of love. Love may be expressed as compassion, kindness, mercy, forgiveness, discipline, empathy, giving, comfort, charity, blessing, mercy, praise, patience, and evens jealousy. For example, to understand that God is love, the mercy offered by God must be explained; for Yahweh is a God of mercy and grace.

As well, his love cannot be understood unless his love is experienced. One must allow the love of God to enter within the mind and heart and spirit. His Love must be felt within one's being. (Deuteronomy 6:5) This relationship requires a personal understanding of love. This relationship also requires a personal understanding and experience with the love of Jesus Christ. As well, a relationship with Jesus depends upon a personal understanding of the tri-unity relationship of truth and love and faith. This is the very reason and purpose of the first commandment. (Luke 10:27-28)

To love God with all our heart, soul and strength and mind seems to be impossible. Even to love our neighbor as we love ourselves seems to be extremely difficult. Nevertheless, all things are possible with God. (Matthew 19:26) As well, we have the mind and heart of Christ. (1 Corinthians 2:16)

Although we know that God is love and that he loves us, the supreme love of God cannot be completely described or explained. We are unable to understand how Yahweh allows love to enter within or how love is felt within his being. The knowledge and understanding required to explain that the love of God is an expression of his supreme perfection is not available. An explanation of how he was able to share his amazing love, as the presence of "love with us" is not available. (John 1:14) We must be able to receive his love, without understanding, in the same way that a child can receive or give love. (Matthew 18:2-4) Although we are unable to understand his supreme love, we can understand and believe that we have been created in his image, to be like Christ, to love and to resist evil. The opportunity to experience his love has been freely offered to us.

His love is experienced in all his gifts of love. (Matthew 22:36-40) (Mark 12:28-33)

Although love is often misunderstood, we as human beings understand the basic premise of love. Love is expressed in respect, kindness, freedom, comfort, blessing, protection from fear, charity, empathy, honor, and truthfulness. Love offers blessings of amazing joy and peace.

The most wonderful aspect of love is that the presence of love is a testimony of the presence of the existence of deity. Love is not a gift of an unknown first cause of existence or of evolutionary development. Love is a gift from God to a universe of creation. Having been created in the image of God we have a natural need for love, and for an understanding of love. The presence of love was given, in the beginning, at the time of creation, when man was created in the image of Yahweh.

Because the love of Yahweh is difficult to define, the relationship or comparison to human love is often misunderstood. How could we possibly understand the joy of love that was placed before Jesus, as he gave his life for us. (Hebrews 12:2) How could we understand the words of Jesus as he explained why he was willing to give his life as a gift of love. (John 14:28-31) The simple truth is that Yahweh cannot be explained or understood without attempting to understanding the love expressed by Jesus. The secret of the blessings of love, is to love as Jesus loved. (John 15:10-11)

Love is simple and complex. The fact that love is simple does not make love any less profound. For example, the simple statement that God is love is profound. As well, the word of God is the written, revealed or expressed love of God. The word, which is the Spirit of Christ, works with our spirit to encourage, motivate, comfort, and inspire actions of love.

As stated, love must be experienced. Love must be felt within the heart. However, love is so much more than a complicated emotion. Love is more than a simple preference or attachment. Love is powerful. Love is essential. Love involves faith and trust and hope. Love is healing, and love is painful. Love may be freely offered; however true love requires trust and faith; for trust must first be given before love is possible. The first commandment, to love God, is not possible without faith; and faith is not possible without trust; and trust is not possible without a simple child-like understanding of love. As well, the first commandment cannot be accomplished without loving others.

Innocent children, who respond with natural or spontaneous trust, are free to love. However, for mature individuals trust must be based upon understanding or experience. We love, because we have chosen to love; and we trust those that we have chosen to trust; and we are able to love those that we trust. As well, with spiritual assistance we are given the ability to choose to be a child of God, to love those who are enemies, that curse us, hate us, or despitefully use or persecute us. (Matthew 5:44)

The apostle Paul said that love is the most excellent way of life. Without love, life would be useless; for the greatest gift of God is life that exist in the unity of love. Yahweh's decision to create life on earth was a choice; and his love for the world is a choice. We have not been told why God chose to create mankind, or why he has chosen to love the world, although we are unworthy of his love. We simply know that he loves because he is Love.

An amazing aspect of love is that life and love can be given as a gift from God. In essence, although we are often unable to trust others, especially our enemies, we can choose to love them, because we trust and love God. Trust and love are gifts of life, offered as a gift from God.

Evidently, the fact that God is Love is difficult for many to accept or appreciate. Because Yahweh is an almighty Deity; fear and awe would be expected. However, one may naturally wonder why the Almighty would be a God of love, kindness, tender mercy, and awareness.

The love expressed by God is patient, kind, and is not jealous. God does not brag and is not arrogant. He does not act unbecomingly and does not seek his own. He is not provoked; and does not take a wrong suffered into account. He does not rejoice in unrighteousness; but rejoices with the truth. As the One who is love, he gives the precious gifts of faith, hope, and love that never fails. (1 Corinthians 13:1-13)

One amazing aspect of God's love is that his love is unconditional. God does not love us because we deserve to be loved; he loves because he has chosen to offer love as a gift of grace and freedom.

God's love is excellent, universal, and unconditional; however, the greatest aspect of his love is that his love is uniquely personal. This amazing aspect of divine love is expressed by Jesus in a simple story about a shepherd and a lost sheep. When the shepherd found the lost sheep, he laid it on his shoulders, brought the sheep home and called his friends and neighbors to rejoice with him.

There will be joy in heaven over one sinner that repents. (Luke 15:1-7)

This parable does not teach that Yahweh discriminates between the lost and the righteous. This parable teaches that God's love is personal and unconditional. This parable is not about the ninety and nine who were safe in the fold. We are all lost sinners; and his love for every one of us is unconditional. The parable expresses the amazing truth of the fact that the love of God is personal. We are all a lost sheep. He knows us, loves us, and is willing to go out into the wilderness to find a single lost sheep like one of us. And when he finds one, he lovingly rejoices with a holy joyfulness that is expressed as amazing incomprehensible love.

As far as mankind is concerned, the greatest aspect or wonder of God's love is that he loves us. Because he is the creator of life and love, he has chosen to give mankind the greatest gift possible, the gift of life.

Another amazing aspect of God's love is that his love is present, in all that he does. Love from God is offered in blessings, mercy, kindness, patience, humility, and friendship. His love is openly expressed in awareness, goodness, judgment, and wisdom. Love influences every decision and every action taken. For example, before Yahweh acts, he is patient, and when he acts, he expresses loving kindness.

The first, second and third person conjugations, present tense, of the verb be or to be, a state of existence or presence, are powerful words. It is important to note that a state of presence or existence is not to be stated in reverse. For example, we may say, "Flowers are beautiful," however, we should not say, "Beauty is flowers." As well, to state that "Love is God" would be incorrect. However, because love is such an integral part of the character of God, it is possible to conclude that without love, God would not be One, the one true God.

Because Yahweh is love, the presence of love on earth and in heaven is of extreme important. Without life, a relationship with existence is not possible. In the same way, without love a true relationship with Yahweh is not possible. (Mark 12:28) Yahweh's requirement for love is clearly stated in the covenant requirement established between Yahweh and the people of Israel. (Deuteronomy 5:1-21) Although our love for God is required as a commandment of honor, love expressed to God is a simple response to his love. The honor of loving Yahweh is a gift of grace; for God has made the act of loving him as simple as turning away from darkness to face the brilliant light of life. Because we are created to love, we can respond to his love in the same way that we may respond to light or to beauty. In other words, loving God is as simple as walking out of darkness into the light. The light of love is beautiful and amazing. A natural response to the love of God is to rejoice, to sing, to shout, to praise God for his love. (2 Samuel 6:14-15) Even for a daily prayer, the thought of his love is worthy of a joyful expression of "hallowed be thy name."

The commandment of love, given to Israel was a blessing of love and protection and strength. (Deuteronomy 6:4-5) The same requirement of love is found in the code of honor that is included in the laws of Israel. (Leviticus 19:17-18) In the same way that loving God is a blessing, loving others is also a blessing, for the joy of giving is greater than the blessing of receiving.

YHWH's love is not contrary to man's love, or completely different from what would be expected. However, one primary difference between Deity love and the common love of mankind does indeed exist. God's love is universal. He is not a respecter of persons. He loves without prejudgment. The love of God is pure and natural, within his very being. His love is expressed as amazing grace to the entire world.

The value and necessity of divine love has been clearly stated in many scriptural passages of prophesy, in verses of psalm, and in statements of praise and teachings of the disciples. Sincere or true love cannot be offered for selfish or self-centered reasons. (1 Corinthians 13:1-13)

Based upon this truth, we could conclude that if Christ Jesus had died on the cross, but did not have love, it would have profited him nothing. The reason that Jesus was offered as a sacrifice was that God is Love. (John 3:16)

Although we are constantly reminded that a complete understanding of the value or beauty of divine love is not truly possible, we also know that the love of God is with us in Jesus Christ. King Solomon poetically described love as expressions of affection between a bride and groom. We read the Song of Solomon; and we fail to comprehend the lesson of love. We do not understand because we do not fully comprehend the meaning of the fact that God is Love. In the same way, the relationship of the body of believers and Christ Jesus is described as a marriage relationship, a relationship of sharing and giving, and sacrifice. This unity of love is a mystery, because the love of God cannot be completely comprehended.

We shall never completely understand why Jesus so loved the world that he gave his life to rescue and to redeem mankind; yet we know that, as an act of love, Yehoshua placed himself on the cross and died for us, for the joy of love set before him, because God so loved the world, and because Jesus loved the father, and because God is Love. We still do not completely understand how or why an Almighty Deity and a loving Son, who are One, would do this as an act of love, for we do not fully understand love. All we can do is to stand in awe of the power and beauty and wonder of Love. We can only imagine what it would have been like to stand before the cross, at the time of crucifixion, to read the words, "Jesus of Nazareth the King of the Jews." (John 18:19) We can only imagine standing before the cross to see the brilliant light of love and to wonder how this could be possible.

Nevertheless, we know the love of Jesus Christ; and knowing the love of Jesus is sufficient. (1 Corinthians 13:12) We can have a relationship of love, understanding, friendship, and fellowship with God through Jesus Christ, for we are drawn to him by love. We are created, in the image of God, to understand life. We have been created to love and to know love.

The passages of love in scripture are awesome. The words contain the precious promises of a loving Father. This enables us to understand the beauty of love. Yet we shall always stand in awe of the power of love; just as we stand in awe of the power of faith. (1 Corinthians 2:9, 13:4-7) Love is awesome; for God is awesome and God is Love. (Romans 8:28, 35)

An interesting representation of love is the number or concept of one. One is life or existence. One is sufficient. One is unity. One is simple yet complex, true, and pure. One is complete within itself, yet able to be unified with one. One can last or endure and be everlasting; for God is One. Yahweh is love, and Love is one!

Yahweh proved that his love is amazing. He sent his only begotten son into the world to give us the gift of eternal life, joy and peace. If we are to love, as he loved us, we must love one another. (1 John 4:8-12)

CHAPTER FOUR

# YAHWEH IS THE TRANSCENDENT ONE

Isaiah described Yahweh as the high and lofty One, that inhabits eternity. His name is Holy. (Isaiah 57:15) Blessings from God have been offered to those who read God's Word and seek to understand the one known as Yahweh. Yahweh is transcendent, perfect, unequalled, and magnificent in person and presence. With these characteristics, together as one, Yahweh is love.

*The attributes or characteristics of Yahweh may be identified as (1) unique descriptions of identity (2) expressions of perfection, beauty and worthiness (3) expressions of purpose of life and existence (4) actions of love, unity, and protection (5) related to his relationship with mankind (6) directly related to his promise of eternal life.*

# 1
# Almighty

The One known as Yahweh is the Almighty. He is known as the God of gods, the Lord of lords, and the King of kings. (Deuteronomy 10:17)

To be almighty is to have unlimited power. Unlimited power includes authority to exercise power at any time or place, or for any reason. To be almighty includes supreme power over life and death, to create or to destroy. To be almighty is to have absolute power over the universe, the heavens, the earth, and mankind.

The word almighty is used to describe kings or rulers. Omnipotent is the descriptive word used to define an all-powerful deity. The Abrahamic name, the Almighty, is the biblical description of the omnipotent power of YHWH. Yahweh is the Almighty and he is the only omnipotent One.

Yahweh is not simply the Almighty; he is the supreme Almighty. He is known as El or El-ohim, the God of gods, the strong and mighty, the almighty God of Abraham, Isaac, and Jacob. Yahweh is Jehovah in the highest. Yahweh is king of the universe. YHWH, the Lord of lords and King of kings, has supreme authority over life and death and everything in Heaven or on earth.

Yahweh has absolute control of power and might; however, the use of authority is always influenced by attributes of love and compassion. For example, God protects the fatherless and widows and the stranger, to give them food and clothing. (Deuteronomy 10:16-18) Yahweh is also the loving Father of Israel.

As the creator of the universe, the father of the universe, and the rightful owner of the universe, all of creation is subject to his almighty voice. (Revelations 4:11) By the word of the Lord, the authority of Deity, the heavens were created. (Deuteronomy 10:14)

Within the historical accounts of Israel, the omnipotent authority of Yahweh has been clearly demonstrated. Abraham and Sarah were admonished for expressing doubt of God's authority; for the authority of Yahweh is not to be doubted or questioned. (Genesis 18:12-14)

Moses stood before Yahweh and talked with God face to face, but Moses was unable to adequately describe the vision because Yahweh was surrounded by brilliant light and clouds.

In his blessing for Joseph, Jacob prophesied of the supreme love of God for Israel. (Genesis 49:24-25) Because their hearts were hardened, the royal king of Heaven allowed the people of Israel to have an earthly king; however, the prophet Samuel warned the descendants of Abraham to remember that Yahweh is their only true King. (1 Samuel 12:12 & 20) His sovereign authority must always be recognized.

The book of Job is a chronicle account that contains a complete description of the character, desires, and intents of the Almighty. This biblical narrative is used to declare that the Almighty is worthy of honor and love. (Job 42:1-2) Within this account, another being that is unwilling to recognize the authority of Yahweh is recognized. He is called Satan, Lucifer, the devil, a lying spirit, the deceiver, and is also known as the anti-Christ. An explanation of why Yahweh allows Satan to challenge his authority is not offered in the account. As well, an explanation of why Yahweh tolerates the existence of this evil one has not been revealed. Perhaps the reason is related to the fact that Yahweh is a compassionate Deity. Perhaps Satan is present because he is useful for Yahweh's extended plan for mankind and for all of creation.

On one unidentified day, the ones called the sons of God came to present themselves before Yahweh, and the one called Satan was among them. (Job 1:6) This passage of scripture should not be used to teach that Satan is a son of God. The verse states that he was among God's sons, not that he was one of them. As well, the sons mentioned are not born of God, for Yahweh has only one begotten son. However, the Lord God was willing to communicate with this evil one. Yahweh spoke to Satan and said, "Where have you come from?" Satan answered, "From going to and fro on the earth, and from walking up and down in it." (Job 1:6-7)

Almighty God, the Lord of all wisdom, offers a challenge with Satan. And the Lord said to Satan, "Have you considered my servant Job? There is none like him in the earth, a perfect and an upright man, one that fears God, and turns away from evil." (Job 1:8)

The Lord God allows Satan to grievously afflict Job, for Yahweh clearly understood that Job, who was perfect and upright, would remain faithful. Job's response is to acknowledge the almighty authority of God and to worship Him. (Job 1:20-21) Strengthened by the power of love, Job recognized the sovereign right of God, to give or to take away, to bless or curse. As well, Job understood that God would respond with love and compassion.

Job acknowledged the authority of God and believed in his heart that God is love. However, this account is not about a man who was so aware of the power and authority of a supreme being that he fearfully submitted to his authority. The story of Job is an account about a supreme Deity who used Job to demonstrate his own sovereign authority, and the power and authority of divine love.

In the second chapter of this incredible story, Satan is once again before Yahweh and God asked, "Have you noticed that Job still holds fast to his integrity, although you have harmed him without cause?" Although Job was in the hands of Satan, without loving protection from the Father, Job was able to remain humble before God. (Job 2:10)

Of course, without understanding and without an explanation for what had happened, Job was disheartened but not despondent. He knew that ultimately the Lord God the Almighty was responsible for his affliction. At the same time, Job was required to endure the admonishment of his friends. Eliphaz the Temanite reminds Job that every man is required to reap what has been sown. Without any expression of sympathy, his friends remind Job that God is a god of justice, and that only God has pure wisdom. (Job 4:12-21) Eliphaz, assuming that God's honor must be defended, said to Job, "You must have admonished someone without cause, or at least you have done something wrong. Your affliction must be God's judgment; for God cannot be at fault."

Zophar, the Naamathite, was anxious to point out that God is Almighty, and that there is none to compare to him. (Job 11:1-12) Although Job has already offered a poetic description of Yahweh's majesty, his young friend Elihu is compelled to shares a frustrated defense of God's honor. (Job 36:1 - 38:24)

The conclusion of the story is for Yahweh himself to offer an accurate almighty explanation of the fact that Yahweh, the one and only Deity, is indeed a God of authority. (Job 38: l, 39:1-30, 40:1-24, 41:1-34)

Yahweh has authority to reveal his power and might and authority to anyone. His presence and his power are never hidden, even to a royal Babylonian monarch. (Daniel 4:34-35) His almighty sovereign authority is also illustrated in the story of judgment against the sovereign king Belshazzar. (Daniel 5:1-31)

Yahweh used the prophet Isaiah to declare his authority to the nation of Israel. (Isaiah 40:6-31) Isaiah clearly understood the majesty of the authority of Yahweh. As well, because Yahweh is a God of loving kindness Isaiah is directed to offered words of comfort. (Isaiah 40:1-2 & 41:1) The interesting fact about the authority of Yahweh is that although he has the authority and the power to demand that every individual being, in heaven and on earth, should stand before him, in honor and in fear, to acknowledge his omnipotent power, Yahweh allows all of us a choice to acknowledge his authority and to accept his love. For the Almighty, this is an act of grace; and for any individual, the choice is an act of faith and honor.

The Apostle Paul says that eternal life has not been offered as an act of authority, or to affirm or prove authority. Eternal life is a gift of God's amazing grace. If the act of faith that is required to receive the gift of eternal life is an act of yielding to the commands of authority, or even if the choice is motivated by fear of almighty authority, salvation would not be a gift of grace. Even if we were selected or chosen by the Almighty, eternal life would not be a gift of grace. Freedom from his authority has been given, not only to those who are of the law of Moses, but to all of mankind.

This promise of freedom from authority has also been given to those that are of the faith of Abraham, for Abraham is the one who has been made the father of many nations. (Romans 4:16-17)

Truly, because Yahweh is the Almighty, we should stand in awe and fear him; however, he is more than a powerful supernatural deity. He is more than an amazing powerful force of our natural or physical universe. Yahweh is Love. His love is amazing. His love, like omnipotent power, is supreme. His love is almighty.

To understand how almighty love and supreme authority exist together, within the unity of One, is to understand how love is the essence of Truth. Without love, our state of being has no purpose or meaning. Without understanding that God is love we will be unable to understand the power and authority of love. (1 Corinthians 13:1-8) If we do not understand the authority of love, we will be unwilling to accept the words of life.

(John 3:16) According to God's will, love and truth will have almighty authority. God is Almighty Love! Hallelujah! Holy, holy, holy is God Almighty!

We can stand in awe of the magnificent stars and galaxies and estimate the force and energy involved. We can dream about traveling in space to observe, to interact and appreciate the beauty of light; or we can stand in awe of the size and power and might of a black hole in a distant universe. We can imagine the satisfaction of the discovery for a cure for all human ailments. We can wonder about the beauty and power of this magnificent existence. We can touch and experience and understand the world and our universe, but we cannot truly communicate with this amazing existence. The physical matter in space is still less than a zero and will always remain less than a zero; for the universe has no words of love to express. The stars of the universe do not have the authority to say, "I love you. I will protect you. I will give you eternal life."

The universal principles of love apply to everyone, even with an Almighty Deity. The true supreme greatness of Yahweh's omnipotence, of his power and might is that he is Love. Without love, he would be like a magnificent expanding universe of outer darkness. He would be an almighty enormous beginning and ending. As Love or with love God is a complete one of existence. He is the "I Am that I AM." As Love, he is the almighty One, an awesome, amazing, magnificent Almighty Father of heaven and earth.

Yahweh has the authority to overcome the darkness of evil and death. (Luke 1:37) This is the right of preeminence. With Yahweh, love is strong, permanent, immovable, stable, dependable, and valuable. His love is beautiful. Love is supreme. Love is almighty.

When we pray the Lord's Prayer, we acknowledge the authority of our Almighty Father, who is in Heaven. (Matthew 6:9-10) When we understand that love bears all things, believes, hopes, and never fails, we understand that God is almighty Love. (1 Corinthians 13:7-8)

## 2
## Anger

The anger of God endures but for a moment, and his favor offers life. (Psalm 30:4-5)

Anger is an emotional and physical response to any adverse experience such as annoyance, hostility, or rejection. Anger may be expressed as shock, silence, tears, hostility, exasperation, wrath, or fury. Anger can cause an increase in heart rate and blood pressure or an increased level of adrenaline. As well, during an emotional state of denial, the stress of anger may be present without awareness.

A comprehensive explanation of righteous anger that is expressed by Yahweh is not possible. Anger felt or experienced by a righteous deity is completely different than anger experienced by human beings. Anger expressed by Yahweh is directly related to the existence of holiness or righteousness. Any confrontation to righteousness is unacceptable. An act of dishonor to holiness creates an inherent situation of anger.

Just as anger expressed by humans may reveal aspects of character, the accounts and statements of anger expressed by Yahweh reveal the thoughts and intents of a God of love. The prophet Isaiah stated that Yahweh quickly expresses angry against injustice, hypocrisy, and haughty attitudes and actions. (Isaiah 10:1-4) His anger is moderated by loving kindness and endures but for a moment. In the account of original sin God does not express angry; however, we may assume that he was not pleased. (Genesis 3:1-24) He placed judgment upon the serpent and Adam and Eve, but his wrath was withheld.

Anger expressed by God as an act of righteous judgment is always justified. Although several human attributes are reflections of the character of God, anger is not an attribute of having been created in the image of God. We were created in the likeness of Love, and we have been commanded to put away anger. (Ephesians 4:31-3) The unexplained anger expressed by God is completely different than the exasperation that we might experience. Several accounts have been recorded in scripture that clearly state that Yahweh demonstrated angry, however, the specific reason for anger has not been completely explained. Although an explanation has not been provided, the events or situations when Yahweh has expressed righteous anger are never hidden or discounted.

By an appearance of God, Moses was informed that he had been chosen, as an instrument of the Lord, to free the Israelites from bondage in Egypt. When Moses demonstrated lack of faith or trust, God's anger was provoked. (Exodus 4:1) The anger of the Lord burned against Moses for failure to honor his righteousness. (Exodus 4:14 & 24-26)

Yahweh often appears to be disturbed, disappointed, frustrated, or even angry concerning the conduct or decisions of the children of Israel. Even before receiving the tablets of stone written by the finger of God, the descendants of Jacob demonstrated that they were an obstinate people. Yahweh was angry, righteously angry. (Exodus 32:9-10)

Fortunately for the Israelites, Yahweh repented or turned from the judgment, not the anger, that he thought to do unto his people. (Exodus 32:14) His repentance does not demonstrate indecisive action or lack of will. His choice reveals his primary character of loving kindness and mercy, for his anger that endures for a moment, is easily and quickly controlled.

Although Yahweh decided to not destroy the descendants of Abraham, he remained unwilling to tolerate lack of honor or disobedience. His response was like that of a loving Father. (Numbers 11:1-12)

This situation does not demonstrate that God was so angry that he was emotionally or physically unable to control his actions. Righteous anger is an expression of a complicated response by a complicated almighty being to a complicated situation. The acts or deeds of Yahweh are always accomplished with complete understanding, with complete authority, and always in accordance with the holiness of his character.

Evidently, the Israelites were unable to fully understand the requirements of honor that should be given to a sovereign King. Yahweh deserves honor; therefore, honor will be given to him, without exception or without excuse. When his chosen ones failed to honor him, righteous anger that only last for a moment was provoked. (Deuteronomy 4:25)

A leader of the tribe of Levi named Korah, obviously an outstanding individual, decided that he would be a better leader than Moses. He had most likely observed that Moses was timid or humble. He obviously did not understand that his own actions demonstrated a lack of honor to the almighty Lord of Hosts, the one who had specifically chosen Moses. He convinced two hundred and fifty tribal leaders to join him in protest. Korah said to Moses, "You have gone far enough. All of us are holy and the Lord is in our midst, so why do you and Joshua exalt yourselves above the assembly of the Lord?" Korah failed to realize that his words were a challenge to the authority of the Lord of Hosts.

Moses was disturbed, but Yahweh was angry. (Numbers 16:21) When Moses humbly intervened, God chose to limit the consequences for this lack of honor. The earth opened and swallowed up Korah and all the leaders with their families and possessions. (Numbers 16:32-33) Fire also came down from the Lord and consumed two hundred and fifty who were offering incense. (Numbers 16:35) God's anger may last only for a moment, for justice is required.

Interestingly, after this conflict, the sons of Israel continued to blame Moses and Aaron. The anger of the Lord was expressed once again. (Numbers 16:45) Yahweh, the God of loving kindness, finally used a miracle, a sign to help the people understand that He had chosen Moses, and that He expected his choice to be honored. God caused the almond wood staff of Aaron to sprout with buds and blossoms. (Numbers 17:8)

Nevertheless, for several reasons demonstrations of anger by Jehovah were not sufficient to teach an obstinate people to fear the Lord. While the tribes of Israel were in Shittim, the people committed evil acts with the daughters of Moab. They went with them to their sacrifices to their gods and ate and bowed down to their gods. The anger of the Lord was kindled against Israel. (Numbers 25:1-5) Obviously, the consequences of Yahweh's angry are severe, but his loving kindness and willingness to forgive are always present. (Numbers 25:11)

Although Moses and Aaron had learned to respect the authority of Yahweh and clearly understood the anger of the Lord of Host, they allowed frustration to cloud their judgment. In the wilderness of Kadesh, Moses was commanded to speak to the rock, that represented the grace and salvation of God, to bring forth water. Because he was unable to control his own frustration, Moses struck the rock twice with his staff. (Numbers 20:12) Later, Moses offered a simple, rather incomplete explanation of this event. (Deuteronomy 1:37)

Yahweh was often angry or upset with the judges, prophets, and kings of Israel. An account of God's anger was recorded in the accounts of 1 Samuel. The children of Israel decided that because all other kingdoms had a king who was able to gather an army to defend the nation, they should also have a king. Yahweh relented and gave them a king; but he also gave a sign of his anger. (1 Samuel 12:16-20) During the time of wheat harvest, God sent a storm of thunder and rain across the land. And the people pleaded with the prophet Samuel to pray to God for mercy. Through the words of Samuel, Yahweh gave Israel words of assurance of protection, but he also offered a just warning. (1Samuel 20-25)

Yahweh does not become angry for any unjust cause. His anger was provoked by the unrighteousness of the people or by the unfaithfulness of the kings of Israel and Judah, but his anger was righteous and justified, and his loving-kindness was always present. As an example, king Ahaz constructed high places to burn incense to other gods, and provoked Yahweh to anger. (2 Chronicles 28:16-26) As well, the anger of the Lord was turned away when the Kings or the Hebrew people were faithful to honor him. (2 Chronicles 29:10)

Although all of Israel and Judah had previously celebrated in Jerusalem with great joy, king Hezekiah's son Manasseh, who reigned for fifty-five years, did evil in the sight of the Lord. He even placed carved images of idols in the House of the Lord. Yahweh allowed the captains of the king of Assyria to bound Manasseh with fetters and carry him to exile in Babylon. (2 Chronicles 33:9-11) (2 Kings 17:18)

Because of his loving-kindness, Yahweh has continued to be with the children of Israel even when they were unfaithful; for the Lord Jehovah is always faithful. When the prophet Ezekiel expressed deep concern about the future of Judah, the Lord answered with words of compassionate assurance for the family of Israel. (Ezekiel 11:16-21)

Yahweh has also declared that a time will come when his anger will be removed from the house of Israel. (Romans 11:25-26) This passage of scripture is a direct promise of blessing to the house of Israel. This commitment is not an open offer to any other past or present or future nation or group of people. This is not a direct blessing or promise of covenant to the followers of Christ or to the gentiles that have professed faith in Christ Jesus. The covenant of faith established for us is a new and different covenant. The new covenant is a covenant of grace.

Obviously, Yahweh can be provoked to anger and wrath; but he remains compassionate. (Psalm 69:34-36) Gifts of love are never taken away. The Lord our God is not easily provoked. His anger is often restricted by his own will;

for Yahweh is always slow to anger. God's anger is fierce and just, but never long lasting. (Psalm 30: 4-5) (Psalm 2:4-5) (Jeremiah 3:12) When Jesus drove the money changers from the temple his disciples remembered a passage of scripture concerning the anger of Yahweh. (John 2:13-17) (Psalm 69:9)

The primary theological lesson concerning anger is that although anger may be expressed, Yahweh is a God of love. In like manner, if we are to be like God, we are not to be controlled by anger. (James 1:19-20)

Perhaps if we were attempting to create a god, in our own image, we might choose to remove this apparent conflict of character. Surely, we would purposely limit the number of recorded events within our holy scripture when our assumed god became angry, and especially when wrath is expressed. However, the actions of Yahweh are openly recorded. Nothing concerning his anger is hidden, discounted or excused. His anger has been openly revealed.

Perhaps one might prefer to have a god that never became angry, was never jealous, and never punished or allowed vengeance to fall on anyone. This false god, made in the image of mankind, could be a god of love and peace; but the world would still be filled with men who are lovers of self. (2 Timothy 3:2-7) Yes, we would have a god that could be accepted without judgment; but the world would still be filled with family and friends that need spiritual redemption, who need to be rescued from an evil world.

Instead of creating our own god, we can accept the grace of God by faith in Jesus Christ. We can be made holy and acceptable to God. We can be free from his anger and wrath and know that someday the world and all of existence will be set free from anger and wrath.

## 3
## Authority

Yahweh has said, "I live forever." This is a statement of supreme authority. (Deuteronomy 32:39-40)

Authority includes the power and right to give orders, enforce the order and to rule on the legal requirement of the orders. Authority includes command, control, influence, and privilege. The power of authority includes the right to give freedom or to place in prison. Sovereign authority is the right to legislate or to establish laws, to enforce the laws and to rule on the justice of such laws. Supreme authority is determined by the authority and the power to rule over life or death.

Supreme authority is the inherent right of being omnipotent, of existing in a position of ascendancy, supremacy, and dominance. The authority of Deity is the inherent right of being Almighty. The One, who is "the Almighty," has absolute authority, without limits or restrictions. Authority includes the right and privilege of judgment. All power, dominion and authority has been given to YHWH. Having autonomous authority, means that everything is under his authority. All order, power and might, belong to him. As well, everything that Yahweh does is justified and right.

The Almighty, the God of mercy and meekness, kindness and compassion, patience and purity, beauty and wisdom, truth and freedom, has the authority to bless the world with love and grace. He has complete authority over every mind, body, and soul on the earth and within heaven and the universe beyond. He has the authority to bestow wisdom or to withhold wisdom. (Job 12:13-25) Yahweh is the King of kings with the authority to rule over every citizen in every kingdom in heaven or earth.

In the same way that almighty power and might has been demonstrated, the authority of Yahweh has been affirmed in numerous biblical accounts.

In the book of Job, the authority of Deity has been clearly explained. At the end of the testing of Job, Yahweh had a personal conversation with Job to instruct Job about the relationship of an almighty Deity to mankind. Yahweh said to Job, "I will ask you, and you instruct me. Will you alter my judgment? Will you condemn me, that you may be righteous?" (Job 40:8) (Job 41:11) Job humbly acknowledged the authority of Deity by stating that no purpose or plan of God can be altered or changed. (Job 42:1-2)

The prophet Isaiah offered prophesies and warnings concerning Yahweh's authority of judgment and justice. (Isaiah 30:1)

Hannah was rewarded for her declaration of the power and authority of Yahweh. (1 Samuel 2:1-10)

King David praised Yahweh for his authority and thanked him for blessings. (1 Chronicles 29:10-13)

Yahweh's privilege of authority was also demonstrated by the story of Balaam. (Numbers 21:18)

Although king Solomon understood the responsibility of having authority, the king questioned how God's use of authority could always be just and righteous. King Solomon failed to consider the fact that Yahweh's acts of judgment are always influenced by his amazing love. (Ecclesiastes 9:1-3)

Although Yahweh, by a sovereign act of almighty love, has chosen to offer life instead of death to the world, his decision for punishment of those who fail to accept his gift of love may be judged by some to be unjust. Nevertheless, judgment of mankind is Yahweh's choice in accordance with his right of supreme authority.

According to the words of prophecy, in latter times the authority of Deity is to be specifically given to a new ruler, the King of kings and the Lord of lords. Jewish scholars identify this one to be the promised Messiah ben David. An accurate interpretation of prophecy concerning the Son of Man and the Ancient of Days, and the identification and acceptance of the Messiah is of extreme importance. (Daniel 7:9-28)

The fact that every aspect of the character of Yahweh is influenced by love has been previously stated. The relationship of sovereign authority and love is an appropriate time to explain this statement.

For those who reside in a nation that has a governmental system that does not include a national king the thought of being ruled by a King is somewhat disturbing. The problem is a basic misunderstanding of the necessity of authority. Authority is a requirement of political and social order and stability. Within the universe or within a national government the total amount of authority cannot be increased or decreased. Because civil or moral authority can be separated into areas of authority or responsibility, such as legislative, judicial, and executive, or shared in various ways, different types of governments may be instituted. One nation may choose to have a sovereign ruler. Another may choose to democratically agree to write and accept a written constitution as the replacement of a sovereign ruler.

Nevertheless, there is only One deity, who is YHWH. The sovereign authority that God has cannot be increased or decreased or shared. This almighty sovereign Deity cannot separate his authority, for there is no other to share his authority. Whether Yahweh is the King of kings, or the Constitution of constitutions makes no difference. He is the King of the universe. Therefore, the true essence of authority is that God is Love. In the Kingdom of Heaven, Love will be the sovereign ruler. Love will be the King of kings.

Yahweh did not initially intend to remove civil authority from the judges of Israel and give this responsibility to the kings of Israel; however, because the children of Israel had hardened their hearts, God chose to allow the children of Israel to have a national king. Nevertheless, just as sovereign authority of deity was not given to the prophets, authority was not given to the kings of Israel. Yahweh is the only Father and King of Israel. He will always have sovereign authority over the nation of Israel. (1 Samuel 12:22)

In accordance with his choice to establish one fate for the righteous and for the wicked Yahweh did at times choose to give authority to foreign rulers that were chosen for his purpose. The foreign kings, under the direct authority of God, were used to discipline Israel and Judah. (2 Chronicles 36:22-23) (Ezra 1:1-3) For example Artaxerxes, king of Persia, was given authority by God. (Ezra 7:21-23) The complete account of Yahweh's presence and interaction with the king of Persia has been recorded in the book of Nehemiah. (Nehemiah 2:1-20)

God may give authority to rulers on earth, but his sovereign authority is never relinquished, shared, or given away; and can never be taken away. He delegates authority and is prepared to remove authority when necessary; however, as a Father and as One, Yahweh is unable to share the authority of being the Father. This Father authority cannot be taken away or given away, for there is no other father to take his place.

Although Yahweh has given authority to kings and prophets and priest, the King of kings and Lord or lords who is One with the Father is the only one that has authority with Yahweh. The Lord of lords, the righteous King of Israel is a jealous God, and he reserves his right of sovereignty; however, Yehoshua the Christ does not share authority, Jesus has sovereign authority with the Father. This relationship of authority is a unique relationship of the oneness of Deity. (John 3:35)

Elisabeth, the barren wife of Zechariah, was allowed to give birth, because with God nothing would be impossible. (Luke 1:37) Of course, this was also for a greater purpose, for providing the one who would fulfill the words of prophecy. (Matthew 11:7-10)

According to the words of the New Testament, the authority of God is specifically demonstrated in the account of the birth of Jesus. At the time of this event the ancient world, from Rome to the far East was under the authority of the Roman Empire. The ruler of the empire had sovereign authority over all citizens and inhabitants of Palestine and the surrounding territories. This authority included the power of life or death. However, although not recognized or acknowledged, all true authority of life was in a small child, in the little town of Bethlehem.

Herod the Hebrew Tetrarch did not recognize the authority of the newborn King; however, the Angels in Heaven and the Magi, the wise men of the East, offered worship and praise because they understood that this infant was the sovereign King of Heaven and earth. The monarch in Rome and Pilot the ruler of Palestine did not recognize the authority of Jesus. Jesus was arrested and tried for treason, for disobedience to the authority of Rome, but no one had the authority to take his life. (John 19:11)

This One, the son of man, was placed on a cross, to be crucified, for the sins of the entire world. The Roman ruler placed a sign above his head that read, "This is Jesus, the King of the Jews." (Matthew 27:37) Those who were standing at the foot of the cross, "who did not understand," said, "He saved others; therefore, can he not save himself? If he is the sovereign King of Israel, let him come down from the cross, and we will believe in him."

Although Jesus had the authority of life and death, he gave his life as a gift of love; and the One who is the Father did not interfere with this choice of authority and love. (Matthew 27:46)

Nevertheless, before Jesus died, he shouted forth the greatest declaration of authority ever presented, "It is finished." He cried out again and yielded up his spirit. (Matthew 27:45-50) No words of authority are greater than these words shouted by Jesus. This is a shout of freedom and peace and joy. By the authority that was given to him by the Father of the Universe, the kingdom of Heaven was established. Nothing else would be required. The new Sabbath was presented. Love was given supreme authority.

On the third day, Jesus arose from the grave. He was resurrected. He was and is alive. And when he appeared to his disciples he spoke with authority and gave instructions with authority. (Matthew 28:17-20) The Apostle Paul said that all authority, not just a mighty portion, had been given to Jesus. The divine sovereign authority of Deity has been given to the Son. (Luke 10:22) This is a sovereign choice of authority made by the Almighty Father. As an act of supreme love, Jesus was faithful, even unto death.

The apostle Paul said that all the authority of love has been given to Jesus. Jesus has been placed in a position of authority "far above all principality and power and might and dominion and every name that is named, not only in this world but also in that which is to come." (Ephesians 1:19-23) (1 Timothy 6:15-16) (Philippians 3:8-11)

No one except Yahweh, who is One, has the sovereign authority of eternal life or death or the authority to forgive sin. Jesus has the authority to forgive sin; and has been given the authority to offer eternal life. Jesus has authority to forgive sin because he is One with the Father. (Mark 2:1-10)

The one called Satan, or Lucifer, thought that he would be able to convince God that he deserved to share the authority of deity. (Matthew 4:9) Satan did not understand that no other except the Son, who from the very beginning of existence has deity with the Father, would be worthy. Because Yehoshua is One with his Father, all sovereign authority has been given to him. This truth does not require explanation or defense. (Mark 11:33)

Jesus did not choose to explain or defend his relationship of authority with the Father. (Luke 20:8) The authority of the baptism of John was verified by his deeds and by his life. An explanation of his authority or purpose was not required. As well, Jesus does not choose to offer an explanation to those who doubt his deity. His authority does not require an explanation or defense. His relationship to the Father has been verified by his life and gift of love. (Matthew 11:25-27) (Luke 10:22)

Before a choice to believe that that Jesus has been given authority only on earth is believed or accepted, the words of scripture should be carefully considered. (Luke 12:1-5) (Philippians 2:5-10.) The Father and Son are in complete agreement concerning the use of supreme sovereign authority and justice. Having supreme authority means that Jesus has absolute authority over life and death. (Luke 12:1-5)

As stated, the most important aspect concerning authority is that supreme authority is determined by the authority and the power to rule over life or death. This fact was declared by Jesus. (Luke 22:69) All authority concerning life or death has been given to Jesus the Christ, because he is worthy. Although he has the authority of condemnation, Jesus has chosen to use authority to forgive sin. (John 3:17) (Mark 2:10) He is the door for the sheep, the way, the truth, and the life for all of mankind. He has the authority to offer eternal life to those who have faith in him. (Luke 10:20) (Romans 14:11-12) (Matthew 9:4-6)

When we honor the Son, we honor the Father who has sent him. We believe that the One that sent Jesus, has given everlasting life to those who accept Jesus as the Messiah. Those who believe will not come into condemnation. We have passed from death unto life. (John 5:17-24) (Luke 10:23-24) (John 5:30)

As One with the Father, Jesus also has authority to give authority to others; however, he and the Father have not relinquished authority to any man or angelic being. (Matthew 10:1) Jesus gave instructions to his disciples with authority; he did not give authority to give instructions, or authority to rule over others. (Matthew 10:8) Jesus the Christ has authority to give eternal life to those who accept his gift of love. (Romans 10:9) Yehoshua the Messiah is the one who has the power and authority to change our state of existence. (Philippians 3:21) This is the power and authority of Love.

Accepting the authority of Jesus is an act of faith. (Matthew 8:8-10) (Luke 7:8-9) Jesus recognized the Roman officer's accurate understanding of authority as an act of faith. The reason for this acceptance is clearly recorded in scripture. (Philippians 2:5-10)

All authority, the inherent right of deity, of ascendancy, supremacy and dominance has been awarded to Jesus Christ. YHWH has declared, as an act of his own sovereign authority, that the authority of Jesus Christ must be recognized and accepted. (Matthew 28:18) We should not be afraid of those who can kill the body; but should fear the one who has authority to destroy both the soul and body. (Matthew 10:28)

Jesus Christ is the one who has gone into heaven and is on the right hand of God.

Angels and authorities and powers have been made subject to him. (1 Peter 3:22)

# 4

# Awareness

"Our Father, who is in heaven" is aware of everything and everyone. (Matthew 6:9-10)

Awareness is a state of cognizance and attentiveness. Awareness may require alertness, acceptance of the reality of the situation and responsive action; however, complete awareness requires knowledge or understanding.

Adam and Eve were unaware of exposure and of the consequences of evil. With a revised state of understanding, they were aware that they were exposed before an Almighty God.

The understanding and awareness expressed by God is amazing and unique in every possible way. The Lord searches all hearts and understands the thoughts of everyone. (1 Chronicles 28:9) He is aware of everything that has happened in the past and present. He is aware of what will happen in the future and is prepared to respond. He hears our prayers. (Psalm 139:6-16)

Yahweh knows us. Yahweh knows you. He is aware of everything and has loving concern for everyone. (Psalm 34:12-22) In essence, this is the mystery of miracles.

Before our present age of science and artificial intelligence the thought that one might know everything would have been difficult to accept. In this era of advanced technology, the thought of supreme information is somewhat acceptable; nevertheless, the fact that God understands the unknowable remains difficult to accept.

The scholars of Israel expressed amazement concerning the fact that God is aware of everything that happens on earth and in heaven. (Job 22:12-20) (Psalm 1:6)

Several of the authors of the psalms testify of God's supreme discernment. (Psalm 13:1) The authors express belief that God is aware of their need and that he hears prayers or accepts praise. (Psalm 88:1-18) In this psalm, although the psalmist does not receive an answer, the truth that God is aware is acknowledged.

The knowledge of divine awareness can be inspiring or disturbing. (Hebrews 4:13) As well, an awareness of God's presence may offer comfort and joy. (Psalm 16:11) We may be concerned that Yahweh is aware of our hidden thoughts, but we are comforted by the presence of love and protection. (Psalm 23:1-6).

Awareness can make a difference in response or acceptance of any situation. When our prayer is not answered, in a manner that we would expect, we may assume that God is unwilling to offer a response or an explanation; however, Yahweh is always attentive. He knows what has happened, what is happening, and what will happen, and he cares.

When strict judgment is required for justice, the bitter reality of judgment may be unpleasant. Although Yahweh is aware that the justice of such action would be questioned, the righteous acts of Yahweh are never hidden or discounted. Many acts of judgment have been recorded in biblical accounts.

The chronicles of Israel include accounts about God's character, concerns, awareness, and plans for the children of Abraham and for the world. The prophecies included in scripture were not words given by the prophets or authors of scripture, for the holy men of God spoke as they were directed by the Holy Spirit. (2 Peter 1:20-21) Yahweh was always present and aware of what the children of Abraham needed.

God was aware of non-disclosed actions of the king of Bashan and his people that required judgment instead of kindness or forgiveness. (Numbers 21:33-35)

Yahweh was aware that Zippor, the king of Moab, wanted to annihilate the nation of Israel. God also knew that Balaam wanted to obtain the monetary fee of divination. When the king of the Moabites tried to convince the prophet Balaam to curse Israel, Yahweh protected Israel. (Numbers 22:4-9, 12)

Yahweh was aware that the older brother of king David was unworthy of being chosen as king. (1 Samuel 16:6-7)

Although Jehovah is aware of the imaginations and thoughts of the nation of Israel, he is also aware of the commitment that he has made to Israel. God has established a covenant relationship with the children of Abraham. God has made a commitment to king David, and to his children. This is an everlasting covenant, sealed by the word of God. (Psalm 89:1-4)

Although Yahweh wanted to bless the nation of Israel, he clearly perceived that the people would be unfaithful. (Deuteronomy 30:16, 31:21) Because the children of Israel had often built altars for worship of foreign idols, God used the prophet Habakkuk to admonish them. (Habakkuk 2:18-20)

Yahweh understood the desires and the plans and the needs of king Nebuchadnezzar; and he was aware that Daniel would be a faithful prophet. (Daniel 2:1 - 4:37) As well, God was aware that judgment was required for king Belshazzar. (Daniel 5:1-31)

Yahweh was also aware that the scribes of Israel, who have a strong faith in the absolute unity and singularity of deity, would not be able to accept Jesus as the Messiah. Jesus was fully aware that many of the children of Israel would reject his gift of salvation. (Mark 12:10-11)

Yahweh understands and is completely mindful that as earthly beings we are not completely aware of his presence. We are unable to completely comprehend his majesty.

For this reason, the only way to obtain an understanding of God, is for Yahweh to reveal himself to us. His precious Son Jesus Christ is that revelation. God has offered a gift of grace so that awareness is directly related to faith in Yehoshua, his son. If we wish to be aware of God, to know or understand Yahweh, we must know Jesus Christ.

By faith, the ability to accept the words of scripture and to believe that all men are worthy of Yahweh's attention can be received. The rule of awareness and the rule of faith is that if we seek him, we will find him. God has provided the possibility of knowledge and awareness by offering faith as the way to hear his voice. Simply stated, awareness of God is a gift from Yahweh through faith in Jesus Christ, the living word of God. By faith, when we hear his voice, confusion and doubt can be taken away. This mystery of the gospel of grace or faith in Jesus Christ, which was for past ages hidden in God, who created all things, also includes an offer of eternal life to the Gentiles. (Ephesians 3:9) (Ephesians 3:4-6) Even when we doubt, when we lack faith, God is aware of our need. Because he understands our weakness of faith, he is able and willing to strengthen our faith and trust. (1 John 3:18-20)

God sent the Holy Spirit as a presence of awareness, to strengthen the faith of believers. He knows those who believe; and He is prepared to meet their needs.

The story of Cornelius is an account that has been offered to emphasize the awareness of God. A Caesarea called Cornelius, who was a centurion of the band called the Italian band, was a devout man that feared God and who gave alms to the people and prayed to God. In a vision, Cornelius saw an angel of God that told him that God was aware of his prayer. Because of his faith, God sent the apostle Peter to witness to Cornelius concerning the Gospel. Because God was aware of their faith, the centurion and his family and friends received the gift of the Holy Spirit. (Acts 10:1-48)

Many events recorded in scripture clearly show that God is aware of the past, present, and future. Words of prophecy also reveal the awareness of God. According to words of scripture, in latter times some will depart from the faith. They will listen to seducing spirits that will be speaking lies in hypocrisy. (1 Timothy 4:1-2)

We are completely aware that we are no longer innocent. We know that we are exposed before an almighty God. We may not sense his presence or accept the fact that God knows what is in our heart; but the most amazing aspect of the awareness of God is that He knows us. God loves us. He hears our prayers. (Luke 12:6-7)

# 5
## Beautiful

Out of Zion, the perfection of the beauty of God has appeared. (Psalm 50:2)

To be beautiful is to be pleasing to the senses or mind. Beauty is alluring, excellent, attractive, elegant, lovely, radiant, divine, and magnificent. True beauty is expressed outwardly and inwardly and is never hidden or distorted.

Although beauty may be seen in sound or movement, arrangement or design, the physical beauty of our world depends upon the presence of light. Every sparkling object, and every shimmering star is visible light. Beauty is seen in the variations of the intensity of light and within the contrast of darkness to light.

Darkness may hide or cover visible beauty; however, inward light and beauty, such as love, is never hidden or overcome by darkness. God is light. There is no darkness in the existence of Deity. (1 John 1:5) (Revelation 21:23)

In the beginning, God said, "Let there be light!" And there was light. And God saw the light, that it was good. (Genesis 1:3-4) In the beginning, God said, "Let there be beauty, and there was beauty; and God saw the beauty and said, "This is good."

Beauty is a natural inherent expression of the existence of Yahweh. God is beautiful and all that he creates is beautiful. Because there is no darkness or evil within Yahweh, his beauty cannot be hidden or taken away. Because he is light and dwells in light, his beauty will never be diminished. The universe above and our amazing world are evidence of the beauty of his creation. (Psalm 19:1)

Although the primary word to describe the appearance of Deity is the word majestic, in the words of scripture the word beauty is used to describe a unique aspect of God's majesty and of his character and actions.

The prophet Zechariah related God's goodness to his beauty. The prophet stated that both God's goodness and his beauty are great. This may be interpreted as meaning that the goodness of God is as great as his beauty. The beauty of God is beyond description and the goodness of God is beyond measure or understanding.

Moses asked Yahweh to reveal his glory. (Exodus 33:18) Moses wanted to see the beauty and glory of Deity. Because Moses had found grace in his sight, Yahweh agreed to reveal a small part of his glory. The fact that God had a personal relationship with Moses is also given as a reason for the revelation of his glory. (Exodus 33:19, 34:5-7) Evidently, Moses did not have words to adequately describe the beauty and majesty that was revealed.

Nevertheless, a revelation of the glory of Yahweh is seen in the beauty of the earth and the shimmering stars of the heavens. The world and all of existence is an expression of the beauty and glory of the Father. (Romans 1:20) In the same way, the existence and beauty of Heaven will be an even greater expression of the beauty of Yahweh and of his son Jesus Christ. Although the beauty of God has been openly displayed on earth, this beauty has not been recognized by everyone. In the kingdom of Heaven God's beauty will be openly displayed and everyone will recognize his beauty.

Just as beauty of light is a natural inherent expression of the existence of Yahweh, the inward beauty of God has been declared to all who are able to see his glory. There is nothing more beautiful than love. The beauty and majesty and glory of the Father is abundantly shown in all that has been created; however, the beauty of his character and nature has been specifically expressed in the gift of grace through his precious son, Jesus the Christ. (2 Corinthians 3:18)

The shimmering beauty of Yahweh has been revealed in his Son who came to share his radiant love. The beauty of the one, who is seated at the right hand of the Majesty in heaven is amazing. (Hebrews 1:3)

Yahweh is beautiful. All that is blessed is beautiful. All gifts from God are beautiful. All that God thinks or plans or accomplishes is alluring, excellent, elegant, lovely, radiant, and magnificent. Yahweh is the magnificent God of splendor and majesty. The light of life is displayed in his gift of creation; and the beautiful light of his love has been offered in his gift of salvation. (Isaiah 52:7)

# 6
# Blessing

The Lord of Host spoke to Moses and told him to have Aaron bless the sons of Israel with a blessing of love and protection. (Numbers 6:22-27)

A blessing is a gift of special favor or benefit. A blessing may be intended to offer praise, appreciation, approval, love, and joy. A blessing may be offered as a reward or as a gift of prosperity and success. A blessing may involve a public declaration of a favored status or given as an act of grace and mercy, and love.

Yahweh is the Father of blessings, of life, liberty, and eternal existence.

A blessing may be given as words of comfort or encouragement, or even as a statement of approval; however, a true blessing requires sincere concern and positive action. When one says to the poor man in need of food or a place to rest, "Go in peace, God bless you." a true blessing has not been offered.

As well, the value and worth of a blessing depends both upon the reason for the gift and upon the one who offers the blessing. For example, a man of honor may bless his children with the benefits of honor. A wealthy yet dishonorable man may offer only the benefits of wealth. Blessings offered by a sovereign Deity of honor and holiness are valuable and worthy.

Yahweh has offered blessings of love to the world. He has also promised to bless those who understand and recognize his authority. (Isaiah 62:1-12) Hannah, the mother of the prophet Samuel, was rewarded because she understood that Yahweh is a God of love and blessings. (1 Samuel 1:17) Hannah was baren but God answered her prayer and allowed her to conceive. After Hannah had given birth to Samuel, she prayed a prayer of thankfulness and offered words of prophecy concerning salvation and protection. (1 Samuel 2:1-10)

Through Abraham, Yahweh offered a blessing to the nation of Israel, to those who are in Zion. (Isaiah 61:1-11) Because Abraham trusted Jehovah, his descendants were given special favor. Israelites, those who are the children of God through Abraham, were given the blessings of the laws of Moses. They were also given an everlasting covenant, and prophecy of a Messiah. (Romans 9:4-5) The historical and chronicle accounts of the children of Abraham include accounts of special blessings of protection, discipline, honor, and loving kindness offered by a God of love.

With words of prophecy, Moses told the children of Abraham that God would circumcise their hearts so that they might love the Lord their God and obey his voice. (Deuteronomy 30:1-20)

Yahweh is also a Deity of spiritual blessings. Yahweh has supreme authority and supreme knowledge, and the power and authority to bestow everlasting spiritual blessings. Like taking five fish and feeding thousands, Yehoshua has chosen to offer the spiritual blessing of sanctification, righteousness, justification, and eternal life to anyone who chooses to be a Christ-one.

In the story of the feeding of the five thousand, Jesus looked up toward heaven and blessed the bread and fish. (Matthew 14:19) This account has not been recorded as a theological lesson about the power of miracles or a lesson about faith, Jesus was teaching that he is the promised Messiah, the bread of life, the one who would be a blessing to the entire world. Jesus is the One who offers the blessing of sanctification and eternal life to anyone who believes that he is the Messiah. (Matthew 16:8-11)

In the story of temptation, the devil challenged Jesus to perform a miracle, to turn stone to bread. The response that Jesus offered included a teaching concerning the blessings of Yahweh. The blessing of life is to understand that the word of God is Jesus Christ. He is our strength and joy of life. He is our daily bread. (Luke 4:3-4) Anyone who desires the bread of life shall be filled. (Luke 6:20-21) Anyone with an open heart, who seeks to know God, will be given the promise of the Holy Spirit. (Matthew 7:7-8)

This gift of eternal life has been promised as a spiritual blessing through Abraham, because Abraham demonstrated faith. (Genesis 12:3) Abraham trusted God, even to the point of being able to offer his own life through his son Isaac, his biological seed, his only son, and his life. Yahweh was pleased because Abraham chose to be a God-one, to give as the Father of Heaven was willing to give. As a blessing from God, Abraham has become the father of many nations and his seed, who is Christ the Messiah, is a blessing to the entire world.

The promise of the blessing was delivered to Abraham by the angel of the Lord, who was instructed to offer the blessing directly from Yahweh. God promised to greatly multiply Abraham's descendants as the stars of the heavens, and as the sand that is on the seashore. All the nations of the earth would be blessed through the faith of Abraham. Yahweh chose to bless Abraham because Abraham believed in the miracle of existence, love, and eternal life. (Genesis 22:15-18)

Years later, Yahweh reminded king David of this promise of blessing. The promise was that the children of Abraham would be as abundant as the stars of heaven. (1 Chronicles 27:23)

In the New Testament, the apostle John recognized that Jesus was the son of David, the seed of Abraham, the one who would be a special blessing for Israel. John recorded a story of the words of Jesus, spoken to a woman of Samaria, to clearly state that this blessing of salvation from God is from the Israelites, the children of Abraham. (John 4:22)

The right to bestow blessings is God's sovereign privilege; however, Yahweh is anxious to bless and not to curse. Because God loved the world, he gave his only son, as a gift of love. Yahweh is anxious to bless those who love him and have faith in him. (Matthew 5:45) This amazing blessing has been offered, with words of comfort and encouragement and worthy actions, as a true complete gift of love by his precious son, Jesus the Messiah. (John 3:16-18)

As well, a unique blessing of joy will be given to those who live by the law of liberty. (James 1:25) This gift of liberty is offered as a blessing of freedom and joy. To follow the law of liberty is to live in the light of love, forgiveness, goodness, and charity. We have been given spiritual life, and the privilege to live in the light of his love that chases away the darkness of evil. (2 Corinthians 4:3-6)

We have been blessed by a God of blessing, for we live in the presence of truth which is the light of righteousness. We know the truth; and truth has set us free to be children of the light of Christ. (Ephesians 5:8-9)

The apostle Paul prayed that we would be given the blessing of knowing the love of Christ, and that we would be filled with all the fullness of God's love. (Ephesians 3:14-21)

Rejoice! I say again, rejoice! (Philippians 4:4)

# 7
# Charity

Charity is the kindness of love. The one who offers charity is not self-centered, selfish, or easily provoked. (1 Corinthians 13:4-5)

Charity is love, expressed with kindness and tolerance. Charity is an act of compassion. Charity is a virtuous act of honoring others.

Yahweh is a God of charity. (Proverbs 19:17) This characteristic of Deity has been demonstrated by many scriptural accounts, in the words of Psalms, and in the teachings of the disciples of Jesus.

According to the laws of Israel, charity is a way to honor God and to be a true child of Abraham. (Romans 2:28-29) A code of honor and respect, that was intended to regulate or guide normal every day social and political interaction, was included in the Laws of Moses. A social order of charity was also established. The citizens of Israel were required to honor God by offering gifts of welfare to those who had fallen into a state of poverty. Foreigners that lived within the cities of Israel, slaves and others with special needs, were to be protected by the Mosaic laws of honor and charity.

According to the rules of social welfare, tithes were to be collected and shared with those in financial distress. This act of charity was required by God so that the nation of Israel would be worthy of his blessings.

(Deuteronomy 15:27-29) As well, the time that a Hebrew citizen could be kept in an absolute state of servitude was limited. (Leviticus 25:39-44)

Additional protections of charity were offered for financial protection of all citizens, and even for the foreigner that resided in Israel. At the end of seven years, the nation was to grant a remission of debts, according to a system of redemption. (Deuteronomy 15:11)

The comment, "for the poor shall never ease out of the land," is often taken out of context and used as an excuse to tolerate the existence of poverty. God has not chosen to accept poverty. Yahweh does not bless or tolerate the existence of poverty. His rule of charity is the opposite of tolerance. Definite action should be taken to alleviate the suffering of poverty or dishonor of social disparity. (Deuteronomy 15:4-8)

Specific instructions are given to the Israelites concerning the poor and others who might be defenseless against economic or legal mistreatment. (Deuteronomy 15:1-18) (Deuteronomy 26:12)

Yahweh, the God of charity, is pleased when those with special needs are protected. Yahweh praised the honorable Job for his acts of charity. (Job 1:8) The story of Job has been offered as an example and testimony concerning Yahweh's expectations of honor, compassion, and charity. (Job 29:1-25) Even when tested by Satan, Job proved to be an outstanding man of honor and charity, a defender of the poor and distressed. (Job 29:14-17) As a blessing, Yahweh rewarded Job for his faith and trust and acts of charity and honor. (Job 42:12-17)

Jesus was greatly concerned about economic situations that would cause lack of social unity. Jesus said that a true act of charity is to give to those who are unable to repay the cost of the gift. (Luke 14:12-14)

The rules for charity that are recorded in scripture should not be labeled as socialism or identified with any political or economic system. The legal requirements for Israel included an uncomplicated plan that provided for limited charity and was not a comprehensive plan for social justice or welfare. According to the rules of charity, although no fellow citizen or foreign worker was to be treated as an economic slave, all residents of Israel were to be treated with respect and love.

John the Baptist was instructed by the word of God that charity should be offered, as an act of repentance. (Luke 3:2, 8-14) A certain tax collector named Zacchaeus was rewarded for his act of repentance and gifts of charity. (Luke 19: 9)

Yahweh is truly a God of charity. Yahweh is thoughtful, considerate, kind, non-judgmental, fair, honest, willing to not consider a wrong, and never openly critical but always willing to offer forgiving grace and love, even to his enemies.

Surely, all of us would prefer to have neighbors, friends, or family members, that are thoughtful, considerate, kind, non-judgmental, willing to forgive, never proud or arrogant or assertive, always honest, willing to avoid arguments, never openly critical but always positive and able to respond with social grace.

Charity and loving kindness should be an identifying characteristic of everyone who has chosen to live as a Christ-one. (Luke 6:27-38) (1 John 4:21) The poor should never be neglected. (James 2:6) We are required to love our enemies and do good to those that hate us. We are to bless those that curse us and pray for those who abuse or dishonor us. Loving kindness requires leniency in judging others or rejecting relationships. Charity is motivated by humility; for humility is part of forbearance. (Philippians 4:5)

The teachings of Jesus should be accepted and followed as an act of love and appreciation to our God of love. (Luke 14:12-14) We are expected to have the same attitude of love that was expressed by Jesus. (Philippians 4:8) "And above all things have fervent charity among yourselves, for charity shall cover the multitude of sins." (1 Peter 4:8)

# 8
# Choice

For mankind, a choice is not an undetermined act of chance. (Proverbs 16:33) This specific aspect of our relationship to God requires an extensive examination.

When presented two or more possibilities, the opportunity or freedom of selection is a choice.

Every decision or physical movement …to select an object, to take a step, to elect a representative, to indicate a preference, to interact with any object or individual is determined by a choice or a reaction. According to Newton's law of physics, for every action there is a response or opposing action. According to the laws of social interaction, every choice includes consequences.

Before a choice can be made, an emotional and intellectual evaluation, or instinctive response is required. The choice or reaction may be made as a matter of necessity, a preference and even by compulsion or deception. Individual choices are determined by mental and physical stimuli that may include cognitive awareness or instinct. However, a choice may also be a completely random decision.

Although a choice may be a simple action, to state that Yahweh is a God of choice is not a simple statement.

A choice may be simple, complex, or complicated. There are often limitations, restrictions, or additional choices to be made for every initial decision or choice that has been made. When physically able, we may choose to climb a mountain, cross a river, or walk through a desert; however, when obstacles are encountered, we may need to take an alternate route or turn around. Freedom of choice, physical, mental, or intellectual, is required before a personal decision can be made.

All such limitations or restrictions do not apply to Yahweh. Yahweh has unrestricted and comprehensive will. He can make any decision or take any action that he wishes or desires. Almighty God has complete freedom or liberty; therefore, he has complete freedom of choice. As well, because his actions are truthful and just, he has no need to seek alternate choices.

In the words of scripture, this sovereign right of choice has been given to the one called "the Truth." A complete theological explanation of this word or concept is as difficult as attempting to describe love or faith. The One, who is Christ, is Truth. Truth provides the freedom of choice; and truth or righteousness justifies the decision.

Although faith is not a simple action of choice, every man must make a choice to accept or to reject the statements made by Jesus. (John 14:6, 8:28-29) Jesus has said that he is the Christ, the Son of man. He is the truth. God as the right to choose to give us eternal life. He has chosen to offer this gift of life through his son, Jesus the Christ. The choice, of accepting the life and freedom that has been offered, must be acknowledged. (John 8:36)

This choice of life and freedom, offered by the living word of God, may be difficult to understand. The reason is related to a limited understanding of our need to be set free. As well, the choice made by God to give mankind the freedom of choice is extremely difficult to comprehend. Although we do not completely understand the reason for this gift of freedom, freedom of choice is a blessing of love.

According to the teachings of scripture our freedom is restricted. We are bound by sinful nature. Even if we believe that we are not separated from God; we live in a world that is afflicted by acts of evil. We do not have complete mental, emotional, physical, or social freedom. We also live in a physical body that cannot be self-sustained, yet we have a desperate need to be free from death. Our choice of having a self-determined life has been taken away by the lack of authority over the social order of the world in which we live, and by the fragile structure and mortality of our human body.

As well, because every decision is determined by authority and ability and presence of mind and spirit, our choices are limited by lack of authority. We are unable to become invisible; therefore, this choice does not exist. We cannot choose to rule the world. We have not been given sovereign authority.

In contrast, Yahweh has all power and authority in heaven and on earth. As well, he is a Deity of truth and freedom. As the God of truth Yahweh can make any choice that he wishes. The accounts of the decisions that Yahweh has made concerning mankind have been abundantly recorded in scripture. Every choice or decision illustrates the power and authority and love of One.

Yahweh may justly alter or reverse any choice or decision. For example, he allowed the tribes of Israel and Judah to be taken into exile and he allowed them to return to Jerusalem. (Ezra 1:1-5) He gave permission to the Chaldeans to defeat Judah and to exile the king of Judah to Babylon. He also chose to remove sovereign authority from Nebuchadnezzar, the great Chaldean king, and to leave him with the cattle in the open fields for seven years, and later to restore the king to a position of honor. As well, he chose to convince king Cyrus that he should choose to honor the Lord God of Israel. (Isaiah 45:1-6, 41:2-4)

The Israelites that were In Babylon were given a choice, to return to Judah or to remain in Babylon. The Father of Israel has also given the children of Abraham the choice of accepting or rejecting the Messiah, the King of kings. (Romans 9:31-33)

Before the world was created, God chose to give man free will. Realistically, when considering the unlimited will of YHWH this freedom is a limited choice. Every decision that mankind is allowed to make has been pre-determined according to the will of God. Nevertheless, mankind has been given the freedom to love and to have faith or to deny the existence of deity and the truth of love. And even when existence of deity is denied, the choice of being worthy or unworthy, wise or foolish, loving or indifferent has been given to every man.

As an anointing and blessing of the Holy Spirit, knowledge or understanding of Yahweh's perfect will was revealed to many prophets and priest and kings, and even to several warriors of Israel. As well, through scripture, knowledge and understanding of Yahweh has been provided so that we are without excuse; for we have been given the freedom to accept the words of the prophets of Israel or to reject their testimony concerning the Almighty.

Because God decided to bless one man, the nation of Israel was chosen. An unknown Chaldean citizen of Ur was anointed with the Holy Spirit because he had faith in God. This is God's sovereign choice, according to his unquestionable will and his supreme authority. He is entitled to any choice that he prefers. For his own personal reasons God has chosen Israel. (Psalm 132:13-18)

Jehovah, the Lord of Hosts, recognized Moses before Moses was born. Although Moses considered himself to be unworthy, and even when Moses proved to be less than a perfect leader, Yahweh admonished and defended Moses. Although the nation of Israel may prove to be less than perfect, Israel will be defended and protected. It is also God's sovereign will for Abraham, and his descendants, to be a blessing to all nations. (Deuteronomy 4:7) Israel has been chosen as a people of inheritance. (Deuteronomy 4:20)

Many statements and events in the chronicles of the Old Testament demonstrate Yahweh's special favor for the nation of Israel. (Psalms 135:4) Yahweh has no need to offer reasons for any decision or the choice that he has made. He is not required to defend his choice of Israel. (Romans 9:4-5)

The reason or reasons for the choice of Abraham are not specifically recorded. In contrast, specific characteristics of honor and worth were recorded for Job, a man in the land of Uz. (Job 1:1) Abraham was not required to meet specific requirements. Abraham was uncircumcised. He was an unknown Chaldean. The reason for the choice was determined by God. (Romans 9:16)

In essence the choice of Abraham does not make Abraham special. (Deuteronomy 7:7) (Matthew 3:9) The choice makes Yahweh an almighty Deity of grace. Nevertheless, the choice does make Abraham a unique chosen one, through whom Jesus is the only special one. (John 4:22) (Romans 1:16)

In the same manner, those who profess faith in Jesus are called chosen ones. However, we are not chosen because we are unique ones; we are chosen by an almighty God of grace and love. (1 Peter 2:9) The apostle Paul was chosen to serve as a unique disciple, but Paul was aware that being chosen did not make him special. (Acts 9:15) (Ephesians 3:8) We who believe are chosen saints, only because we are children of an almighty God of love and grace. (Ephesians 2:8-10)

Because the children of Israel were his own possession, Yahweh chose to defend them against nations that intended to destroy them. The prophet Balaam fully recognized this choice when he attempted to curse Israel by giving a blessing of war to the king of Moab. (Numbers 23:7-10)

Because of lack of proper respect, Moses was not allowed to enter the land that was promised. This was a choice made by Yahweh, who has the authority of choice. However, because God is compassionate, he allowed Moses to view the land from a high place. (Deuteronomy 3:23-27)

Yahweh chose king Saul and anointed him as the sovereign ruler of Israel. (1 Samuel 10:1) Because the people of Israel understood that Yahweh has authority to choose, Saul was accepted as their ruler. Then Jehovah revised the choice, and sovereign authority was removed from Saul. (1 Samuel 14:45) When Saul tried to reason with the prophet Samuel, to convince Yahweh to revise his choice, Samuel informed Saul of one important fact. (1 Samuel 15:9-29) Yahweh is an almighty God; he has no need to revise or alter a choice. He has no need to correct any injustice. Yahweh's decisions are pure and justified and true.

David was chosen as the king of Israel, instead of his brothers, because Yahweh was aware that he had a strong trust in the faithfulness of Yahweh. (1 Samuel 16:13, 17:36-45) Yahweh chose Solomon because he knew that he would prove to be a faithful and capable ruler for the nation of Israel. (1 Chronicles 28:5-7)

Because a choice is an act of free will, God also gave the nation of Israel an unrestricted choice, to accept or reject his blessings. The unrestricted choice that God has offered is a choice of life or death. (Deuteronomy 30:6) The primary requirement for Israel was to love and to obey Yahweh. (Deuteronomy 30:19-20)

Jesus, the Christ, the Messiah, the mediator between God and man, was sent as a gift of love to the chosen of Israel. (Matthew 15:24) When this relationship between Yahweh and Israel is not acknowledged, scripture may be incorrectly interpreted. (Matthew 10:5) Certain passages where Jesus is speaking directly to the children of Israel are often taken out of context and used to teach performance theology. For example, when Jesus told the disciples to allow the little children to come to him, he was referring to Israel as little children. (Mark 10:14) And when he spoke to the wealthy youth and beholding him, loved him, he was expressing love for Israel. (Mark 10:17-22) Because Jesus was speaking and teaching directly to the children of Abraham, such passages should not be interpreted, misapplied, or used as direct teachings concerning religious expectations, or instruction for religious or moral behavior.

However, the good news of the gospel is that because God so loved everyone, he chose to give his love, for us. (John 3:16)

In the same way that Yahweh chose to honor Abraham he has made a pre-determined choice to adopt others into the family of Abraham. (Ephesians 1:4-5) (Romans 9:23-24) The New Testament covenant, the covenant offered by faith in Jesus Christ, provides the same choice, a choice that is directly related to free will. Before any individual can choose between two alternatives, the individual must have the power and authority of free will.

The good news is that Yahweh has given mankind free will, the liberty to choose life or death, freedom or destruction. The gospel has been freely offered; nothing is hidden, so that all will have a free unrestricted choice. Yahweh is truly a God of choice and freedom. God has given everyone a choice to accept the truth and to be set free. (Mark 8:34-36)

Jesus explained the situation by using the parable of the sowing of seeds in an open field. (Mark 4:1-34) (Matthew 13:24-58) The offer of salvation through faith in Jesus Christ is offered, in the same manner that a farmer may sow or broadcast seeds for a planting in a field.

The gospel is also like the light of a lamp. One does not light a lamp and then put the lamp under a large basket, or under a bed. The light is put on the lampstand. Nothing about the gospel has been hidden. The gospel is the revelation of the fact that God is love. (Mark 4:21-23) (Luke 8:8) (John 7:37-39)

According to his perfect sovereign will, God appointed his only begotten Son, Abraham's seed, as the promised Messiah the King of Israel, to be a way of salvation and a gift of life to all man. (Psalm 118:22) Jesus has come as a light unto the world, that whosoever believes should not abide in darkness but will have the light of life. (John 12:43-46)

The gospel is a gift, freely offered, that may be chosen or rejected by anyone. Through Abraham God has chosen to offer a blessing to the entire world. Through Abraham, eternal life has been offered to you, and to all the gentiles of the world. We have been given a choice of being adopted into the family of Abraham.

Jesus offered a parable to the religious leaders to teach them a lesson of choice. (Matthew 21:27-46) He admonished them for not accepting him as the Messiah and offered them a scriptural prophecy concerning the children of Israel. (Matthew 21:42)

The apostle Peter also admonished the Israelites for their lack of understanding. (1 Peter 2:6)

Yahweh has given everyone a choice of life or death. (Matthew 11:26-27) (John 3:14-15) We are challenged to make a right choice. (Psalm 2:10) We must decide to whom the Lord was speaking when he said, "I have set my King upon my holy hill of Zion." (Psalm 2:6-8)

If we decide that this is the nation of Israel, we must accept the fact that the psalmist is stating that the nation of Israel will be the ruler of the entire world. If we decide that the one called the Son is a promised Messiah ben David, a ruling prophet and king of Israel, we must be prepared to give homage to him, for he will have the power of God's wrath.

Perhaps we will be unable to decide or unwilling to choose between the alternatives. Perhaps we should decide that this is only an ancient Hebrew poem, without meaning or importance or consequences for anyone. Whatever we believe, a decision, a personal choice is required. We have been given the physical, mental, and intellectual freedom that is required for a personal choice. Yahweh has given everyone the freedom of accepting or rejecting faith in Jesus Christ.

Even if one decides to not read the Bible, a choice will be made. A choice has been freely offered by a sovereign God; however, this choice requires a response. Yahweh has chosen to offer a blessing of eternal life for the entire world, although we do not deserve his gift of grace. However, every man is free to believe or not believe that Yahweh exist. Every man is free to accept or to reject faith in Jesus Christ.

Yahweh has chosen to require the only possible gift or performance that could be offered to an omnipotent deity that would be worthy of the blessing of eternal life. A choice of faith and trust is required.

The choices that God has made for mankind reveal his reasons or purpose for the world. Jesus came to offer the choice of life and freedom, made by Yahweh. (Luke 8:8)

Of his own free will Yahweh chose the twelve Apostles; he chose Judas; and he chose Matthias. (Acts 1:26) Of his own will he created the kingdom of Heaven. (James 1:18) (1 Peter 2:9-10) As an act of love, God has chosen to set us free from the curse of the law of sin and death, by allowing his Son to be a curse for us. (Galatians 3:13)

Even for those who accept his gift of love, Yahweh has not chosen to take away individual freedom of choice. For those who have chosen to be Christ-ones, the choice to enjoy life has been given. (Philippians 4:4) The choice to be faithful, or to grieve the Holy Spirit has not been taken away. For this reason, the Apostle Paul urges believers to continue to honor the right choice. (Romans 12:1-3)

Yahweh chose king David; and he chose Joseph and Mary. He chose the children of Abraham; and he chose to give his Son as a gift of grace to the world. As well, Yahweh the Almighty One has chosen us, so that we may choose to be a gift of love to others.

# 9

# Comfort

Yahweh is called the Father of mercy and comfort. He comforts us in all our trials and struggles. For this reason, we are expected to offer charity and comfort to others who are suffering. (2 Corinthians 1:3-5)

To comfort is to aide or assist others, to lessen pain, grief, or distress. The intent of comfort is to lessen suffering or to offer encouragement with words of wisdom or actual physical deeds of compassion. To be able to comfort may require empathy, patience, or the ability to expressed compassion without words.

Yahweh joyously offers loving kindness and comfort. (Psalm 34:17-22)

Jesus offered a parable, to a certain lawyer of Israel, as a lesson concerning the importance of loving kindness, for compassion is required by the Laws of Moses. (Luke 10:25-37)

Although many passages of scripture are words of comfort to the children of Abraham, the religious leaders of Israel did not express an understanding the blessing of compassion and loving kindness that had been offered to Israel by Yahweh. (Isaiah 49:14-15) (Zephaniah 3:17) (Psalm 23:1) (Deuteronomy 31:7-8) (Joshua 1:9)

Yahweh has also offered words of wisdom and encouragement to all of mankind. (Ecclesiastes 3:22) (Isaiah 40:31) Therefore, take courage; God is in control of everything. (Ecclesiastes 3:1-22)

God understands the needs of those who are discouraged or broken hearted. (Psalm 147:3) (Matthew 22:30) He is present, to comfort us. (Psalm 23:4) The valley of the shadow of death is a poetic description of our present life on earth, where our true adversary is evil, the enemy of love.

God has chosen to offer blessings of protection and comfort to anyone who will choose to accept his gift of love. (John 16:20) (Matthew 6:25-32, 11:28-30) We are blessed by God's empathy and protection and with the knowledge that he keeps the promises that have been made. (Philippians 4:4-8) (1 Peter 5:6-7)

Jesus prayed to the Father, that the Holy Spirit would be sent as a comforter, with the gifts of peace and freedom. (John 14:16-17) We are comforted in our inner being by the Holy Spirit; for the Spirit is a spirit of comfort. This comfort comes in the form of assurance, the same assurance that a child may have when in the presence of a father. (Hebrews 11:1) (2 Corinthians 4:8-9)

Therefore, we should humble ourselves under the authority of God so that he may exalt us in due time. (1 Peter 5:6-7)

An abundance of comforted has also been offered in the words of scripture. (John 16:33) (1 Thessalonians 5:16-25) (2 Thessalonians 3:5) According to the truth of scripture, the gift of eternal life is the ultimate gift of comfort and peace. (Isaiah 49:10)

We live in a world of travail, with wars and conflicts, poverty, and natural disasters. Yahweh has not chosen to take us out of this world of trials and tribulations; however, he has by the power of the Holy Spirit provided comfort and protection. (Matthew 10:28-29) As well, we have been given the privilege of offering comfort to others; for the privilege of offering comfort to others is part of the requirement to love others as ourselves. (2 Corinthians 1:4)

Although God is so much more than just a God of loving kindness, he is indeed a God of comfort and assurance. (Revelation 7:16-17)

# 10
# Commitment

According to the inspired words of scripture, YHWH is one who keeps his covenant and his loving mercy with those that love him and keep his commandments, to a thousand generations. (Deuteronomy 7:9) This promise was made to the children of Abraham and has been shared with all nations by Jesus Christ.

Commitment is to be devoted or dedicated to a cause, a person, or a relationship. A commitment is a pledge of loyalty, an obligation that must be fulfilled. Synonymous words or actions include dedication, devotion, allegiance, loyalty, faithfulness, fidelity, and unity. A commitment is a voluntary action that establishes an obligation that limits freedom or makes one liable for conduct. The value of any commitment depends upon the ability or worth of the one who has made the promise or pledge. In essence, a commitment is a firm or unaltered choice.

The almighty God, the Father of Abraham, Isaac and Jacob, the God of Israel is a God who makes pledges and promises that are guaranteed by his word. When a covenant is establishes; the agreement is made with an everlasting pledge and with the absolute assurance of a promise. The word of God includes an extensive record or testimony for the firmness and dependability of commitments made by Yahweh.

Yahweh's firm unalterable commitment to Abraham affirms the truth of his promises to mankind. The Almighty, the God of truth, made an

ONE

everlasting commitment to Abraham, to Isaac and to Jacob, and firmly re-established this commitment to Abraham's descendants. This commitment has been reaffirmed many times through the words of prophets and the accounts of scripture.

The commitment made to Israel is an everlasting commitment. Even a strong plea from the king of the Moabites was not able to persuade Yahweh to change his choice. Although king Balak had constructed seven altars of sacrifice, in three different locations, God promised to defend Israel. (Numbers 23:22-23) The prophet Balaam, moved by the spirit of the Lord, also prophesied that Yahweh would bless those who are defenders of Israel. (Numbers 24:9)

As a firm act of commitment, Yahweh established a covenant with Israel, and he required a proper response of honor and respect and acknowledgement of this firm commitment. (Deuteronomy 10:12-13) The primary requirement of the covenant was for Israel to make a firm commitment to love God. (Deuteronomy 1:1) Yahweh reaffirmed this covenant commitment to Israel with a promise. (Deuteronomy 26:18-19) As well, the prophet Samuel reassured the people of Yahweh's commitment. (1 Samuel 12:22) The intent and purpose of this covenant relationship was acknowledged. (Deuteronomy 30:6) As well, the people of Israel understood that they were making a commitment to God. (Deuteronomy 24:9-28)

In the New Testament the apostle Paul affirmed that this commitment was made only to Israel. (Hebrews 8:6-13) However, the apostle Paul also taught that God has made a promise to all who are willing to believe that he is a God of commitment.

The covenant made with those who profess faith in Jesus Christ is called a new covenant. However, this covenant is not a second covenant with a new people. This commitment is the fulfillment of the original covenant made with Abraham. For a second covenant to be made, there would need to be a second Abraham. The covenant made with Moses and David, and the New Covenant are a continuation or fulfillment of the original commitment made to Abraham.

The establishment of a new covenant, or the fulfillment of the original covenant, does not take away blessings that have been given to Israel. The relationship between God and Abraham, and between God and Israel has not been altered or changed. (Romans 3:1-2)

Yahweh's commitment to Abraham was made with a promise of a blessing that is completed in Jesus Christ. This is the primary reason that Jesus was sent only to the house of Israel and not to the Samaritans or to the gentiles. Jesus clearly stated that he was sent only to the lost sheep of the house of Israel. (Matthew 15:24)

The new covenant, the covenant made through faith in Jesus Christ, is a commitment of love that is firm and everlasting, just as every commitment make by the Almighty is firm and everlasting.

Because Yahweh is a God who requires faithfulness, the nation of Israel was required to honor his commitment; and believers in Christ are required to make a similar response, a pledge of honor and love. An insincere commitment will not be accepted. (Luke 9:57-62, 14:25-35)

A sincere, firm and lasting profession of faith is required. This act is a single act of commitment to a loving Christ. This choice is an act of honor to a Father who is love. (Romans 12:1) This is not a commitment to live a life of religious devotion. A simple sincere commitment of faith and love is the only act that is required.

Although Peter affirmed that he would lay down his life for his master, Jesus knew, that without assistance by the power of the Holy Spirit, Peter would deny him. (John 13:37) Jesus is also aware that without the assistance of the Holy Spirit our ability to keep our pledge would be insufficient. After the resurrection, Jesus offered Peter an opportunity for redemption. (John 21:15-17) Jesus was teaching Peter that the strength of commitment is from the Holy Spirit, and the power of commitment is love. Later, God strengthened Peter with the gift of the Holy Spirit, and Peter was allowed to encourage the commitment of other believers. (Acts 2:25-36) (2 Peter 3:4-8)

Although there were individuals and prophets and a few kings that understood the requirements of love to Yahweh, the children of Israel were often unfaithful. (Psalm 78:36-37) The children of Israel thought that religious zeal would enable them to honor their commitment.

As well, Christians will not be able to please God through religious zeal. A commitment of devotion to Christ must be empowered by love. (Luke 14:33) Comfort, encouragement, and assistance from the Holy Spirit is required to accomplish the requirements of faithfulness. Just as the strength of Yahweh's commitment is love, a true commitment to Yahweh must be a pledge of sincere love, empowered by the Holy Spirit, and offered as joyful appreciation for the gift of freedom from the law. (Romans 8:4) A profession of faith must be a firm and faithful commitment. (Luke 14:27) (Matthew 10:38-39) (Luke 9:62) This commitment is not to be a life of spiritual restitution or repayment. (Matthew 11:28-30) This commitment is to be a gift of love offered to others, in the name of Jesus.

Although we may be weak in faith and may struggle to maintain a relationship of love, we can be encouraged by the example of the apostles Paul and Peter, who were able, by the power of the Holy Spirit, to make a humble commitment to God, as a gift of love to Christ. (Ephesians 3:16) (Philippians 1:20-21) The apostles were Christ-ones.

In the same way that a father is pleased when his children are loving and honorable, Yahweh is pleased when we keep our promise of love that has been made to him and to others, for commitment is an expression of love.

Those who keep their commitment of love will share the joy offered by God. (Matthew 25:23)

# 11
# Compassion

Jesus was not sent by God to be a religious ruler of Israel. He came to call Israel to repentance. This was an act of mercy, grace, and compassion. (Matthew 9:13)

Compassion is a unique aspect of love. Compassion is sympathy, kindness, and consideration. Compassion is not only the intent to help but involves actual deeds of assistance and charity. Compassion is the physical evidence of love.

Yahweh is a God of loving kindness. He is a father of mercy, forgiveness, and forbearance. Yahweh is a God of compassion and forgiveness.

God's compassion has been demonstrated in his relationship with the nation of Israel. (Psalm 106:44-46) Yahweh has declared that although the children of Abraham have been unfaithful, his loving kindness will never be withdrawn. (Psalm 145:7-9, 78:32-37)

Yahweh is a gracious and compassionate God. (Nehemiah 9:30-31)

In several New Testament accounts Jesus acknowledged the compassion that Yahweh offered to Israel. At the pool of Bethesda several of the afflicted were lying beneath the five porches; but Jesus chose a man who had been waiting for thirty-eight years. (John 5:1-15) In the same way, Yahweh had chosen Israel, a people who had been waiting for many years for a Messiah. And Jesus said to the afflicted, and to the nation of Israel, "Rise and take up your bed, and walk." (John 5:8)

Jesus went up to Jerusalem, the city in which the prophets had been killed. And when he was near, he observed the city and wept over it. (Luke 19:41)

Jesus also stood before the tomb that held his beloved friend Lazarus. Jesus wept for Lazarus, for the children of Abraham, and for you and me. Jesus has the power and authority to command anyone to stand and walk, or to come forth from a prison of death. Yahweh has chosen, as an act of compassion, to heal the sick and lame, to give eternal life to mankind.

Yahweh has expressed compassion, not just for the children of Abraham, but for all of mankind. The gift of his one and only Son is an awesome act of benevolence. This is a gift of loving consideration that has been offered to Israel and to us. Jesus died for the world, the children of his creation. Emmanuel, "God with us," has been able to express empathy because he completely understands our suffering. (Psalm 68:5-6, 72:12-14, 103:8-14)

The Lord of lords and the King of kings has compassion, even for those who do not believe in him. (Matthew 5:43-48) His compassion is expressed as amazing perfect love.

As Christ-ones, we are commanded to be non-judgmental and compassionate to all men. (Luke 10:29-37) In this way, Yahweh intends to use us to express acceptance and concern to those who doubt his love. Love requires forgiveness and understanding and compassion that is to be offered not only for believers but for all of mankind. We must not receive the grace of God in vain; we are to be servants of God. We must be prepared to use the weapons of righteousness and compassion, to bring honor and glory to our God of sincere love. (2 Corinthians 6:1-8)

Jesus offered clear instructions for loving kindness in the parable of the returning King. (Matthew 25:40) In the say way, we are required to express love to all men. (1 John 3:16-18) We have been commanded by our God of compassion to offer non-judgmental empathy to fellow believers.

(1 Peter 3:8) We have been commanded to have compassion on some who are doubting, or unfaithful. (Jude 1:22-23)

We are to love as God loved and to have compassion on all men; for Yahweh is a God of righteous compassion, forgiveness, and grace.

# 12

# Covenant

Yahweh is a God of commitment, and he is a God of covenant. He is faithful, and He is love. He keeps his commitments of love and mercy forever. (Deuteronomy 87:9) (Psalm 144:15)

A covenant is an agreement that is binding on all parties or participants that have made pledges of commitment. A covenant may be defined as a formal and legal commitment, as a binding contract that includes both promises and pledges with stated consequences for a breach of agreement or commitment. A covenant may be made by words of honor between friends; or a covenant may be a binding legal agreement as though written in tablets of stone.

A beautiful, amazing, wonderful relationship has been established by the fact that Yahweh has chosen to make a covenant, a pledge of love with mankind. In much the same way that a pledge of love brings assurance, comfort and joy are magnified when we understand that God has made a firm promise to mankind.

Making a covenant is an act of honor, and keeping a covenant is an act of integrity. As well, making a covenant of love, requires a commitment of love.

Yahweh made a covenant promise with Adam and Eve. He made a covenant with Noah; and God made a covenant of faith with Abram, an uncircumcised Chaldean. (Genesis 12:1-2) By establishing a covenant with Abram, God committed his honor, worth and name and his love. According to his own free will, for reasons that he preordained, Yahweh established the covenant with Abraham, with his son Isaac, and Isaac's son Jacob, the fathers of King David, the king of Israel. This was an everlasting covenant. (Genesis 17:7) Yahweh testified, with his own words, that the covenant would be an everlasting commitment. (Psalm 89:1-5)

This covenant was a firm commitment by a sovereign Deity clearly stated with specific promises and requirements for a proper relationship. (Deuteronomy 5:1-22) Other requirements, including the Sabbath, were given as a blessing to the people. These requirements were designed to establish a system of honor and love for social unity. The first commandment, the requirement of love for God was restated in a different way. (Deuteronomy 6:4-5)

Moreover, this was an unconditional commitment of love, by the One who cannot be untruthful or unfaithful. Yahweh has clearly declared that this covenant would not be violated, and the words of commitment would not be altered. (Psalm 89:30-37) In the words of a song, king David praised God for his loving kindness and faithfulness; and by the spirit of the Lord, the king prophesied concerning the God of Israel, the rock of Israel and the light of the morning, who had made an everlasting covenant with king David and the house of Israel. (2 Samuel 22:1-23:5) The covenant also included the adopted children of Abraham who were to be grafted into the tree of life. (Romans 11:17)

The covenant with Abraham is a covenant of love; however, the covenant was not faultless. The laws of the covenant were written in tablets of stone; however, the children of Abraham did not write them in their hearts. Yahweh was aware that the children of Abraham would not be able to keep the law. A mediator, one that would be able to establish a better covenant, a renewed covenant of love and forgiveness that was to be a fulfillment of the original covenant, would be required. This new covenant is not a replacement of the old covenant. (Romans 11:1-2) An explanation of the majesty of this new covenant, made with the house of Israel, was given by the writer of Hebrews. (Hebrews 8:6-12)

This covenant promise has been given to Israel by the sovereign Authority of heaven and earth. Yahweh is the One who is allowed make a covenant or to show mercy to whomever he has chosen. (Romans 9:15-16)

The authority and guarantee of this new covenant will be placed within the hearts of the children of Israel by the power of the Holy Spirit. This is a blessing of love and mercy to the house of Israel. (Ezekiel 36:26)

Jesus is the priest, the sacrifice, the mediator, and the redemption of the New Testament. (Hebrews 9:15-16) As an act of love and grace this new covenant has also been offered to the gentiles, to all who believe the word of God.

As a fulfillment of the covenant given to Israel, as a blessing to Israel and to the world that he created, God has also chosen to extend or to share this new covenant with the ones who have faith in the words of the King of Israel, a king like king David, the One known as Emanuel, the King of kings and Lord of lords. By becoming participants of the original covenant, those who have professed faith in Jesus have been adopted as children into the family of God, as though they have been grafted into the tree of life. Yahweh has, in like manner, put his Spirit within the hearts of those who believe, who profess faith in Jesus Christ. (Hebrews 10:16-17) Those who believe are sealed with the Holy Spirit, as a down payment of this covenant. (Luke 22:19-20)

Although amazingly different, the new covenant is a fulfillment of the original covenant made with Abraham and promised to his descendants. (Genesis 17:7) This new covenant, a covenant of faith and mercy is a better covenant, a covenant that by fulfilling the requirements of the original covenant has made the first obsolete. (Hebrews 8:6-13, 9:1-28)

Although the new covenant is not a founded upon laws, the covenant does include specifically stated requirements and expectations. (Romans 12:1-21) The new covenant is based upon the truth of love, compassion, and grace. (Matthew 9:13) (Deuteronomy 6:4) The new covenant is a gift of grace, from the One who is Lovem, to those who do not deserve the gift of life.

The new covenant has been made with a firm promise, a sovereign commitment of love, offered as a gift of grace by the Almighty who is a God of covenant and commitment. (2 Corinthians 5:1)

# 13
# Creation

The heavens and the earth declare the glory of creation. (Psalm 19:1-4)

Creation is the action or process of bringing something into existence. As an action of creation something is produced out of nothing or something valuable is created out of what exist. Creation implies the use of design, formation, order, and purpose. As well, our present existence of order and design strongly implies the use of intelligence and purpose in the process of creation.

The originator, or any spontaneous action of creation, would be the agent of determination of the value and purpose of whatever is brought into existence. Any identified first cause of a sustainable existence would require the power or authority to predetermine the state of existence. In any situation of creation, evolution, or alteration of matter, if or when the first cause does not have "the power and authority to predetermine the state of existence" that which is created or established will exist in a state of disorder or chaos. The existence of sustainable life, order and stability, and the existence of love, are evidence of the existence of a creator with the power and authority to predetermine or design our present creation.

Awareness of existence is not possible without life. Life is the primary evidence of existence. The probability that the beginning of life was caused by physical interaction of material objects or by chemical or electrical interaction is less than zero. As well, the existence of our present universe depends upon uniform laws of physics. Although the first cause of this order and mathematical precision is unexplained, the requirement of predetermined design is obvious.

Light, gravity, atoms, and DNA did not come into existence by an explosion in outer space. The evil of hate did not originate as a natural consequence of evolution or insufficient development. The universal biological need for reproduction and preservation did not originate as a chemical, biological, or evolutionary process. The presence of love is not a miracle of a cosmological expansion of chemical elements. Love is the presence of Deity. As well, the presence of evil, the enemy of love, was not created or established as a process of evolution. Evil, darkness, and destruction exist only in the absence of love, light, and life.

As a reasonable choice, based upon logic and scientific fact, and by faith, every believer chooses to believe that Yahweh, the God of Abraham, Isaac, and Jacob, the One true God of Israel created mankind, the earth, and the universe. (Romans 1:20)

As believers, we trust the words of Scripture, we accept God's word by faith, and we believe in our heart that God created the world. According to his word of truth, a cornerstone firmly set in place, we believe that Yahweh is the God of creation.

The Lord God made the earth and the heavens. (Genesis 2:4) (Hebrews 3:4, 11:3) (Colossians 1:16-17) (Psalm 33:6-9, 104: 5-9)

The order of One made the world by the Word, the Son, our Lord and Master, the one called Yehoshua, the Christ, Yahweh with us, the Savior of this created world.

The order of One created everything for himself. The Lord has made all things for himself, even the wicked for the day of evil. (Proverbs 16:4) All that God created is valuable. (1 Timothy 4:4) Yahweh is the God of creation; and everything created is beautiful, functional, and intricately designed. All has been created according to his design and for his purpose. (Psalm 24:1-2)

YHWH not only created the earth; he is in complete control of what has been created. He alone has the right to create or destroy, to eliminate or to recreate. Yahweh created the heavens and earth in a natural state. Then he created humans in his likeness, male and female, to rule over the earth. With this creation he gave mankind the ability to love. With the ability to love, he gave the right to choose good or evil. Adam and Eve made an unnatural choice, and the destiny of mankind was altered. The presence of evil, the enemy of love was introduced into a wonderful natural creation. The story of love and evil is not the story of creation. The story of love and evil is the story of mercy and forgiveness. (2 Peter 3:12-13)

Be still and know that I am God. (Psalm 46:10)

# 14
# Defender

The protection offered by God is described as a fortress or stronghold where refuge can be taken. (Psalm 144:1-2)

An act of defense is action taken to prevent or to delay harm to one that requires assistance.

The actions of defense and aggression may appear to be similar; however, the actions are completely different. The difference between vengeance and revenge is also obvious.

An act of defense may be a planned act of prevention of harm or a spontaneous action of protection. In contrast, the basic intent of revenge is to obtain just or unjust compensation for an injury, insult or assumed harm. To retaliate, to punish, regardless of whether the act is justified, would be an act of revenge. Although an act to avenge could be compensation for injustice, God has not offered any form of aggression as a means of defense.

God has no need to defend his righteousness, and he has no need to retaliate with harmful actions. As well, although he has a strong desire to establish justice, Yahweh is not a God of vengeance.

One of the best know biblical accounts concerning protection for Israel is the story of David and the Philistines. Yahweh used an ordinary youth to demonstrate his commitment to the nation of Israel. (1 Samuel 17:1-58) Yahweh defended Israel so that all would know that there is a God in Israel. (1 Samuel 17:46)

The account offered by king David is a testimony of Yahweh's defense of Israel. (2 Samuel 22:1-51) These words of a song are records of military defense and are also words of prophecy concerning the covenant promise to the nation of Israel. This passage of scripture is also a prophecy of salvation from evil which is death and destruction. (2 Samuel 22:51)

Many of the writers of the Psalms are obvious defenders of God's righteousness. Their judgmental attitude toward the wicked often seems to be contrary to the basic principles of love and forgiveness that are central aspects of God's character. These writers seem to fail to understand that Yahweh has no need for revenge. (Psalm 68:1-3)

God's judgment against the enemies of Israel has at time been severe; however, his judgment against nations that were used, in the hands of God, to bring judgment against Israel and Judah has at times been delayed. Evidently, God did not need to retaliate or to bring swift judgment upon these nations. Nevertheless, all nations and individuals will reap the consequences for their actions; for all nations will be righteously judged. Yahweh is patient and compassionate; however, he is also willing and able to avenge injustice.

Yahweh is a God of loving-kindness; but he also requires justice. He is a defender of the poor, the afflicted, and all who are defenseless. (Psalm 140:12-13) God is a loving defender of those who may be weak in faith yet still have faith in him. (Romans 8:31-32)

Yahweh is truly a guardian of those that he loves; however, his defense for the disciples of Jesus Christ is somewhat different than expected.

(Matthew 10:28) Although defense against evil is offered as a promise, defense for the Christian is not necessarily protection from harm or from death. (2 Thessalonians 3:3) As well, protection from the one who is roaming about the earth is directly related to spiritual awareness and wisdom. (Job 1:7) (Ephesians 6:10-18)

According to the words of scriptural prophecy, there will be a time of persecution in which the children of Israel and believers will require spiritual protection or defense from evil. Although the prophecy is about "fearful sights and great signs," assurance has been offered that we will be protected by God. (Luke 21:10-15)

Specific accounts or times for the need for protection from evil have not been offered; however, assurance of defense has been given as a promise by the one who has all power and authority. (Matthew 28:18-20)

Although we live in this world of shadows of death, we will fear no evil, for Yahweh is with us, and he is a God of commitment and protection. (Psalm 23) We have been promised protection by the power of the Holy Spirit. Our defense is faith; and our faith is strengthened by the power of the Holy Spirit. By faith, we humbly declare with the Apostle Paul that we know that God is love, and we are persuaded that he will keep his promises to us. (2 Timothy 1:12)

# 15
# Discipline

Yahweh is the Father of Israel. Yahweh disciplines those that he loves, in the same way that a worthy father instructs or disciplines his children. (Proverbs 3:11-12)

Discipline is to have knowledge or understanding obtained by a controlled process of study or training. To be disciplined is to obey rules or follow a code of conduct. To be disciplined is to be in control of actions and emotions.

The word discipline may have different definitions and may be used in different context or for contrasting purposes. The intent of the word is also altered when used as a verb, noun, or adjective form.

To be disciplined is to be mentally alert, mentally prepared, and emotionally stable. When used to describe an action of training or correction, discipline is a practice of training in the ability to obey rules or a code of conduct. Discipline, as training or correction, may include encouragement or punishment, that may be used to prevent disobedience or to correct traits of character. To be disciplined means that one can control actions or behavior, or that one is self-disciplined. One who has been disciplined or trained may be referred to as a disciple of the training or the code of behavior, or of the program of the one who controlled the process of discipline. The ultimate positive goal of discipline training is for the one who is instructed to be self-disciplined.

Because lack of discipline implies the absence of control or proper function, corrective discipline may be a necessity. For example, when a father neglects to discipline his children, he has failed to love or to honor his children. The obligation of a worthy father is to teach his children to be self-disciplined. As the Father of Israel, God disciplines his children with strict discipline, but always with loving-kindness. His desire for Israel is for his children to be self-disciplined. As well, the Holy Spirit's goal of discipline is for the disciples of Christ to be self-motivated. However, the most important aspect of spiritual discipline is for the disciple to be motivated by love. (Hebrews 12:5-8)

Teachings or descriptions concerning Yahweh's discipline are abundantly offered in scripture. The need for positive chastisement is expressed in the explanation given to the nation of Israel for their time of testing and discipline. (Deuteronomy 8:2-6) Yahweh guided and encouraged the Israelites with instructions of wisdom and gentle warnings offered through anointed prophets. (Deuteronomy 13:1-4)

Discipline may be offered as harsh correction, persuasion, admonishment, or encouragement; however, Yahweh's discipline is always just, honorable, and acceptable. (Hebrews 12:5-11)

Discipline is a blessing. Discipline is strength. To be self-disciplined is to have wisdom. (Proverbs 12:1) Discipline is not to be controlled by fear. God has not given Christ-ones the spirit of fear. We have been given the power and strength of love.

(2 Timothy 1:7) We can be thankful that discipline is an act of grace. (Psalm 106:1-48) (Job 5:17-18)

The story of Job teaches a lesson of Yahweh's honor, discipline, and love. This account about an honorable man is an illustration and verbal testimony of Yahweh's compassionate relationship to the world that he has created. His love is never separated from discipline; his discipline is never offered without love. The fear of the Lord is the beginning of wisdom and wisdom is never without honor and love.

Yahweh has spoken through prophets, such as Malachi, both to warn the people of Israel concerning lack of honor, obedience, or faithfulness, and to clearly declare his love for Israel. (Malachi 1:2)

As a matter of wisdom and honor a worthy father's actions should seldom be questioned. Acceptance of discipline is a matter of honor and respect. (Malachi 1:6)

When disrespect has been expressed, honorable discipline is required. God never hesitates to discipline; for lack of discipline is lack of love. (1 Corinthians 11:32)

Yahweh offers correction and guidance and discipline through corrective teachings of scripture. All scripture, written by inspiration of God, is useful for doctrine, reproof, correction, or instruction in righteousness, so that we may be prepared for acts of love to others. (2 Timothy 3:16-17)

The Lord admonishes us, so that we might be partakers of his holiness. In other words, he corrects us for our own benefit, and to make us a blessing to others. He does not discipline for his own benefit or to defend his righteousness. As well, we are not disciplined so that we might live for Jesus; we are to live with Jesus. (Matthew 1:29-30) To be yoked with Jesus, is to bear the burdens of others with him. We may state that we are "living for Jesus" but we are actually living for others. (Matthew 10:42)

The apostle Paul explained the blessings of discipline. Discipline or sufferings are temporary. Blessings will be everlasting. (2 Corinthians 4:17-18)

The apostle Paul also offered inspiration to his young friend Timothy concerning endurance and acceptance of discipline. The apostle Paul, the assumed author of Hebrews, also sent a letter of encouragement or exhortation to other brothers in Christ. Although the entire passage (Hebrews 12:1-12) is worthy of reflection or study, several thoughts are especially encouraging. (Hebrews 12:3)

A basic rule of life, concerning discipline, is that discipline is not required for the one who is self-disciplined. As well, we are not disciplined for righteousness, or for any religious reason; we are disciplined so that we might be worthy instruments of love for others. We should praise God and be thankful that Yahweh is a God of discipline; for to be disciplined as a Christ-one is profitable, valuable for this life and for eternity.

The discipline given by the Holy Spirit is not offered as a difficult program of religious performance. The discipline required is simple and easy. Our burden is light. (Matthew 11:28-30) We who have professed faith in Jesus Christ are encouraged to rejoice, pray, and give thanks; for this is the will of God for us. (1 Thessalonians 5:16-24) To be a disciplined Christ-one is to live a life of freedom in the light of the beauty of love. (John 8:32) We are forgiven. We have been set free to let the light of Christ shine in a world of evil. (2 Corinthians 4:3-5) As children of light we live by the law of liberty, free from religious restrictions or principles of men. (Ephesians 5:8-9) We are free to be what God originally intended for mankind to be.

To live as a Christ-one is profitable for the present life and for the life to come. (1 Timothy 4:6-8)

## 16
## Empathy

God is the one who does many unsearchable marvelous things. (Job 5:9-27)

Empathy is understanding, compassion, identifying, feeling, involvement, and lack of indifference. The one who expresses empathy must be able to understand the thoughts and emotions, fears or regrets, and the pain of the one who needs compassion, kindness, or forgiveness.

Although empathy is an expression of love, empathy is an unexpected aspect of the transcendent nature of Deity.

Theological questions concerning the true nature of deity are indeed interesting; however, our task is not to debate theological questions or to determine the limits or restrictions of the character of Deity. In scripture, human descriptions are used to express both the nature and character, actions and responses of Yahweh. Having been created in the image of God, we share a sense of justice, love, knowledge, truth, and faith. (Genesis 1:27) In essence, the honest way to truly understand or appreciate Yahweh is to be able to understand the true character and nature of human beings. (Proverbs 2:1-10)

We would expect an omnipotent deity to be a God of light and beauty, knowledge, and awareness; however, should we expect Yahweh to be a God of forgiveness? Would empathy be our first thought about his character? Surely, we should not be judged for wondering why the Almighty would choose to have empathy for imperfect human beings. The primary reason for such doubt is most likely that we know that a personal relationship is required to understand fears or regrets or pain that may be experienced by other individuals.

The answer to this complicated situation is to be found within the simple statement that God is Love. Yahweh is more than a magnificent sovereign creator or an omnipotent power, his existence is fulfilled and completed by the presence of faith and hope and love. Empathy is basically an open expression of love. As One that is Love, the Father of Heaven and the Son of man express empathy. The Christ, who is called the Advocate with the Father, is the one who intercedes for us with the Father. (1 John 2:1)

Simply stated, Yahweh is a God of empathy because he is Love.

The author and date of the unique book of Job is unknown. The first verse or sentence is a simple introduction of Job. "There was a man in the land of Uz, whose name was Job: and that man was perfect and upright, and one that feared God, and eschewed evil." (Job 1:1) Nevertheless, the Book of Job is a story about Yahweh. The account could have been correctly titled The Book of Yahweh, for the central character of the account is Yahweh. Although this story is a presentation concerning the authority of Deity, the account also includes a lesson concerning empathy. The statements made by the participants of the story, as well as the responses made by Yahweh, are primarily lessons of discipline and honor. Within these instructions, a teaching of empathy has been provided.

The story of Job is an account of Yahweh's interaction with an honorable man, known for deeds of honor. Because Yahweh has chosen to use Job as an object lesson to illustrate love, honor, and empathy, the evil one called Satan is allowed to tempt and to test Job's honor, loyalty, and love for God.

While Job suffers from the afflictions that are placed upon him, his friends confront Job concerning his relationship to Yahweh. Obviously, these associates do not realize that they, as well as Satan the evil one, are being tested by God. As shown by actions and comments, their lack of empathy is quite evident. These scholars obviously understood that Yahweh is the Almighty; however, they seemed to have been unable to comprehend that Yahweh is also a God of empathy. Obviously anxious to emphasize the fact that God is omnipotent, one who does great things without number, these men of wisdom fail to properly consider the human-like nature of deity.

This religious emphasis upon the holiness of God and upon what God requires is evident today among many disciples of several different faiths who have read the scriptures and have decided to follow God's will. However, as we honor God, we must not fail to honor our brothers in faith, and our enemies as well. This is the lesson of empathy that is found within the character of a loving Father. Honoring others by offering understanding, compassion, feeling, involvement, and lack of indifference is a specific requirement of living in the light of love.

Job's friends compassionately gathered to pray with Job, to counsel with him, to express concern about his tragedy; however, they failed to offer actual empathy. Because their primary concern was to defend God, the faithful friends were unable to recognize their lack of compassion. Even when Job, who was more righteous, openly expressed a need for understanding, their failure to offer empathy was obvious. Job noted that true friends should offer pity, so that the one who is suffering would not forsake the fear of the Almighty. (Job 6:14) Instead of loving concern and emotional support, his friends legalistically offered admonishment and advice for proper religious performance.

Job described his friends as miserable comforters with vain words. They had failed to offer sympathy with actions and words, to ease the grief and suffering of their friend who was in desperate need of comfort. (Job 16:4-6) Because his friends had chosen to admonish, rather than to comfort, Job's suffering was multiplied or increased. (Job 16:20)

As a faithful servant of the Living God, Job was willing to rejoice in suffering and would not deny the words of the Holy One. Job understood that Yahweh is a God of justice; and he also knew that Yahweh understood his need for empathy. (Job 6:10) (Job 7:11) Although Job was being tortured in flesh and spirit, he believed that the Lord is a God of mercy. (Job 7:17-20)

Then Bildad the Shuhite, offered his words, to acknowledge that everyone knows that the Lord is compassionate, at least to those who are pure and upright. (Job 8:5-7) And Zophar the Naamathite agreed with this concept of prosperity theology. (Job 11:13-19)

An assumption that we will find favor and will be directly rewarded for good deeds, or that rewards are directly offered by God for spiritual performance, is the basic error of the teachings of performance theology. Such religious performance causes believers to be judgmental. As well, an inability to accurately judge oneself can result in self-righteousness. Such action is a definite way to grieve the Holy Spirit. For example, when Job continued to offer defense, his friends became resentful and angry. They agreed that Job must be guilty, for he was being treated the same as the wicked should be treated. (Job 18:1-21)

Job continued to plead for understanding, for a small measure of sincere compassion, but his friends were unable to offer empathy. Yahweh was not pleased. (Job 19:18-22) God does not require compassion as an obligation to the law; compassion is required because we are to be disciples of love. Having been made righteous by the Holy Spirit within us, we have no excuse when we are not compassionate. A believer may be able to quote scripture, live a morally righteous life, tithe and attend a worship service every week and be called a faithful Christian, but religious performance is useless if empathy is not understood and accepted. Yahweh requires compassion that is from the heart. He requires all works, or good deeds to be actions from the heart.

Faith without works is dead. Works without faith is worthless. Love without empathy is not worthy love.

The lesson of the Book of Yahweh is that only God, a God of empathy, is holy and righteous. The believer does not earn the gift of righteousness; does not deserve the gift and will not be rewarded for receiving the gift of righteousness. Our reward is eternal life; nothing more and nothing less. Of course, this everlasting life, this new life in Christ does include present and future blessings of love and peace and hope. The believer's state of blamelessness, having been justified and sanctified by the Holy Spirit is a gift of God's grace; therefore, righteousness has not been, and cannot be, obtained by moral, religious, or spiritual performance. Without love, any action, thought or deed, religious or non-religious, becomes worthless. As well, even an act of love that is not of oneself, is not worthy of being rewarded. This is a truth that the honorable Job clearly understood. (Job 9:20) Even Eliphaz scornfully reminded Job that even if a man is perfect in all his ways, this does not offer pleasure or profit to God. (Job 22:3-4)

As Jesus taught the disciples about the Kingdom of Heaven, he was teaching them about their relationship to others and about every man's relationship to the Heavenly Father. In every account, with patience and compassion, empathy is expressed. When the disciples lacked faith, his words expressed frustration, but his actions showed compassion and empathy. (Matthew 17:16-18)

In several accounts Jesus expressed empathy for the children of Israel. (Luke 5:12-13) (John 11:35) (Luke 19:41) And Jesus was especially pleased when one believer expressed empathy, that was offered to Jesus. One day when Jesus was sharing a meal in the house of Simon the leper, a woman, brought a box of precious ointment and poured it on Jesus. Jesus said that this act of empathy would be a lasting honor for her. (Matthew 26:6-13)

Jesus was also pleased when a criminal was willing to expressed empathy.

And Jesus rewarded him for his act of empathy and faith. (Luke 23:39-43)

God requires his disciples to be compassionate and understanding and non-judgmental, even to their enemies. Acts of love must be works of love and not merely words of sympathy. (1 John 3:16-18)

Hope is God's gift of empathy to believers. And these three remain: faith, hope and love. (1 Corinthians 13:13) Yahweh is truly a God of empathy. He is pleased when we are truly Christ-ones, when we are compassionately involved with others, willing and able to meet their needs.

Yahweh is a divine being of light and beauty, knowledge, and awareness; and he is an amazing sovereign Deity that is allowed to express empathy. For God felt such empathy, for those in need, he gave his only son as a sacrifice, as a gift of love, for eternal life, to a lost world. (John 3:16-17)

# 17
# Eternal

For Yahweh, time is eternal. (Psalm 90:4) All of creation may pass away, but Yahweh will remain, his days will never end. (Psalm 102: 25-27)

The meaning of the word eternal is to be lasting or existing forever, without end or beginning.

By faith, we believe that Yahweh is eternal, everlasting with no beginning and no end. Yahweh is the life that gives meaning to time. Yahweh is also the life that gives meaning to the existence of Heaven and earth.

Before anything can be eternal, the anything must exist, in a state of time. Time is defined as the indefinite or unaltered continued progress of existence. Time is also identified as a state of existence in the past, present, and future. A state of eternity implies that for anything to be eternal the anything must never, at any point of time, become nonexistent. Everlasting life is the essence of eternity.

Without intelligent life, awareness of time or existence would not be present. Without awareness of existence, eternity would have no meaning or purpose. A distant planet may be everlasting in time; however, eternal existence without life has no true meaning. Existence without life and light is meaningless. Existence without life is an absolute zero.

A basic explanation of eternity is all that can truly be understood about eternity. Although we may define and debate the possibility of eternity, an actual understanding of eternity lies within the realm of the unknowable, for we are unable to accurately scientifically explain that which we are unable to experience. Therefore, because we are not able to experience eternity, a state of eternity must be accepted by faith. As well, without knowledge or understanding, the fact that Yahweh is eternal and has everlasting life, must be accepted by faith.

We, who are disciples of Christ, believe that Yahweh and Yehoshua and the Holy Spirit, as the One who is I AM, is an eternal divine Deity who has the power and authority to give eternal life to anyone who believes that he exists and that he is willing to reward those who believe in him. We who believe in the existence of eternity, are those who are being spiritually born again, by the Word of God, which lives and abides forever. (1 Peter 1:22-23)

Eternal life is a gift of Jehovah through Yehoshua the Christ our Lord. (Romans 6:23) Faith in Jesus Christ offers a state of existence that will last forever. (Isaiah 51:6)

A small group of Sadducees, who believed that there is no resurrection, came to Jesus and began questioning him. As a test of scriptural interpretation, the religious leaders proposed a difficult theological question concerning marriage relationship in heaven. Jesus answered by reminding the scribes that God resides in a state of eternity. Jehovah is not the God of the dead; he is the God of the living. (Mark 12:18-27)

When God said to Moses, "I am that I am, and I will be what I will be," he was saying, "I am Everlasting. I have always existed. I am present now and I will be with you in eternity."

Yahweh understood that man would never be able to discover the scientific knowledge that would be required to understand the state of eternity. As well, the One who created the universe knew that we would never have enough knowledge of this world and of existence to be worthy of establishing eternal life. He understood that knowledge was not the answer of salvation for mankind. Because Yahweh knew that the knowledge and awareness of eternity lies within unsearchable or unknowable wisdom, he decided that acceptance of the reality of eternity must be established by faith rather than by knowledge or awareness. Because our power of faith is weak, the only alternative was for Yahweh to offer strengthened spiritual faith through the power of the Holy Spirit. (Matthew 5:3)

For those who believe, the good news about faith is that because Yahweh is the everlasting Father, he has the right to bless those who believe in him with eternal life.

Yahweh is our God of eternity. His word is the living and eternal word of life.

(1 Peter 1:22-23) He is the King eternal, immortal, invisible, the only God. He deserves to be honored and praised forever and ever. (1 Timothy 1:17)


# 18
# Existence

In the beginning the earth was created by or through Jesus, because he had the power and authority of life. (Genesis 1:1) (John 1:1-4)

Existence is a state of having objective reality, to be alive or to be active.

Yahweh said to Moses, "I am, and I will exist." (Exodus 4:14)

A logical state of reality is established by the fact that we are alive. Therefore, life is a state of awareness of existence. However, the essence or purpose of existence, cannot be adequately explained by the simple statement, I am alive.

The purpose of existence within a world or universe that came into existence in a spontaneous or chaotic fashion would not be identifiable.

In contrast, existence in the presence of Yahweh provides meaning and purpose for life; and our present existence establishes the presence of everlasting life. Yahweh is the One who gives meaning and purpose to existence. (John 1:4)

Therefore, Yahweh is the One of existence. Yahweh is the I Am, the one and only Deity of existence. (Colossians 1:16) Everything, in our existence, was created by and through the One who is the Son of God. (John 1:3-4)

The beginning of existence for mankind has been recorded in the beautiful words of scripture. The account of creation is simple and complex, magnificent and beautiful, and full of light and love. (Genesis 1:1-3)

Yahweh, our God of order and purpose, designed an amazing world, and placed man and woman, made in his image, in this amazing world of objective reality, to be alive, to live, and to love.

## 19
## Faith

The one who wishes to understand Deity must believe that Yahweh is the one and only Deity. We must believe that God is love. (Hebrews 11:6)

This statement of scripture clearly establishes Yahweh as a God of faith. Faith is trust or confidence in something or someone. Spiritual faith is belief and trust in God.

A complete explanation of faith or adequate defense of the requirements of faith is not possible in a brief presentation; therefore, the following comments concerning faith are offered as simple statements, without complete theological explanations.

Yahweh is a God of faith.

This truth is one of the most amazing aspects of the character of Deity. Yahweh is a God of faith, hope, and love. Although the greatest is love, faith is one of the greatest aspects of Deity. Faith can only be explained by making statements about faith.

For mankind, faith is a simple yet complicated action that requires knowledge and understanding. An act of faith also involves emotion and will. Therefore, one would assume that when absolute proof of what must be believed is provided, trust or confidence is not required; however, the acceptance of truth or reality always requires trust. Although trust is required, the reason for trust or confidence does not need to be completely understood. The required assurance may be offered without complete understanding. (Job 19:18-22)

An absolute understanding of faith is not possible. Faith is too complicated to be completely understood. Faith is even the substance of miracles. (Matthew 17:20) (Mark 12:24) The apostle Paul offered an extensive historical record of the relationship of faith and miracles. (Hebrews 11:1-40) Faith is also an amazing gift of love from God.

The miracles of spiritual faith are demonstrated by the actions are deeds of Yahweh; however, the amazing deeds of Yahweh are often difficult to describe or explain. Nevertheless, every act, from creation to the present or future, has been or will be a demonstration of faith.

Although faith is not easily defined or understood, love and hope and faith are primary characteristics of the very being of Deity. Life and the presence of love would not exist in a world that came into existence only by physical or chemical action. Our amazing state of existence was not created by an unidentified force of chance or by any form of evolution. In contrast, Yahweh's acts of faith and hope and love give meaning and purpose to our present existence. As stated, all of Yahweh's works or deeds, from creation to resurrection, have been acts of faith, love and understanding. For spiritual faith, the knowledge and understanding of the truth of the existence of Deity is proven by what has been created, and by the presence of love and evil. By faith Yahweh is the I Am, the one of existence.

By faith Yahweh created the heavens and earth.

For Yahweh, faith is a precious substance of value and beauty that cannot be measured. (Matthew 13:44) In the same way that Yahweh honors love, faith is honored. (Luke 7:47-50) Faith and love are obviously interrelated. (Luke 8:15) We shall not truly understand faith until we are able to love God with all our heart. (Mark 6:52)

Love offers strength to faith, and faith strengthens love. (Ephesians 6:6)

Faith and trust are also interrelated. (Luke 8:25) (Mark 4:40)

Faith is a mystery. (Luke 8:48) The relationship between mankind and God is a relationship of faith that has not been completely explained. (Mark 6:5-6, 10:52, 11:22-26) The relationship of friendship between a believer in Jesus Christ and the lord of Lords is a mystery of faith. Faith has also been described as an extremely complex accomplishment. (Matthew 17:19-20) (Romans 16:25-27) Even the scriptural statements about faith are amazing. (John 20:29) (Luke 16:31)

Yahweh has chosen to establish trust and faith as a requirement for acceptance, a state of being counted as righteous. Yahweh has not chosen wisdom, power, beauty, service, worship, religious or moral acts of devotion, or anything else in heaven or on earth for which man can achieve a status of righteousness or acceptance. Faith, and only one kind of faith, a faith that is a gift of his grace, is required. (Mark 10:15) Yahweh is a God of purpose and wisdom and love and understanding; however, he has chosen faith as a way of acceptance. (Hebrews 11:6) Although the dynamics of the power and wonder of faith have not been completely explained, we are required by a God of faith, to have faith in Jesus Christ.

Spiritual faith, belief, and trust in God, has been revealed only by Jesus Christ. This is the faith that makes all things possible. (Mark 9:23) Spiritual faith is belief, trust, and acceptance of Yahweh, the Holy Spirit and Jesus as One. (Mark 9:37) Spiritual faith is the miracle of eternal life. (Mark 10:27)

The faith required for the gift of salvation is simple. (Romans 10:9) As stated, the gift of spiritual faith has been compared to the simple faith of a child. (Matthew 18:3-4)

The act of faith that meets the requirements of salvation is also specific. (James 2:26) (1 John 2:4) Thankfully, the faith of the believer is protected by "the power of God" through spiritual sanctification. (1 Peter 1:2-6)

Spiritual faith may be a gift from God by the Holy Spirit. (1 Corinthians 12:9) As well, spiritual faith may be restricted in a time of tribulations. (Luke 18:8-9)

Yahweh requires his children to be children of faith, and hope, and love for "neither death, nor life shall be able to separate us from the love of God." (Romans 8:38-39)

## 20
## Faithful

Many of the psalms are beautiful expressions for the faithfulness of Yahweh. (Psalm 36:5-9)

Faithfulness is to be loyal, steadfast, dependable, true, devoted, reliable, and trustworthy. To be faithful implies that one is steadfast in affection or allegiance or ability to keep a promise. Faithfulness may require a commitment of trust. Faithfulness may also require strength of purpose and determination. Faithfulness is an act of honor, respect, and love.

Our Father who art in Heaven is a faithful Father. He is never less than faithful. He will never withhold faithfulness. This is a matter of honor; for Yahweh is love.

Yahweh made a promise of faithfulness to Abram. (Genesis 15:5-6)

And Abraham named the place where the promise had been made, Jehovah-jireh, the Lord will provide. (Genesis 22:14) Yahweh also sent the Angel of the Lord to tell Abraham that by his seed all the nations of the earth would be blessed because Abraham had faith in God. (Genesis 22:15-18)

Yahweh's very nature is to be trustworthy. He has proven his faithfulness by remaining faithful to Israel. Yahweh was faithful to Joseph. (Genesis 50:24) Yahweh was faithful to Moses. (Deuteronomy 7:9)

Yahweh was faithful to Israel although he knew that the kings and people would often be less than faithful. Moses prophesied that they would "provoke God to anger" and that evil would fall on them in latter days. (Deuteronomy 31:29)

The requirement of the covenant for the children of Israel was to honor Yahweh by being faithful. Because the kings of Israel had assumed the position of mediator for the One who will always be the true king of Israel, the anointed kings were directly responsibility for keeping the requirements of faithfulness. When the king was faithful, Yahweh protected Israel. When the king or the people failed to honor the Lord of Hosts, God removed his hand of protection. When lack of faithfulness was a direct insult, Yahweh brought severe judgment against the nation of Israel, or any other nation that failed to honor the Almighty sovereign king. (Daniel 9:4)

ONE

In the later years of his reign, king David's love and attention to Yahweh was diminishing. As expected, many of the people of Israel were offering worship to foreign gods. Because Yahweh was concerned and angry, king David was allowed to take a census, to number the people, to find out how strong his army would be in battle. (2 Samuel 24:1) This act was a direct lack of faith in the Father of Israel that had sworn to protect the nation. (2 Samuel 24:10) The discipline for the king's act of pride was severe. (2 Samuel 24:13)

Yahweh, the Lord of hosts and the Father of Abraham, Isaac and Jacob, strongly desired to bless the nation of Israel. When the kings of Israel were faithful, God continued to bless and protect the Israelites. Hezekiah was a faithful king. He served God with all his heart and prospered. (2 Chronicles 31:20-21) Josiah was also a faithful king. (2 Kings 23:25-26)

When his children are unfaithful, God remains faithful; he never changes. He is a God of blessing. (Psalm 121:1-8) Many direct promises of faithfulness, of blessings and of salvation for the children of Abraham were recorded by the prophets of Israel. For example, the "word of the Lord" was sent to the prophet Ezekiel with instructions to offer words of judgment but also promises of faithfulness. (Ezekiel 34:1-31)

The book of Hosea is a story and an illustration of God's special relationship with the children of Abraham. Although God knew that the kings and citizens of Israel and Judah would be unfaithful in the same way that Hosea's wife was unfaithful, he used Hosea to tell Israel that his love would remain firm. Yahweh promised that he would take Israel back into a loving relationship. (Hosea 14:4-8)

An account in the book of Luke about a Pharisee named Simon and a certain woman, who was a sinner, is also a lesson of faithfulness. (Luke 7:36-50) We might assume that the Pharisee represents Israel, and that the woman represents those who have faith in Jesus Christ; however, both the woman and the Pharisee represent Israel. The Pharisee represents the unrepentant citizens of Israel when Hosea prophesied concerning the judgment of God; and the woman represents the Israel that God loves. Jesus said to the woman, "Your sins are forgiven; your faith has saved you; go in peace!" In the same way that Jesus expressed love to this Hebrew woman, Yahweh loves Israel. When the children of Abraham have learned the meaning of forgiveness, Yahweh will say to Israel, "I love you freely, for my anger has turned away from you; I will receive you back as a husband who loves a harlot, a sinful woman. Although you were unfaithful, I remain faithful. I shall redeem you from slavery to sin. My love is supreme love. I am Love." This is part of the mystery of the gospel that the apostle Paul identified. The apostle plainly stated that the gifts and the calling of God are irrevocable. (Romans 11:25-30)

God loved Simon the Pharisee in the same way that he loves the unrepentant of Israel. He did not judge or condemn Simon, for he had not been sent to judge anyone. (John 3:17) Simon might have been one who joined with Nicodemus to accept Jesus as the Christ. Simon might have been one who stood before the Roman ruler to shout, "Crucify, crucify him!" However, Simon was also one for whom Jesus prayed, "Father, forgive them; for they do not know what they are doing." (Luke 23:34) Yahweh is a faithful Father.

Jesus used the parable of the vine-growers to illustrate Israel's lack of faithfulness. (Mark 12:1-11) Because they have rejected the Son of God, Yahweh has chosen to give the vineyard to others, to those who believe that Jesus is the Christ. However, we must quickly add that this is a temporary situation only for the age of the gentiles; for God is always faithful, and the gifts and promises made to Israel will never be taken away. Those who are citizens of the kingdom of Heaven have become adopted children of the family of Israel. (Matthew 13:24) However, because Yahweh is faithful; the children of Abraham will always be protected, for all of Israel will be in the kingdom of God. (Romans 11:26-28)

Yahweh has also made a new covenant, a covenant of faithfulness, with believers, through his son Yehoshua the Christ. Faithfulness is the binding requirement of this new covenant, for both believers and the heavenly Father. (2 John 1:9) (1 John 2:23)

This is not a covenant of works or rewards. (Luke 17:10) The new covenant is a covenant of love. (Luke 16:13) We will be unfaithful if we fail to keep ourselves free from the world, if we love the things of the world rather than Christ Jesus. We will be unfaithful if we fail to love others, as Christ loved. We cannot be self-centered and love God at the same time. We are not to be double-minded or lacking in faith and deeds. We are required, by reason, to be faithful to spiritual standards of honor and love. (Matthew 10:38-39)

The new covenant is not a covenant of religious works. The new covenant is a commitment of faithfulness. Faith has been given as a gift;

and the requirement of faithfulness has been fulfilled by the faithfulness of Christ; therefore, the requirement has been fulfilled by Christ and not by man. (1 Corinthians 1:9)

The wonderful blessing and joy of the new covenant is that the covenant is not guaranteed by our faithfulness and not by our deeds or good works. The covenant is guaranteed by the blessed faithfulness of our Lord and master, Jesus Christ. He has been faithful for us. Whether we are faithful or unfaithful, Yahweh is still a faithful father; and nothing will separate us from his love. This is a gift of immeasurable joy and assurance. We will always be able to depend upon him for protection and for provisions. (Psalm 23:1-6) He will never disown or disinherit us, and he will never give a task that is too difficult to accomplish. We will be required to endure trials and tribulations, but he is with us as a faithful shepherd. We may be required to live out our salvation, but we will never be required to work for our salvation. God is faithful. (1 Corinthians 1:7-9)

As disciples of Jesus Christ, we are not called to accomplish great feats of faith, or amazing tasks of religious works, we are only required to trust Jesus. Several theologians have offered worthy teaching concerning discipleship, principles of life, relationship to God, or spiritual warfare; however, the best teaching concerning faithfulness has been offered by the apostle Paul. (Hebrews 4:1-16) When we are tired or when we feel that we lack faith, the best solution is to stop, and rest.

In the Kingdom of Heaven, Jehovah-jireh!

## 21
## Father

Yahweh is the Father of Israel. (Exodus 4:22)
Yahweh is our Heavenly Father. (Isaiah 63:16, 65:1-20)

A human father is the genetic provider of a living child. A child is one of a father and mother.

YHWH is the unique One who is a father of Heaven and earth. He is a father to whom we are allowed to pray. (Matthew 6:9-10)

The bond between a father and a child, of love and discipline and protection, is a relationship that is recognized in every society. The value, worth and honor of every social entity is dependent upon fathers who honor responsibilities for the proper care of their children. For this reason, fathers and children share a relationship of honor and responsibility; for honor is only obtained when responsibilities are fulfilled.

Jesus said that we should pray, "Our Father, who art in heaven, blessed be your name." This is a statement of respect and honor; however, although Isaiah and other prophets of Israel acknowledged that YHWH is the Father of Israel and of the universe and all of existence, the religious teachers would not have used this personal name for Yahweh. (Isaiah 63:16) Although they understood that Yahweh is the Father of every family in Heaven and in earth, they would have addressed God as Adonai, the God of the Universe.

In Israel, respect and admiration is given to the patriarchs of Israel, for these renowned leaders, chosen by God, were men and female prophets to whom Yahweh, by the power of the Holy Spirit, spoke face to face. Yahweh chose Abram, established a covenant pledge, and gave Abram the name of Abraham, father of multitudes. God changed the name of Abram's wife, from Sarai to Sarah. Sarah was to be a mother of nations; kings of nations would come from her. (Genesis 17:15-16). Through Moses, the Lord of Israel gave the Law, the way of life to the Hebrew people. These patriarchs were men of whom Yahweh chose to bear his name. God plainly told the children of Israel that he was the Lord of their fathers, the God of Abraham, Isaac, and Jacob. (Exodus 3:6) These patriarchs are known and recognized to be "the fathers of Israel."

Although the fact that the Almighty could be a father of the nation of Israel might have been recognized, a personal relationship would not have been an emphasized theological teaching. Respect was given to the patriarchs, but great reverence, or veneration was reserved for the Lord of Israel. Yahweh was known as YHWH, or the Lord God Almighty, or the Lord God of our fathers. The Pharisees and Sadducees would not have used the words "Our Father" to identify the Almighty God of Heaven and earth. (Luke 18:11)

God told Moses to tell the Israelites that he was to be known as "I am that I am." He also instructed Moses that he was to be identified as "the

God of their fathers." This was to be his memorial name forever. (Exodus 3:14-15) God's relationship to Israel is complicated. A carefully reading of the book of Deuteronomy would be required for a proper explanation or understanding of the fact that Yahweh is the Father of Israel. An extensive theological understanding of the character of Deity would also be required to understand why Abram was chosen, blessed, and defended.

Deuteronomy includes historical accounts as well as words of prophecy, admonishment, warnings, encouragement, judgments, blessings, covenant statements and promises of a Father to his children. The statements of Moses that is referred to as the Song of Moses (Deuteronomy 31:1-32) is especially revealing. In this account, much of the character and attitude of the Heavenly Father is clearly revealed. The reasons for discipline, anger, frustration, jealousy, judgment, and protection are explained as expected attributes of an honorable father. (Deuteronomy 33:29) In fact, none of the accounts of relationship between God and Israel can be fully understood without understanding that Yahweh is the Father of Israel.

When Jesus attempted to explain to the Jewish leaders that he and the Father are One, the Pharisees responded with accusations and questions. (John 5:1- 8:58) The religious leaders demanded that Jesus should identify his authority to teach lessons about the Laws of Moses. (John 8:25) Jesus answered, to tell them that his authority was directly from his Father. The teachers replied by saying, "Abraham is our father!" (John 8:38-39)

Notice that the scribes or teachers did not say, "YHWH is our father." The words spoken by Jesus were assumed to be disrespectful to YHWH. Jesus was accused of breaking the law of the Sabbath day, and of blaspheming the name of YHWH. The Pharisees and rulers were obviously offended when Jesus said, "My Father is working until now, and I myself am working." (John 5:17-18)

The Jewish leaders strongly rejected the teachings of Jesus. When Jesus opened the eyes of a blind man, the leaders brought the one that had healed to trial, and said to him, "What do you say about this man, that opened your eyes?" The man answered, "He is a prophet." (John 9:17) Of course the Jewish leaders had declared that Jesus should not be accepted as a teacher of Israel, for he did not keep the Sabbath. (John 9:16) And they said to the man who had been blind, "Give glory to the Lord; we know that this man is a sinner." (John 9:24) Then the man answered, "I have told you already, and you did not hear; why do you need to hear it again? Will you also decide to be his disciple?" This was too much for the religious leaders to tolerate. (John 9:29)

This theological attitude of defending the honor of Yahweh is evident today in the defense of monotheism. Understanding that there is only one true God is a logical theological conclusion; however, this Father has a son, a very unusual son. Jesus is the one who has claimed to be Deity with the Father. He has clearly said, "The Father and I are One." (John 10:14-15, 27-30)

Yahweh is the Father of the Son, the Messiah the Christ. He is the Father, to whom Jesus prayed. (Matthew 14:23)

Within One, the son is the image, presence, and revelation of the invisible God. He is identified as the first born of all creation. (Colossians 1:15) (Luke 2:49) He is called Wonderful Counselor, Mighty God, Eternal Father, and Prince of Peace. (Isaiah 9:6-7)

The Father and the Son have a unique, divine relationship of unity of Deity. As well, the authority that Jesus shares with Yahweh cannot be denied. (John 5:19-26) (Matthew 11:25-27) (Mark 8:38)

Yahweh is the Lord of Hosts, the father of the whole world in whom every family in Heaven and on earth is named. (Ephesians 3:8) As a father, he desires obedience from his children, because he knows what is best for them. He has the power and authority to bless the children who have faith in him. (1 John 3:1) (Proverbs 3:11-12)

Although we are allowed to address Yahweh as "our Father in Heaven," the relationship that we have with the Father of Heaven is not a simplistic human relationship. The relationship is a spiritual relationship, a gift of grace. (Matthew 12:49-50, 5:16) Those who do the will of the Father are accepted as brothers and sisters of Christ.

Jesus told the disciples that all authority in heaven and earth has been given to him. Jesus instructed the disciples to baptize those who profess faith in Jesus in "the name of the Father and the Son and the Holy Spirit." (Matthew 28:18-20)

Jesus is the only begotten son. Jesus is always the Son; and the Father is always the Father. (Luke 22:41-42) (Mark 14:36)

Jesus is the one who taught us how to pray to the Father. (Matthew 6:8-13) Yahweh is the Father of Heaven and earth, Adonai, the God of the Universe, and the only One who is our Father.

As a theological footnote we must be aware of the necessity of reverence for YHWH. A lesson from Jewish scholars concerning a proper attitude should be acknowledged. The privilege of praying to our Father in Heaven is a gift of grace, provided through Jesus Christ. We should not use a liberal translation for the word, Abba. (Romans 8:15) (Galatians 4:6) We are allowed to pray to Abba, Father, just as Jesus prayed, but always with respect and honor that is appropriate for an almighty Father who is Lord of Heaven and Earth.

Yahweh never fails to fulfill his promises; he is always a faithful father. He deserves honor, praise, adoration, and love because he is our worthy Father. As well, unless we offer love and respect to one another, and to our enemies, we cannot offer love and honor to our Heavenly Father.

# 22
## Feared

Yahweh is a great King that is worthy of being feared. (Malachi 1:14) (Hebrews 10:31) All the inhabitants of the world should stand in awe of him. (Psalm 33:8)

Fear is an emotional response to an actual or perceived threatening situation. Fear can cause anxiety, distress, panic, or apprehension. Fear can also cause anger and physical and emotional defense.

The Lord of heaven and earth, the Almighty, is not a deity to be feared. He is a loving Heavenly Father who takes away fear. Yahweh does not wish to cause fear or to be feared.

Angels that were sent to bring a heavenly message offered words of comfort, "Fear not, for I have..." This greeting is given because honor or respect cannot be adequately offered when fear is present.

Although fear of Yahweh is closely related to respect and honor, fear and respect are entirely different. For the announcement of the birth of Jesus, wonderful words of great joy were given, not words of fear. (Luke 2:10) Although fear or respect of God is the beginning of wisdom, Yahweh is not a God of fear. (Proverbs 9:10)

If emphasis is placed upon the attributes of wrath, vengeance, righteousness, judgment, might, or firmness, without considering the love and majesty of Yahweh, fear would be a natural response. An attitude of fear, untouched by respect or love, would imply that Yahweh is inaccessible or unapproachable. Because of the presence of power and might, Yahweh is indeed physically unapproachable; however, as an act of grace, God is completely accessible through Christ Jesus. The presence of the Holy Spirit and love of Christ takes away the fear of the Lord.

The Egyptian warriors, that were pursuing the tribes of Israel, did not respectfully fear the Lord. Tragically, the warriors of Egypt failed to comprehend or to understand the power and might of an almighty Deity. When God caused their chariot wheels to swerve, so that driving them was difficult, the Egyptians said, "We should flee from Israel, for the Hebrew God is fighting for them against the Egyptians." However, the brave soldiers resisted fear and continued in pursuit. When Moses stretched out his hand over the sea the sea returned to its normal state, while the Egyptian army was fleeing into the path of the sea. (Exodus 14:25-27)

On the other hand, when the Israelites saw the great power that the Lord had used against the Egyptians, they feared the Lord and believed in the Lord and in his servant Moses. (Exodus 14:31) Respect was present with fear, and a song of praise and honor was offered to the God of Israel. (Exodus 15:1-18)

Yahweh established the Sabbath, a day of rest and remembrance, as a way for the people of Israel to offer respect for their covenant relationship with God and to remember his blessings and promises to them. Yahweh is a God that demands respect; however, he is also a God of comfort and protection. (Exodus 31:12-13)

The laws of Moses were given to Israel to take away fear. The Laws were given as a warning and as a blessing to the nation of Israel, so that the Israelites would be able to live in peace, to love God rather than to fear the wrath of God. (Psalm 19:7-11)

Most of the words of comfort in scripture have been given exclusively to the children of Abraham. The fact that Jesus was sent only to the Israelites and that his words, even his words of prophecy, were given directly to the nation of Israel must be clearly understood. Jesus was speaking directly to Israel when he told them to watch and pray. (Luke 21:28, 36)

For the Christian disciple, the fear of affliction and death has been removed by faith in Jesus Christ. (Romans 8:1-2, 15) We do not fear because we love the One who first loved us. (I John 4:18-19)

Yahweh is the good shepherd who takes away fear. He is a God of grace and love and forgiveness. (1 John 4:4)

# 23
## Firmness

God is as firm as solid stone, his work is perfect, and just. He is a God of truth without iniquity. (Deuteronomy 32:4)

Firmness is the quality of having a solid, stable, or unyielding structure or surface. Firmness of character is to be confident, positive, and determined. Firmness is the primary quality of dependability.

Yahweh, the Lord of lords and King of kings is firm, stable, immovable, and worthy of trust. Yahweh is firmly dependable.

Firmness is the foundation of trust and faith. Stability is the cornerstone of truth.

Jehovah's steadfast offer of salvation is compared to a firm foundation, and a corner stone that has been firmly placed within an enduring construction. (Isaiah 28:16-17) (Psalm 118:21-24) Jesus was referring to these passages of scripture as he admonished the Jewish leaders for not identifying as the Messiah. (Matthew 21:42)

Yahweh is love. His love is firm and immovable and everlasting. His love never fails. (Lamentations 3:22-23)

Yahweh is as firm and stable as absolute truth. (John 14:6)

His determinations or decisions are firm and unmovable. Every good gift, and every perfect gift is from God. (James 1:17)

As Christ-ones we are required to stand firm in faith; however, our firmness is a gift of the power and strength of the stone that was rejected, and not of ourselves. This requirement of steadfastness not a religious or spiritual requirement. Our firmness must be found in spiritual freedom offered as an act of grace, through the gift of the Holy Spirit.

The apostle Paul says that we have been set free from the restrictions of the law. Christ has set us free. We should stand firm and not be subject again to a yoke of slavery, to legal restrictions. (Galatians 5:1)

If we attempt to stand firm by seeking to be justified by the law, we will fall from grace. We must be led by the Spirit so that we may stand firm in faith. (Galatians 5:1-18) The spiritual strength to do the will of God from the heart is provided by the Holy Spirit. The full armor of God that includes truth, righteousness, peace, faith, salvation, and the privilege of prayer are strengths or protections given by the Holy Spirit. We are not required to depend upon our own strength or firmness. We are allowed to depend upon the firmness of the promises of our loving God of truth and firmness.

We can rejoice in the Lord always, because we can do all things through Him who strengthens us. (Philippians 4:1-13) Our gracious loving Heavenly Father is almighty love.

## 24
## Forgiving

At a place called Calvary, Jesus was crucified. On the cross Jesus prayed to his Father that forgiveness would be given to those responsible. (Luke 23:34)

A man who was paralyzed was brought to Jesus. Jesus saw the faith of the man and his friends. Jesus said to the afflicted one, "My son, take courage, your sins are forgiven." (Matthew 9:2)

Forgiveness is to be forbearing, to overlook faults or imperfections. Forgiveness may require tolerance, compassion, and understanding. Forgiveness is to pardon or to grant relief from payment of a debt or obligation. The forgiveness of a debt may require a financial sacrifice or a financial gift of payment.

True forgiveness is to be free from resentment or anger. As well, although compassion is not always required, an act of forgiveness may also be an act of love and compassion.

Forgiveness that is worthy, valuable, or acceptable must be offered without condemnation, without judgment, or without requiring change or a response from the one that is forgiven.

Forgiveness does not require agreement or participation with a fault, imperfection or harm that may have been forgiven or overlooked. The forgiveness of a debt does not require one to discount a wrong or to agree with any action or thought that is an untruth. Forgiveness does not require dismissing or giving away honor or respect.

An act of forgiveness may be difficult to explain or to understand; however, revenge, which is the opposite of forgiveness, is clearly understood. In essence, forgiveness may be a rejection of revenge or vengeance.

Forgiveness is commonly considered to be difficult or painful. When one has been insulted or offended, the requirement of forgiveness seems to be unacceptable. For this reason, the positive aspects of forgiveness should be considered.

Forgiveness may be a blessing to the forgiven. Forgiveness may also be a blessing of freedom, to be received by the one who forgives. An act of forgiveness sets one free and opens one's heart to love. Because the necessity of forgiveness, as well as the benefits are not clearly understood, the blessings for acts of forgiveness may not be fully appreciated. The concepts and blessings of forgiveness may be described or explained, but a true understanding of forgiveness can only be obtained by experience. The experience of forgiveness is like taking a breath of fresh air, after having been pulled out of a deep dark dungeon. The ability to forgive is a blessing that than has been offered from a loving Heavenly Father. As well, because forgiveness often requires humility, blessings for acts of humility have been promised from our Heavenly Father.

The ability or willingness to forgive can be obtained simply by asking for the wisdom to choose to forgive. Anyone can forgive, at any time. Forgiveness is a choice, made by a loving God of peace and love. (Luke 17:4) Forgiveness can also be a simple choice by one who chooses to love, or to reject a desire for vengeance. An act of forgiveness does not require acceptance, dismissing, forgetting or any other mental or emotional action concerning the individual or the reason for forgiveness. The ability to forgive does not need to be learned or practiced or perfected. Forgiveness does not require a strong will or emotional control. Forgiveness is possible without understanding, or without expecting recognition or understanding or appreciation for the act of forgiveness.

YHWH is truly a God of forgiveness. For Yahweh, forgiveness is a choice, a righteous decision. His forgiveness is based upon justice, love, kindness, tolerance, compassion, understanding, and mercy.

God is an almighty supreme sovereign; therefore, he may choose to give any form or degree of forgiveness. Yahweh has the freedom to bestow any forgiveness that he wishes to offer.

Yahweh made a choice to forgive mankind. As an amazing supreme act of forgiveness, Yahweh offered his only son Yehoshua the Christ as a gift of life and freedom. (John 3:16-17) Almighty Jehovah is an amazing God of forgiveness. The story of the Gospel, the crucifixion, death, and resurrection of Jesus, is an act of forgiveness, that required an act of humility. (Philippians 2:6-7)

The entire Bible, the Story of God, clearly illustrates the willingness of God to forgive mankind. However, the story of the children of Abraham has been specifically used to illustrate the loving kindness and forgiveness offered by our Heavenly Father. One account that includes recognition of God's forgiveness and mercy for the nation of Israel has been recorded in the chronicles of Nehemiah. (Nehemiah 9:7-32)

A brief or concise history of the nation of Israel has also been recorded in scripture. (Psalm 105:8-106:48) The passage begins by stating that God has remembered his covenant forever, the words that he commanded to a thousand generations. The passage ends with an emphasis on forgiveness for Israel. God regarded their affliction, when he heard their cry. He remembered his covenant and repented according to the multitude of his mercies. He also made those who had taken them captive to have pity on them. (Psalm 106:44-46) In other words, although the children of Israel were continually unfaithful, and although they were unable to keep the requirements of the covenant, and because Yahweh is a God of compassion, he remained faithful. He offered the nation of Israel grace, that which they did not deserve and would never be able to earn, simply because he had the supreme right to forgive. Yahweh has also offered the children of Abraham complete forgiveness, not a limited or qualified forgiveness.

The promise of the fulfillment of forgiveness for Israel has been offered as words of prophecy. God intends to give Israel peace, not evil, and a future with hope. When they choose to search for God with all their heart, they will truly know that God is love. (Jeremiah 29:11-13) When Israel will humble themselves, pray and turn from their wicked ways, Yahweh will hear their prayers and will forgive their sin and heal their land. (2 Chronicles 7:14)

This promise of compassion, mercy, and forgiveness was sworn unto the fathers of Israel from the days of old. (Micah 7:18-20)

The choice of forgiveness offered to Israel is illustrated by the two criminals that were crucified with Jesus. Neither of the criminals deserved forgiveness, but one who did not judge Jesus was offered the gift of grace. (Luke 23:39-43)

From the account recorded in Luke we may assume that Jesus asked for forgiveness for all of Israel, for those who stood to watch his crucifixion. (Luke 23:34)

Jesus Christ, the only begotten son of God, is truly One of forgiveness. For the promised Messiah has come to offer forgiveness that is worthy, valuable, and acceptable. His forgiveness is offered without condemnation or judgment.

A devout Pharisee who would have been considered by the followers of Christ to be unworthy of forgiveness, experienced Yahweh's loving forgiveness in a unique way. This young religious leader met the Son of God, in light and power, and experienced the forgiveness of a loving Father. The story of the apostle Paul is an amazing account of the loving forgiveness of Yahweh. (Acts 9:1-22) In the same way, God reaches out to all of us, to offer forgiveness, acceptance, and unity in Christ. (Colossians 2:13) (1 Timothy 1:15-17)

God, by his own free will, has chosen to offer forgiveness to all of mankind, even to the enemies of Israel. All who are willing to accept his gift of grace will be set free from death, because the Father of Israel is a God of forgiveness and freedom.

In forgiveness, Yahweh has also been set free. Yahweh is free to love and to be loved. He set the example of forgiveness. His son Yehoshua prayed for Israel, "Father, forgive them; for they do not know what they are doing." (Luke 23:34)

The forgiveness of God is an act of compassion and love; however, his forgiveness also establishes a situation of honor. Forgiveness is a requirement of honor to a forgiving Father. Forgiveness is to be offered as a blessing to others. (Luke 17:3-4) (1 John 1:9) (Micah 7:18-19) An attitude of forgiveness is required for a proper relationship to a God of love. (Mark 11:25-26) We are required to forgive, because we have been forgiven by God. (Ephesians 4:31-32) (Colossians 3:13)

The blessings of forgiveness cannot be overemphasized. When we forgive; we become imitators of God. (Matthew 5:23-24) To forgive is to be Christ-like. When we do not forgive, we grieve the Holy Spirit.

Yahweh gave his son as a gift of forgiveness. Yahweh did not offer forgiveness, because forgiveness was required, or because the world deserved to be forgiven. Although forgiveness by Yahweh cannot be completely comprehended, the gift of eternal life is a gift of love and forgiveness. (John 3:16) (Matthew 9:2)

In the words and accounts of scripture, a glimmer of understanding of the blessing of forgiveness has been given. We are reminded that Jesus is the one who for the joy that was set before him, endured the cross, despising the shame; and is at the right hand of the throne of God. (Hebrews 12:2)

In this supreme act of forgiveness, God gave a gift to creation. He set himself free from the necessity of judgment and condemnation. He offered his son as a gift of joy and peace and fulfillment to all of creation. We have not been offered understanding of how Yahweh benefits from acts of love; nevertheless, we do understand that forgiveness is a blessing, even to the one who forgives. Forgiveness offers freedom and liberty.

As Christ-ones, we are commanded to be children who love and forgive. Because Christ loved us and gave himself up for us, as an offering and a sacrifice to God, like a fragrant flower we are commanded to forgive. (Ephesians 5:1-2) Having freely been forgiven, how could we not forgive others? (Matt. 6:14-15)

On the other hand, lack of forgiveness, and mercy and honor will result in dire consequences. Jesus taught a lesson of forgiveness to his disciples by telling them a parable about an unworthy, unforgiving servant. (Matthew 18:21-35)

There is only one circumstance or situation in which forgiveness will not be offered. While Jesus was teaching that he has full authority to forgive sin, he explained this situation. (Matthew 12:30-32)

Yahweh is a God of forgiveness because he is Love. He is also a God of honor because he is YHWH, the God of the Universe.

# 25
# Freedom

The Spirit of the Lord lives in a state of freedom. (2 Corinthians 3:17)

Freedom is defined as the state of not being imprisoned or physically restrained. Freedom is also a state of being free from harm or affliction, fear, hunger, or death. Political or social freedom is a state of having self-determination. Peace is a requirement of liberty, for freedom without peace is not true liberty. Freedom from fear or restriction is possible only in a state of peace.

Yahweh is a God of life and liberty; for life cannot be enjoyed without liberty. Yahweh is a God of liberty. He lives in supreme liberty and peace. He is free from everything. His blessing, Peace be with you, is a blessing of the legal right to have both freedom and peace.

Through his one and only Son, Yahweh has offered eternal life to mankind. This "new life" is a life of spiritual freedom, for Israel and for all of mankind. Spiritual freedom is freedom from death and separation from God. This time of peace was prophesied by the prophet Isaiah and announced by Jesus. (Luke 4;18-19, 21)

The hope and faith of this promise of freedom to the children of Abraham was expressed by the multitudes who shouted outside the city of Jerusalem and by the children at the temple who cheered, "Hosanna in the highest, he sets us free, he is the Messiah who saves us." (Matthew 21:16)

Because Yahweh understands the blessings of freedom, his desire is for all mankind to be set free in every possible way, to know the truth that is Jesus and to be truly free. His gift of life, of freedom and peace, is offered to everyone; for true peace is only possible when everyone and all of existence resides in a state of liberty. This liberty is not merely a state of righteousness, our Sabbath is a life within the love of God.

His offer of peace and rest has been offered to everyone. (Matthew 11:28-30) Luke and John have said that when we know the truth, the truth of the gospel of Jesus Christ shall make us free and if the Son makes us free, we shall be truly free. (Luke 4:18) (John 8:32)

The promise of eternal freedom that God offers is for a future age or time. In this present chaotic world, the peace that Yahweh desires for all of creation is not possible.

To accurately or properly explain why anger and conflict, evil and war are present today, an understanding of the story of creation, of original sin, of conflict in Heaven, of the corruption of men in the days of Noah, of the lack of communication in the days of Babel, or of the lack of honor given by the tribes of Israel to their King of kings would be required. The story of creation and of the trials and tribulations of mankind are only part of an extended chronical account found in the Bible.

The historical story of mankind is complicated by the fact that God has chosen to allow a state of mental and emotional freedom of choice to exist, so that love may be given or received. As well, the present conflicts between good and evil, the sufferings of this present time, are related to the fact that love cannot be offered or received unless love is freely given and freely received. The value of existence and life depends upon the presence of freedom, so that love may be freely given and freely received.

The sufferings of this present time are obvious. We are all anxious to experience true liberty. Spiritual liberty will be revealed by the son of God, and the world will be delivered from the bondage of corruption into the glorious liberty of God. (Romans 8:18-23)

On the cross, the offer of life and freedom was announced with a shout, "It is finished." (John 19:30) "It is completed," is a shout of freedom. Jesus was announcing to the world that the prisoners are set free. The doors of the prison of sin and death were opened. Separation between man and God has been taken away. The price of freedom has been paid. The lost have been redeemed. Freedom for all of creation has been offered. Jesus is free to offer the gift of eternal life to the whole world ...Liberty!

Someday this world will be free from evil. We will be free from fear, hunger or pain or any possible earthly affliction. We shall be free from doubt or lack of faith. We will be free from the frustration of not being able to understand the unknowable. We will be free from conflicts of thoughts or beliefs. The theologian and the scientist, the unconcerned and the intellectual will stand together; for all who believe will be in unity and in peace with God. What has been stated is not a belief in universal salvation; this is a statement of a future existence in the presence of Yahweh for those who have been like Abraham, to have faith in Jesus Christ. (Romans 10:8-12)

Because of the freedom of choice given to Adam and Eve, we have all been separated from God. The story of original sin is recorded in the

ONE

book of Genesis. This account must be accepted by faith. The world has been placed within a prison of doubt and confusion, of rebellion and evil. The one called Satan, the liar and deceiver, is the one who has been given temporary authority over the prisoners. Jesus has come to open the prison doors, the gates of Hell, and to set the captives free from darkness and evil. (Psalm 142:6-7, 143:1-4)

Yahweh has used the children of Abraham to teach his lessons of choice and covenant and forgiveness and faithfulness. (Romans 11:28) The words of prophecy and declarations of freedom offered to Israel are recorded in scripture. (Isaiah 61:1-11)

Many passages of scripture have been recorded concerning the alienation of mankind from God. As well, passages that explain God's plan for restoring a state of peace between God and man have been abundantly offered. The conflict of love and evil in this world is evident; however, Jesus Christ is the gift of grace that sets the world free from the prison of unrighteousness, death and destruction. (1 Peter 3:18-20, 4:6)

Yahweh is a God of Freedom and Liberty. (Romans 6:14) As believers, we struggle against the flesh but yield to the control of the Spirit of life and live by the law of Liberty. (Romans 8:2) (James 1:25) We should not return to the bondage of the law; we are free. (Galatians 5:1) We are alive. We do not need to practice being alive; we are alive. Therefore, we have been commanded to rejoice in being alive.

We who have professed faith in Jesus Christ are those who know the truth, and the truth has set us free. (John 8:32) The law of the Spirit of life in Christ Jesus has set us free from the law of sin and death. (Romans 8:1-3)

An understanding concerning the value of liberty has been offered by Yahweh. Exodus 3:14) To be one, in a state of existence, and to be what we shall be, is a gift of freedom and liberty. Yahweh has offered forgiveness to those who profess faith in his gift of grace, so that we are able to say, "I am what I am, and I shall be what I shall be. I am forgiven. I know the truth. I have been set free from sin and death. Liberty!"

No greater gift can be given than the gift of peace and eternal life. (Romans 6:22-23) Freedom is the theme of the Lord's prayer. After each separate sentence, we could shout the words freedom or liberty. At the end of the prayer we could shout, "I am free, free indeed." (Psalm 23:1-6) We should read the prayer and praise God for the gift of life and freedom.

# 26
# Friendship

The words of the book of Proverbs contain the wisdom of Yahweh. Many of the teachings are simple, others are extremely complex. A simple principle of life is that when we give, we receive. If we wish to have friends, we must offer friendship. Jesus is a friend that stays closer than a brother. (Proverbs 18:24)

Friendship involves understanding, acceptance, and willingness to listen and to care. True friendship involves mutual affection, a bond of mind and spirit. Friendships can be established between any two individuals or groups of individuals ...a mother and son, brother to sister, male to female ...or any combination possible, such as soldiers or classmates or individuals of a community. Although friendships may be established with or without a requirement of love; friendship requires personal interaction, cooperation, and acceptance.

Although the nature of Yahweh should not be described or explained as being human-like, Yahweh is the creator who has placed deity-like characteristics in mankind. Nevertheless, because friendship is universally recognized as a valuable human characteristic, perhaps concerning this characteristic, Yahweh would not be offended when we consider his actions to be human-like.

This characteristic is an amazing aspect of the nature of Yahweh. Even after accomplishing an extensive theological study of scripture, one would most likely not be able to adequately explain or fully comprehend the friendship of God.

For the Lord God of Israel, friendship is a matter of honor and respect. Yahweh cares and communicates, even with those who do not love him, and even with those who do not believe that he exists.

Jesus lived as a common man, eating and drinking with his friends. Some called him a gluttonous man and a winebibber, but he was a friend to all men, even to publicans and sinners. (Matthew 11:19)

The Lord of Hosts has remained as a faithful friend to Abraham, Isaac, and Jacob and to all the children of Israel. He is faithful and forgiving and wishes only the best for the children of Israel. Abraham lived by the principle of giving and receiving. Abraham offered friendship to God and

God accepted the friendship for righteousness, and Abraham was called the friend of God. (James 2:23)

When the nation of Israel is like Abraham, when Israel offers friendship to Yahweh, he has promised to accept their friendship for righteousness, and to give them one heart, a new spirit within them. Yahweh will take the heart of stone and give them a heart of flesh. (Ezekiel 11:19)

His divine characteristic of friendship is shown in open willingness to accept the strangers and foreigners within the midst of Israel without condemnation, without being judgmental or without requiring change.

In the New Testament, this divine characteristic is expressed in his acceptance of gentiles, as the adopted children of Abraham. Cornelius, the Centurion officer, sent for Peter and said, "And I sent for you; and you have come; we are all present before God to hear what you have been commanded." And Peter said, "I certainly now understand that God is not One to show partiality, but in every nation the man who fears him and does what is right is accepted in friendship." (Acts 10:31-48)

To these chosen Caesarean gentiles, God gave the gift of the Holy Spirit, before they were baptized, and without laying on of hands. Yahweh had already recognized their offer of friendship. While Peter was still telling them about the forgiveness of sin, the Holy Spirit fell on all of them. (Acts 10:44, 11:15-18)

In a simple request for prayer and for awareness of God's choice, the apostle Paul declared God's concern for all of mankind. The apostle said that we should offer prayers, petitions, and thanksgivings, for all men, even for kings and those who are in positions of authority, in order that they may lead a life of honor and dignity. Our prayers and friendship are for a higher purpose, for God desires for all men to be saved and to come to the knowledge of the truth. (1 Timothy 2:1-4)

God's gift of friendship is expressed in the story of the wedding feast. The king who was giving the wedding feast instructed the servants to go to the highways, find as many as possible and invite to the wedding feast. The servants went out into the streets and gathered all they could find, both evil and good. The wedding hall was filled with dinner guests. (Matthew 22:1-14)

His loving concern for the lost ones of Israel and of the world, is shown in the parable of the lost sheep. When the Sheppard came home, he called his friends and neighbors and asked them to rejoice with him; for he had found his lost sheep. (Luke 15:6)

His friendship is offered by Jesus Christ, in deeds and actions, for Jesus gave his life for his friends. The highest form of friendship is for one to give his life for his friends. (John 15:13) Jesus offered friendship to his disciples, and he has offered friendship to us. (John 15:15) How could this friendship ever be explained?

Yahweh is a faithful friend; however, one who is a friend of the world, who loves the things of the world, cannot be a friend with God. (Luke 16:13) Anything that would interfere with friendship must not be placed between God and man. (Matthew 6:19-24) The evil things of the world are enemies of God; and the ruler of this world is an enemy of God. Yahweh cannot share friendship with evil. (James 4:4)

Love, honor, charity, and friendship are characteristics that identify one who is a true disciple of Jesus Christ. As Christ-ones, we are truly friends of God when we love one another. (John 15:14-17)

# 27
# Giving

Every perfect gift of life is from God. Perfect gifts are from the Father of lights. (James 1:17)

Giving is to freely transfer the possession of something to someone other than to oneself. A gift may be a material object, or something of intrinsic value of what one possesses and is able to share or to give.

Yahweh is the God of giving. Purpose, value, and consequences of giving have been established by Yahweh. His gifts are pure, valuable, and lasting. (James 1:17) Every good gift from Yahweh is a perfect gift, for the primary aspect of love is giving or sharing of oneself.

Yahweh is a benevolent Father. Every good or perfect gift given to mankind has been given by the Father of life. No greater gift can be offered or received than the gift of existence and life, and the gift of love.

The value of a material gift, such as gold or silver, is determined by inherent value. As well, the value of the gift may be determined by the cost to the giver or the worth or value to the receiver; therefore, any object or act of usefulness or benefit may be offered as a gift. The greatest gift would be for the giver to give his life as an act of service or love.

True giving is defined as an act of voluntarily presenting a gift without restrictions, expectations, or compensation. True giving requires that whatever is given is needed or will be accepted by the receiver. As well, a worthy gift is given to meet a specific need without requirements of how or when the gift is to be used. When a child asks for bread, the child should not give him a stone. (Matthew 7:9)

On a certain day, Jesus sat down at the entrance of the temple and was watching as people put offerings into the treasury. Many that were rich put in valuable coins. Then a certain poor widow put in only two small coins. As a testimony for giving, Jesus called his disciples and told them that the poor widow had placed all that she had for a living into the treasury. Jesus recognized her gift as a true act of giving. (Mark 12:38-43)

Although material objects may be treasured as valuable gifts, the greatest gifts are non-material blessings. Many intrinsic blessings, such as the freedom to make a choice, are often unrecognized or received without appreciation. For example, the gift of honor given to parents by children may not be fully appreciated. According to the laws of Moses, the commandment to give the valuable gift of honor to mother and father is the first commandment with a promise of lasting blessings. (Ephesians 6:2)

As human beings, we often fail to recognize that which is truly good or perfect. Non-material objects such as honesty and kindness or valuable gifts that are worthy of giving or receiving. (Philippians 4:8) Sometimes we fail to remember that the greatest gift of life is love, and life. Everything in this life that is good or valuable, true or honest has been given by our heavenly Father.

Because the gifts of God are worthy of being shared, the rewards and blessings of giving are also special. When giving or sharing is motivated by love, joy may be a blessing to the one who gives and to the one who receives. Those who are selfish or self-centered will miss blessings of joy and peace. (2 Timothy 3:1-5)

Although a true gift must be freely given, the one who has offered a gift may be entitled to certain expectations. Yahweh, who is the rewarder of special gifts, is especially worthy of appreciation. Jesus used a parable to illustrate such expectations. (Matthew 25:14-30) This parable was offered directly to the children of Abraham as an admonishment; however, a basic truth is included that may be applied to everyone. The servants were given talents, according to their individual abilities. Appropriate rewards were offered, except to the servant that did not appreciate the talent. In defense of his neglect the servant offered an unworthy statement concerning the character and will of the Master. When God gives intelligence, wisdom, beauty, health, or any personal gift, he expects that talent to be used appropriately. When the talent is misused, the joy of using the talent will be lost.

There are no greater gifts to be given than the gifts offered by the Almighty Father of Heaven and earth. (Acts 20:35) He understands the amazing blessing of giving. He is the Father of joyful giving. Yehoshua the Christ gave his life for the joy set before him. (Hebrews 12:2)

Yahweh is the only one able to give the greatest of all possible gifts, the gift of eternal life. There is no greater gift than his gift of grace. (2 Corinthians 8:9) The gift of salvation is God's gift of life to the world. (John 3:16-17) (Luke 12:32)

The choice of accepting the gift of eternal life is a choice of faith. The apostle Peter offered a simple statement concerning this gift of eternal life. (Acts 2:38) Eternal life is a precious gift, voluntarily presented without expectation of compensation. The gift is offered generously to anyone who is willing to have faith. Eternal life has been given to meet a specific need, without requirements of how the gift is to be received or used. Every precious or positive statement or fact concerning giving can be applied to the gift of eternal life. (Matthew 20:15-16)

Yahweh's original gift, the light and life that was presented in the creation of the world, has been returned by the true light of life as a gift from the Creator. (John 8:12) Life is best described by contrast with what is not life. Life is existence, not non-existence. Life is light, not darkness. Life is freedom, not imprisonment or slavery.

Eternal existence is a precious valuable gift of joy, not suffering. This is a gift of friendship, not rejection. Eternal life is a gift of love from One who is love. Everlasting life is supreme liberty, joy, hope and love and the absence of hate or suffering. In contrast to eternal life, existence on earth is life in prison, with a glimmer of light from a small window. Our world is the valley of the shadow of death. (Psalm 23:4) Those who profess faith in Jesus Christ will experience the joy and excitement of having the prison doors pushed wide open. (Romans 10:9-10) The true believer is allowed to walk out into shimmering light of spiritual life to experience the joy of true liberty. In Heaven the reality of this spiritual existence will be fully experienced. (1 Corinthians 13:12)

The true meaning of freedom and the joy of giving is to be found only in Jesus Christ. This choice is to believe that the words of Jesus are truth. (John 8:32) Truth is found in the law of liberty. (Galatians 5:1-6) For those who profess faith in Jesus, the gift of the Holy Spirit has been freely offered. (Luke 11:13) As previously stated, the principle of giving is directly related to the principle of retribution. The basic meaning of retribution is that we shall reap what we sow. (Galatians 6:7-8) (Ephesians 6:8) However, the principle of giving, and essence of freedom, is that gifts from God are unmeasurable. Briefly stated, when we give ourselves to be a Christ-one we offer our life to be used as a blessing to others; and a life of freedom is returned, with blessings of joy, and peace, and hope. (Matthew 16:24-27)

The truth of this blessings is illustrated in the story of Zacchaeus, a tax collector who had lived a life of selfishness. By faith in Jesus, Zacchaeus was set free from self-centeredness. Zacchaeus was anxious to be a giver and not a receiver. (Luke 19:1-10)

The greatest gift that Yahweh has been given to the world is love. The greatest gift of love is eternal life. The gift of eternal life is the everlasting gift of faith, hope, and love. (1 Corinthians 13:13) The greatest gift that has been given to those who believe is the gift of the Holy Spirit, that is freely given to those who ask for the blessing. (Luke 11:13) The Holy Spirit is the gift of unity and friendship. (1 John 4:1-7) The greatest gift that we can give to God is to allow the Holy Spirit to inspire us to give blessings of love to others. (1 Corinthians 13:3-7) (Colossians 3:8-17) The greatest gift of being useful is joy and peace. (Isaiah 35:10) The greatest expression of appreciation for having received the gift of eternal life is to joyfully offer oneself as a gift of love to others. (Matthew 28:19-20)

Jesus came into the world as a gift of love and life. Jesus did not come to receive or to be served or to receive worship, he came to give his life as a gift of life to us. (Matthew 20:28)

# 28
# Goodness

The performance of acts of goodness may be beneficial or rewarding, but the value of goodness is not great enough to be given or exchanged for the gift of eternal life. (Mark 10:18) (Luke 18:18-27) (Psalm 24:3-5)

The word goodness is used to identify moral quality of character or actions. The existence or presence of goodness implies virtuousness, to be morally correct, honorable, and honest. The characteristic of goodness also implies that one is recognized or accepted by associates.

When supreme qualities of sovereignty, beauty, and knowledge are considered, the statement that the Lord of Host, the Lord of heaven and earth is righteous and good seems to be an understatement. (Psalm 24:10) Interestingly, statements concerning the goodness of God are used to express characteristics that are easily recognized as human-like characteristics, which in principle are deity characteristics that have been given to mankind. For example, Yahweh is described as a good father who wishes goodness for his children. And as the son of the Father, Jesus performed acts of goodness. (Matthew 11:5)

In essence, goodness is godliness. (1 Timothy 3:16)

The nature of the goodness of God is often misunderstood. Yahweh is holy. He does not need to perform acts of goodness or righteousness. Yahweh does not need to express goodness, to be good; Yahweh is good or righteous by his very nature, because he is deity. As well, the goodness of Yahweh is not expressed by being right or righteous, or even by defending righteousness. The righteousness of God is expressed as love.

In scripture, the goodness of God is not emphasized. This statement must be carefully explained. The holiness of Yahweh is evident; therefore, emphasis is not required. The goodness or holiness of Yahweh is covered by humility, expressed as acts of grace, so that the characteristic of love instead of righteousness, is emphasized. This fact is emphasized by the statement Jesus made to the young ruler of Israel. (Mark 10:18) Jesus did not say that we shall be blessed for calling him good. We are required to honor Yahweh by doing good works of love, but the goodness of the acts cannot and should not be emphasized. (Matthew 19:17)

Yahweh's holiness is expressed by sharing goodness as light and love. (Matthew 12:9-13)

Only God is holy, or righteous. (Psalm 14:1-3) Evidently one man named Job was, as Yahweh testified, humanly good. (Job 1:8) However, Job understood his own imperfection. (Job 9:1) Job also clearly understood that God is love.

YHWH is the only one that is good, and everything that God does is good; this is his nature. Everything that he does for those that he loves is good; this is his choice according to his goodness. Everything he does for all of creation, in heaven and on earth, is an act of goodness. (Psalm 5:4) Simply stated, God is merciful and gracious, long-suffering, and abundant in goodness and truth. (Exodus 34:6-7) (Psalm 100:4-5, 136:1-26)

Yahweh does not tolerate one who is boastful, speaks falsehood, or is guilty of bloodshed and deceit. (Psalm 5:5-6) (Proverbs 6:16-19) Yahweh is a God of loving kindness and truth. (Psalm 25:8-10) (2 Samuel 22:20-26)

Yahweh may allow men to be called good; but only when compared to other humans and not to deity. And Jesus said that there is only One who is good. (Luke 18:19) We inherit evil, within our heart and being, that defiles us. (Mark 7:20-23) For mankind, goodness is not possible. Even to live as a reflection of the radiant glory of God we must be saved by grace. (Exodus 34:29) (Romans 5:1-21)

As well, the purpose of the gift of salvation was not to make man righteous before God; the purpose of salvation was to give eternal life to mankind. The purpose of salvation was to set man free from the prison of death and destruction. (Romans 6:1-10)

Although the purpose of salvation was to give life, a state of righteousness or sanctification was required. A new vessel of life was required, because "the old wineskin," the unholy vessel could not hold the power of the Holy Spirit. Therefore, righteousness is an inherent gift of salvation simply because righteousness was required.

Righteousness is a gift of love and grace offered through the life of Jesus Christ so that the gift of eternal life might be given to those who believe.

We have been given the gift of the Holy Spirit, not to make us good, but to give us the privilege of doing good. (Matthew 5:14-17) Our spiritual goodness is a gift from God, for according to the brother of James we have been "sanctified by our Father." (Jude 1:1)

Nevertheless, if we are to be Christ-ones, reflections of his goodness, we must pray for those who mistreat us and offer acts of love to those who are our enemies. If we wish for our enemies to be our friends, we must offer friendship. (Luke 6:28-33)

Reading scripture is valuable way to learn the lessons or principles of giving, for the rules within the laws of Israel remain as a law of love. (2 Timothy 3:15-17) Yahweh is a God of love that desires good deeds, not religious performance. Although works of faith, that are proof of faith, are required, performance of religious acts or moral or ethical deeds are not required. The requirement of being a Christ-one is to offer acts of love and honor to others. Love must be freely offered from the heart and not as deeds of labor. Religious, moral, or spiritual works cannot produce faith and love. Religious, moral, or spiritual works cannot make the performer righteous or good. (Mark 10:18) Only God is good.

The fruit of love can only come from the seed that falls on good ground. (Mark 4:20) The rule of goodness is love. Goodness must come out of the good treasure of the heart. (Luke 6:45) Goodness, offered by mankind, must be offered in the same way that Jesus expressed love to the world. (Hebrews 12:2)

True goodness is love without hypocrisy. (Romans 12:9)

In the last days, everyone will know and understand and experience the goodness of God. At some time, the children of Israel will repent and will seek the Lord their God and their king. They will come to receive his goodness. (Hosea 3:5)

# 29
# Grace

As an act of grace, Jesus gave his life to allow us to have eternal life with him. He raised us up with him and has seated us with him in the heavenly places. (Ephesians 2:5-6) The gift of eternal life is a gift of love.

An act of grace is to bestow honor upon someone, or to place another in a favored or privileged position. Grace may be given to one who is unable to repay or does not deserve the honor of grace. To be gracious is to be elegant, dignified, refined or charming.

One does not need to be gracious to bestow grace; and bestowing grace does not necessarily make one gracious. Yahweh is the exception. Our Father in Heaven is a God of grace. He is full of grace. He is always gracious and willing to graciously bestow grace on others.

This truth was clearly taught and illustrated in the writings of the Old Testament. The prophets of Israel, scribes and writers of psalms were used to teach the concepts of compassion and grace to the descendants of Abraham. (Psalm 84:11-12) (Psalm 143:10) The accounts of the life of king David and of his son Solomon were historical records that also included lessons of God's relationship to the children of Abraham. The Israelites understood the promises that God made to king David and to Israel. According to the words of scripture, king David said that because he did not turn aside from anything that God had commanded him to do, God promised an everlasting kingdom to the king. (1 Kings 15:4-5)

Without considering the complete history of the relationship of God to Abraham, an assumption could be made that because the king did that which was right, he deserved God's grace. However, the truth is that acts of divine compassion were necessary for an imperfect king that did not deserve grace.

Although the concept of grace may be found within the teachings or laws of Moses and in the life of king David, the Hebrew scholars who challenged the teachings of Jesus did not clearly express an understanding of the amazing grace of a loving Father, or the necessity of God's grace for the salvation of mankind. This apparent situation is understandable, for the doctrine of acceptance by grace is technically in conflict with the doctrine of acceptance as a divine choice made by God. (Romans 4:4, 11:6) As previously stated, this writing is not a study of theology; and this writer is unqualified to explain Jewish theology. Nevertheless, a brief explanation of this assessment is necessary.

The Hebrew scholars understood that the children of Israel had been chosen (John 8:39, 9:28) and had been given a status of righteousness through the Law of Moses. Almost without awareness, the Hebrew scholars seem to have failed to recognize the grace of God, that was expressed as acts of mercy, quickening, strengthening, or kindness. Grace or mercy was offered to the citizens of Israel who were often disobedient, or had "hardened their hearts." As well, the primary emphasis of relationship to Yahweh seems to always be upon keeping the statutes of righteousness instead of being compassionate or honorable. (Psalm 119:9-16, 153-160)

The Mashiach was not identified as one that would bestow the grace of God upon the world. The Mashiach was to be primarily a blessing from God for the nation of Israel, because Israel had been given a promise to be blessed by God. Honor, kindness, and blessings would be given by God, not as an act of grace, but because of Jehovah's relationship to Abraham. In other words, the blessings would be given simply because the Hebrew people are the chosen ones.

According to several theological teachings, this national leader of latter times, a direct descendant of King David, will be an amazing individual. (1 Chronicles 17:11-14) At some time in the future, when the Hebrew people are worthy of redemption, or worthy of God's favor, this person will be directed by God to establish his right to be the Mashiach. The awareness of the need for tender mercies, or grace does not appear to be an integral part of Jewish theology. A comment from Jesus concerning this lack of understanding is offered by the apostle Mark.

The apostle recorded an interesting account concerning comments made by Jesus about the necessity of grace for the Israelites. On a certain day, Jesus was walking by the seashore, and a crowd was following him. As he was talking and teaching, he walked past Levi the son of Alpheus, who was sitting in the tax office. Jesus said to Levi, "Follow me." The tax collector got up and followed him. And later, while he was reclined at a meal in Levi's house, eating with several tax collectors and other unworthy citizens, the Jewish religious leaders began asking, "Why is he eating and drinking with tax collectors and sinners?" Jesus heard their comments, and said to them, "It is not those who are healthy who need a physician, but those who are sick. I did not come to call the righteous, but sinners." (Mark 2:13-17)

The fact that Jesus had also stated that he was sent only to the house of Israel should be emphasized. Therefore, Jesus was stating that he had been sent to Israel, the sick and sinners, who are in need of mercy and forgiveness. Jesus, the Messiah, did not come to restore a nation of righteous individuals who deserve his compassion; he came to bestow grace on Israel, and upon all of us, for we are all sinners. Yahweh is a God of pure complete grace for all of mankind, not limited grace to be offered only to certain chosen ones.

Jesus admonished the Pharisees by telling them that they should understand that God desires compassion, not sacrifice or religious service. He did not come to call the righteous, but sinners. (Matthew 9:13) Although the prophet Jonah understood that the Lord God was gracious and compassionate, he was angry because he thought that God's grace or willingness to forgive the evil deeds of the citizens of Nineveh should be unacceptable. Obviously, Jonah had a limited understanding of love that surpasses understanding. (Ephesians 3:17-19) He failed to understand the willingness of God to offer grace, even when the citizens of Nineveh did not truly deserve to be forgiven. (Jonah 4:9-11)

When God saw that the citizens of Nineveh had repented, he did not destroy them. Jonah was exceedingly displeased. He was very angry. He prayed, and complained, but acknowledged that he was aware that God is a gracious, merciful, slow to anger and of great kindness. Yahweh always repents of evil. (Jonah 3:10-4:4)

The story of Jonah teaches that all who seek to know Yahweh are accepted. As well, no one is acceptable unless God's gift of grace is acknowledged and accepted.

As part of the story of God's grace, the book of Ruth is offered to teach that Yahweh is willing to be the redeemer of Israel. The Hebrew scholars were held accountable for not learning the lessons of grace and forgiveness, and for their need for redemption.

Lessons of mercy and grace were also clearly offered by Jesus to the descendants of Abraham. (Luke 15:1-32) Jesus told them three parables. The characters of the parables represent the children of Abraham. Yahweh will someday, as an act of mercy and grace, run and embrace and kiss the lost sinners of Israel. (Luke 15:20)

The fact that Yahweh loves Israel, that he is a God of grace should be acknowledged with joy and celebration. He has graciously offered a gift of love and compassion and forgiveness and eternal life to all of mankind. For by the transgression of one, who was Adam, death ruled over mankind, but we have received grace and the gift of righteousness through the One, Jesus Christ. (Romans 5:17-19, 21)

The concept of God's grace is the foundation of the faith of the followers of Jesus Christ. (Matthew 11:28-30) This gracious offer of salvation and eternal life has been offered to everyone, by the only begotten Son of God who is One with the Father. This offer of peace and freedom, in this life and for eternity, is a gift of absolute unmerited grace from the One who is love.

We who have accepted Jesus of Nazareth as the Messiah believe that the Word of God, that includes the laws of Moses, has become flesh in the person of Jesus Christ and is the Word of Life. By the power of the Holy Spirit, this gift of spiritual life and love now resides in believers. The disciples of Jesus are not religious adherents who follow laws or commandments; for the requirements of the law, and the condemnation of the law has been fulfilled in Christ Jesus. Christians are followers of Christ and are bound by a law of love, a law of freedom that is to be expressed in Christ likeness, as appreciation for the gift of grace. Christians are free from the legal restrictions of the law. Those who live by the law of freedom are free to live in the light of grace and forgiveness. This does not mean that the law has been discarded or discredited. The value of the law has not changed and those who honor and keep the laws of Moses will be rewarded. (Psalm 19:7-11)

Yahweh's grace has been given as a gift; and keeping the law is no longer a means of gain or of reward. (Galatians 5:4) The requirements of the law have been fulfilled or accomplished, as an act of grace by the loving gift of Jesus Christ. And when his grace is accepted, nothing can nullify his grace. (Galatians 2:20-21) (Ephesians 1:3-7)

Legal or righteous acts have never been God's plan for salvation. Yahweh knew from the beginning that a supreme act of grace would be required. He is gracious and compassionate to sinners. As an act of divine grace, he has given eternal life to those who have faith that he is One and that he has sent his only son as a sacrifice, as a gift of love. (Revelation 3:20) (Romans 10:9)

Salvation is a gift of divine love, freely offered to the children of Israel, to all sinners, who are sick and in need of a physician. Salvation is not a reward for moral or religious deeds. Salvation is also not a reward reserved only for the chosen, or for the good things that anyone is able to do. (Ephesians 2:8-9) Salvation is an unmerited gift of eternal life from the One who is the father of all creation.

Many who heard the witness of the apostles were not able to understand that salvation is not obtained by moral or religious deeds. Indeed, the message of the Gospel does seem to discredit the customs and laws of Moses; however, many of the scribes believed and accepted the truth of their words. (Acts 6:7)

The children of Israel may be judged for failure to understand that the gift of grace is offered with complete freedom; however, the same must be applied to others as well. Several theological interpretations of scripture have been presented that distort or diminish the completeness of God's act of love and forgiveness. Nothing about the gospel, or God's act of grace is incomplete or lacking. To teach that saving grace must be worked out, that sanctification is a process, or to use phrases of scripture to teach that God's grace is restricted, difficult to find, or incomplete, is false teaching. (Matthew 7:14)

We should not simply state that salvation is a gift of grace, or that grace is a gift of divine love, without clearly understanding that amazing grace is fully free and completely complete. In truth, simplistic interpretations may be excused, for the gospel is indeed a spiritual miracle of love, forgiveness, and atonement. We can only attempt to comprehend the amount of love required and the majesty of the gift of eternal life.

The Almighty Creator looked down from Heaven, to see that there was no one righteous. No man or woman would ever be able to keep the law. (Romans 3:19-28) The world, all of Israel and all of creation was destined for destruction. A gift of life was necessary. (Romans 6:3-10) A gift of spiritual life was required. (Romans 8:1-16) This act of giving eternal life is the act of grace that is incomprehensible. The Father, the Holy Spirit, and the Son of God, together as One gave eternal life, as a gift of grace by …being born, in the flesh, as human …and then by dying …as human flesh and blood …and by renewing life …by rising from the tomb …alive! (1 Timothy 3:16) How was this done? Why was such love offered? How can this act of grace be explained? How can such amazing awesome divine love be comprehended? We can only stand in awe, and wonder …why the Almighty God of Heaven and the Universe would do this for you and for me?

On the cross, Jesus shouted, "It is finished." The act of grace was completed, nothing else was required, nothing can be added. Yes, finished. Yahweh is a God of grace, complete grace.

Thankfully, we are not required to understand, we are only asked to believe the words of truth, to have faith, the faith of a child that is strengthened by love. We are only required to believe in our heart and confess that Jesus Christ is Lord. Nothing more can be given. Nothing more is required.

# 30
# Holy

The description of the holiness of Yahweh is awesome and frightening. (Isaiah 6:3-4) (Revelation 4:8)

The essence or nature of holiness is beyond description or comprehension.

Although several affirmative words such as righteous, sanctified, divine, sacred, saintly, and awesome may be associated with holiness, none are truly synonymous. Perhaps a proper way to define holiness is to combine every amazing attribute of Deity into one word. The word would be holy. And then, because God remains incomprehensible, the description would be incomplete.

The presence of holiness, purity, and righteousness of Yahweh creates an inherent problem for an unholy human race. We were originally created in God's image, with some measure of purity, in a state of acceptance and without awareness of the possibility of being separated from a holy Deity. (Genesis 2:25) However, after this privilege was removed, only those who were designated as being holy, the Levite priest of Israel, were allowed to enter the presence of YHWH. All non-anointed Israelites were restricted, and many lost their lives by failure to recognize or to honor this physical and spiritual separation from a holy Deity.

Moses, while tending his flock, saw a burning bush that was not consumed. When God saw that Moses had turned aside and was approaching the bush, Yahweh prevented Moses from entering the presence of his holiness. He spoke to Moses from the midst of the bush, "Moses, Moses." Moses answered, "Here am I." And God said, "Do not come near. Take off your shoes from your feet, for the place where on you stand is holy ground. I am the God of your father, the God of Abraham, the God of Isaac, and the God of Jacob." And Moses hid his face; he was afraid to look upon God. (Exodus 3:3-6)

The very presence of holiness causes everything around Yahweh to be declared holy, even the ground on which he stands. His holiness separates him from anything that is unholy. Nothing that is unholy can enter his presence without being immediately destroyed. Yahweh's holiness is awesome and terrifying.

Even a limited awareness of the presence of God is fearful. In ever appearance of the presence of the Angel of the Lord, the angel said, "Fear not, for..." When Peter saw the miracle of a great catch of fish and realized that he was in the presence of holiness, he said, "Depart from me, for I am an unholy man, O Lord!" (Luke 5:4-8)

Yahweh, the Father of Israel, is holy. The Israelites were to be righteous, as God himself is holy; however, this task was essentially not possible. The book of Leviticus gives specific directions for religious ritual, as a means of atonement, when the nation of Israel or individuals failed to treat God as holy. This action of repentance would allow Yahweh to offer grace or forgiveness to the entire nation.

The requirement for respect and honor for Yahweh was not to be treated as trivial or excusable. And Nadab and Abihu, the sons of Aaron, took their sensors and put fire and incense therein, and offered unholy fire before the Lord, which God had not commanded. And fire was sent from the Lord and devoured them, and they died before the Lord. Then Moses reminded Aaron that this what the Lord meant when he said that He must be sanctified by those that come near him. Before all the people, Yahweh must be glorified. (Leviticus 10:1-3)

As stated, the requirement for righteousness is a natural consequence of the holiness of Yahweh. Yahweh was the Deity who brought the Israelites out of the land of Egypt; therefore, they were expected to be holy as God is holy. (Leviticus 11:45)

This requirement should not be interpreted to mean that Yahweh is a God of worship, or that his primary purpose or relationship to mankind is to obtain worship. God is infinite. He is worthy of praise and worship; however, as an infinite being, he is completely self-sufficient and requires nothing from mankind. (Micah 6:6-8) He loves and appreciates love, because he is Love. He does not require love to be complete. His actions of love and his reception of praise and worship are a natural consequence of his supreme existence. (Luke 19:40) In other words, God is One; he has not been made One by being called One or by being recognized as being One. He is a complete one. He is Deity. He does not become love by being the loving Father of Israel. He is love in the same way that he is "I Am."

On several different occasions and for several different reasons Isaiah offered poetic descriptions of the holiness of Yahweh. One of the beautiful expressions is the statement that the whole earth is full of His glory. (Isaiah 6:1-3) Holiness is beauty, charity, kindness, faith, honor, humility, goodness, grace, justice, freedom, knowledge, truth, perfection, majesty and glory, brilliantly displayed through the amazing light of the joy of life. God is the light of holiness, and in him there is no darkness. (1 John 1:5)

An interesting aspect concerning holiness is that Yahweh is extremely protective of holiness. This aspect of holiness, although not completely explained in scripture, must be understood and accepted. Luke said that if a word is said against the Son of man, the act may be forgiven. However, blasphemy against the Holy Spirit will not be forgiven. (Luke 12:10) YHWH is Holy! He is holy because he is the One true Deity. He is awesome in holiness and righteousness and honor.

Another aspect of holiness is that Yahweh has chosen to bless mankind with his holiness. His gracious gift of salvation is a blessing of holiness. This does not mean that believers have been made holy. Only Yahweh is holy. We have been sanctified so that we may be worthy of receiving the indwelling of the Holy Spirit. We are sanctified so that we may live in the presence of holiness. (Isaiah 12:1-6)

According to the words of scripture, the inspired word of God, the mystery of holiness is amazing. As an act of holiness, Jesus was revealed in the flesh, vindicated in the Spirit, beheld by angels, proclaimed among the nations, believed on in the world, and taken up in glory. (1 Timothy 3:16) Yahweh is holy and righteous, and worthy of praise. (Exodus 15:11) Jehovah is the Lord who shall reign in holiness forever and ever. (Exodus 15:18)

# 31
# Honor

Blessings are also offered from God for deeds of honor.

The word honor has several different meanings for different situations, or when used as a noun or a verb or as an adjective. To be honored, or to receive honor, is to be offered respect, recognition, distinction, or esteem. To honor others or to be honorable is to be respectful, faithful, non-judgmental, forgiving, kind, truthful, admirable, and trustworthy.

Honor is a primary characteristic of Deity. Yahweh is a God of honor!

In much the same way that scripture states that the God is love, we could easily state that the essence of Deity is honor. God is always honorable or willing to offer honor and respect. As well, Yahweh deserves respect, recognition, esteem, and honor. As an infinite deity, Yahweh deserves honor, not simply because he is Deity, but because his is a worthy father.

The most outstanding aspect of honor expressed by Yahweh is loving kindness that is offered to the poor and oppressed. As the father of all nations in heaven or on earth, God is compassionately concerned about trust and love and honor. As a blessing or recognition for acts of honor, Yahweh has established consequences so that rewards are returned to the one who is honorable. (1 Samuel 2:30) (Proverbs 14:31)

Perhaps because the relationship of honor and blessings are so often misunderstood, the value of honor may be discounted. Honorable deeds may be neglected; and acts of dishonor may be excused. Nevertheless, we must not fail to recognize that Yahweh is a God of honor. The followers of Christ Jesus are required to live by a code of honor. We are required to honor God by offering acts of love for others. (2 Timothy 2:19-21)

Legal rules and regulations are based upon what is beneficial for the unity and peace of mankind. Rules and codes of honor are basically common sense. The Apostle Paul said that a woman should not teach or exercise authority over a man, but to remain quiet. (1 Timothy 2:12, 8:15) If one assumes that this rule establishes a status of inequality, the value of the lesson of honor may be misunderstood and disregarded. The key words are "authority over a man." The teaching involves a complicated situation of creation, of Adam and Eve, and a simple matter of honor and respect, of a wife to a husband and to her children. Honor for a man is necessary because God requires fathers to be responsible for the care of their family. A father is required to love his wife, as himself, in a godly way, and to honor and protect his children. Because much is required, the man requires respectful support. Honor given to the husband is necessary to help him fulfill his required responsibilities and sets an example for the children to do likewise. An atmosphere of respect and cooperation is established. If a wife fails to honor her husband, by taking authority from him, she fails to honor her children and herself; and she fails to honor God. As such, the rule of equality between male or female, husband and wife, or children and adults is maintained.

The laws of Israel and the rules of social conduct are laws of honor and love. (Exodus 20:12) (Ephesians 6:2) The law was given by Yahweh as a blessing to the children of Abraham. (Proverbs 14:19-22) The first law of honor is the requirement to honor Yahweh as the Father of Israel. Yahweh is a father who deserves honor; and he is one who requires honor. The words of the Lord's Prayer, "Our Father, who art in heaven, hallowed be thy name." is a statement of honor. (Matthew 6:9) The one who does not honor the Father will experience the same condemnation as the one called Lucifer. (Isaiah 14:12-19) As well, honor is to be given to the Son of Yahweh, because as One with the Father, he is worthy of honor. (Luke 19:39-40)

The second law of honor is that respect is to be given to others, even to non-Hebrew residents and to strangers and neighbors. (Matthew 22:37-40) (Proverbs 23:24) (1 Timothy 5:25)

In like manner, the disciples of Christ are required to honor everyone, even our enemies, as a gift of respect from Jehovah. Honor requires an attitude of forbearance, of forgiveness and tolerance.

Most of what Jesus offered in his Sermon on the Mount concerns honor. (Matthew 4:1-7:29) If we wish to understand that the Lord of Heaven is compassionate, humble, meek, patient, respectful, empathetic, honorable, and loving, we should study the words of the teaching of Jesus. As well, the account in the book of Luke, concerning John the Baptist should be considered. John did not establish a moral religion; he emphasized God's code of honor. (Luke 3: 8)

One who lives a life committed to a code of love and honor will achieve a greater worth than one who is merely religious or moral. The one who is honorable will live in his integrity; and his children will be blessed after him. (Proverbs 20:7)

The admonishment that Jesus offered to the Pharisees and Sadducees was the same that John the Baptist had offered. Jesus did not admonish the religious rulers about religious devotion; he judged them for lack of honor to others. (Matthew 15:7-9)

For us, instructions of honor have been clearly stated. We are to honor one another with brotherly love. As a requirement of honor, we are to give preference to others. (Romans 12:10) All is to be done for the glory or honor of God. (1 Corinthians 10:31) We are required to honor the King eternal, immortal, invisible, the only God, with honor and glory forever and ever. (1 Timothy 1:17

# 32
# Hope

Hope is a gift of love offered through faith in Jesus Christ. Hope is an assurance that we have an inheritance, reserved in heaven for us, that is everlasting. (1 Peter 1:3-5)

Hope is an expectation of the fulfillment of a promise. The joy of anticipation is what a child would experience while waiting to open a precious gift. Hope involves delayed gratification, with full trust in the fulfillment of the wish. Hope involves a true expectation with confidence in the promise.

Hope, like faith, is an assurance of things not seen. The assurance of salvation is a heartfelt awareness of the presence of love and joy and peace. Our hope in Jesus Christ, the expectation of the fulfillment of the promise of eternal life, is a gift of love.

Yahweh is a God of hope. Hope is a gift of love. The gift of hope has been offered with the words of a promise, "Fear not, for behold I bring you good tidings of great joy that shall be to all people." (Luke 2:8-11) Hope is a blessing of peace offered by Jesus. (John 14:3)

The promise of salvation and eternal life was offered as a gift of hope to the children of Abraham. Yahweh promised to bless Israel and make them "a praise among all people of the earth." (Zephaniah 3:14-20)

Hope is a gift from the Holy Spirit, a blessing from our Heavenly Father to those who have faith in his promises. Perhaps, when we read the words, "these three remain, faith and hope and love," we may emphasize faith and love, but fail to consider the wonder of hope. The gift of hope, strengthened by the presence of the Holy Spirit, is a gift of joy, peace, and assurance, that allows us to say, "We know the One in whom we have believed and are assured that He will keep his promises." (2 Timothy 1:12)

Hope is a promise of the faithfulness of Yahweh to the nation of Israel that is to be shared with all believers. (Psalm 37:7-9) Spiritual hope is an expectation of the promise of resurrection and eternal life, offered as a gift of grace from our Heavenly Father. Before Felix, the Roman governor at Caesarea, the apostle Paul explained the expectation of a blessing from Yahweh, that the children of Israel shared, according to prophecies of the prophets of Israel. The apostle Paul also explained this promise of faith and hope of eternal life to king Agrippa. (Acts 24: 10-16, 26:6-8)

God's gift of the hope of resurrection and eternal life brings joy and assurance, peace and strength. (Romans 5:5) Hope takes away the need to perform religious acts of righteousness. (Romans 8:14-17) Therefore, we should sanctify the Lord God in our hearts and be ready always to give an answer to every man that asks for the reason of the hope that we have. (1 Peter 3:15)

Hope is a spiritual connection with our Father of Heaven. When the promise of hope has been fulfilled; there is no longer any need for hope, for the joy of receiving the promise will be experienced. (Psalms 30:5) However, the experience of the hope that Yahweh offers will never be taken away. (Psalm 30:11-12)

Yahweh is a father of hope. He has given hope, in Jesus Christ; and he will fulfill his promise of that hope. Yahweh will always be a father of faith and hope and love.

The gift of hope is a precious gift of love. (Romans 8:20-25)

# 33
# Humility

We can have faith in God because he is love. We can trust God because he is the one who has all power and authority. We can learn to love as he loves, because he is meek and lowly in heart. (Matthew 11:28-30)

Humility is a moral quality or strength of character that is evident when one is not controlled by self-directed needs or desires. Humility is to be able to have a modest estimate of one's own importance. Humility is to guard against being proud or arrogant, haughty, or boastful.

Although humility is an identifiable human character trait that is approved by God, to state that Yahweh is a God of humility would be incorrect. Therefore, his approval of humility can only be identified as an identifiable positive aspect of love. For mankind, humility is a positive trait that is beneficial to oneself and to others. Humility is a valuable and honorable character quality that establishes friendship, and social unity. Humility is a positive trait of character that should not be classified as meekness.

Because humility has been mistakenly identified with traits of weakness or lack of honor, the fact that an almighty, supreme, divine, infinite being would be able to appreciate and honor humility is difficult to understand.

One recorded event, that is obviously used to recognize the fact that God is always loving and kind, also demonstrates God's appreciation of humility. This historical event occurred during the reign of king Hezekiah. Hezekiah posted announcements to all Israel and Judah, Ephraim and Manasseh, telling them to celebrate the Passover in Jerusalem. (2 Chronicles 30:1)

The people of Israel and Judah responded to the King's request. They chose to humble themselves before Yahweh. The event was planned so quickly that many who wanted to participate did not have time for ritual preparation and proper cleansing; however, those who were spiritually willing to humble themselves were allowed to participate although they had not been ritually prepared. King Hezekiah prayed that God would pardon all who had prepared their hearts, though not according to the purification of the sanctuary. God heard the king's prayer and gave his blessings for the celebration. (2 Chronicles 30:17-27)

Obviously, Yahweh considers humility to be a human character trait that is of great value and worthy of being acknowledged. Perhaps because honor is a central aspect of his nature and character, Yahweh also appreciates acts of honor that are expressed with humility.

Another account is about king Manasseh who humbled himself and prayed, and God returned him from exile in Babylon. (2 Chronicles 33:12) The son of Manasseh, king Josiah, also humbled himself before Yahweh, and was rewarded for acts of humility. Yahweh heard the prayers of Manasseh. God also promised to delay the time of his judgment for Israel so that the king would not witness the evil that was to be brought upon Judah. (2 Chronicles 34:26-28)

God is even willing to honor a foreign King or anyone that willingly puts away unjustified pride. Nebuchadnezzar declared that he would praise and honor the King of Heaven, for all the words of God are true and his actions are just. As well, as an act of justice, Yahweh may choose to humble those who live a life of pride. (Daniel 4:37)

Humility is to express modesty, to be respectful, to not be pretentious or assertive. (Luke 14:11) Perhaps for Yahweh, this is a simple act of being respectful to all of creation. As well, because Yahweh has no need to be assertive or prideful, his actions that are expressed as being meek and lowly in heart are simple acts of lovingkindness.

Jesus, who is one with God, clearly expressed the fact that Yahweh is a God who encourages humility and honor. Jesus offered a parable to the religious teachers who considered themselves to be righteous, although they despised others. The parable is about a Pharisee and a publican. The two were praying in the temple. (Luke 18:9-14) The lesson of the parable is that everyone that exalts himself will be abased, and the one that humbles himself will be exalted. (Luke 18:14)

The account of Stephen is another lesson of humility. The power of the Holy Spirit was upon Stephen as he humbly accepted his death and prayed for forgiveness for those who judged him. (Acts 7:60) If we are insulted for the name of Christ, we are blessed. (1 Peter 4:14)

The reason why humility is a primary requirement of those who have chosen to be a Christ-one is clearly understandable. We possess nothings; we have accomplished nothing for which we might be proud. The worth or value that we have has been given as a gift. We are sinners saved by grace. We should not think more highly of ourselves than we should think. (Romans 12:32)

We are required to live a life of humility. We are to submit ourselves to God and resist the devil. We are to draw near to God and humble ourselves in the sight of God. (James 4:6-11) We are to "put on bowels of mercies, kindness, humbleness of mind, meekness, long-suffering, forgiveness and charity, which is the bond of perfectness." (Colossians 3:12-16)

With humility, the apostle Paul graciously acknowledged dependence upon Jesus. (1 Timothy 1:15) With love he committed himself to suffer with fellow Christians. With joy he professed faith in Jesus Christ. (Philippians 1:21, 29) He was able to do only what the Holy Spirit gave him the strength to accomplish. (2 Timothy 4:7)

We should as well pay close attention to the teachings of the apostles Peter and James. (1 Peter 5:5-7) (James 4:8-10) (Psalm 51:16-17)

Although humility and meekness are primary requirements for the disciples of Christ, many are unfortunately missing the blessing offered for acts of meekness and humility. (1 Corinthians 4:1-16) We have been clearly taught that God is opposed to the proud but gives grace to the humble. (James 4:6) As well, the wise will be granted honor, but fools receive dishonor. (Proverbs 3:34-35)

For us, humility must also be expressed by accepting the one who is weak in faith, without the purpose of passing judgment on his opinions. (Romans 14:1-12) Humility is a positive attitude of love. The one who is humble does not judge or condemn. (Romans 14:13-23) The one who is humble is willing to support and encourage others. (Romans 15:1-9) The humble are willing to be the servants of all. (Mark 10:44) The one who is humble should have an attitude of forbearance. (Philippians 4:5) To be humble is to be teachable, patient while suffering and willing to endure injustice.

We should remember that Jesus is the one who, by an act of love and sovereign authority, set the example of the positive value of humility. (1 Peter 2:21)

God placed Jesus in a highly exalted position and gave him a name above all names. (Philippians 2:6-9)

# 34
## Humor

Sometimes, humor may be found, or assumed, in unusual places or situations. (Proverbs 17:1)

Humor is an action or statement made with the intent to cause amusement or laughter. Humor is the ability to understand, express or enjoy what is comical or amusing.

Character traits of any individual may be hidden or non-revealed. Although there are accounts that show that God was pleased, there are no passages of scripture that state that God laughed or smiled. As well, statements or accounts that indicate that Yahweh is opposed to humor are not available.

We are also unable to state that Yahweh has expressed appreciation for anything that was comical or funny.

There is a humorous account about the non-Israelite prophet Balaam and his donkey, but there is no indication that God thought that this was a humorous situation. (Numbers 22-24) (2 Peter 2:15-16) Another comical situation is when the heathen idol Dagon is placed in a position of submission before the Ark of the Lord. (Samuel 5:1-5)

Several other situations are only slightly humorous. We have been instructed to not neglect to entertain strangers, for some have unknowingly entertained angels. (Hebrews 13:2)

As a process of deduction, we could reason that since mankind was created in God's image, Yahweh is One who appreciates humor. As well, because laughter and joy are associated with humor, and because God obviously approves of joy and laughter, we may assume that he does not disapprove of humor.

Obviously, Yahweh, who is a God of loving-kindness, is concerned about attitudes and actions that are beneficial, instead of just being able to make one laugh.

Words of wisdom come forth from the heart of the wise. Pleasant words are like a honeycomb, sweet to the soul and healing to the bones. (Proverbs 16:23-24)

Obviously, concerning humor, we must be satisfied with a limited understanding of the one infinite God; however, it is wise to remember that a joyful heart is good medicine. (Proverbs 17:22)

## 35

## Infinite

The infinite nature of Deity has been clearly described in scripture. God can count the number of the stars and give names to all of them. His power and authority are great, and his understanding is infinite. (Psalm 147:5) The heaven of heavens, cannot contain him. (2 Chronicles 2:6)

Infinite is to exist in limitless space, that cannot be calculated or measured.

The essence or meaning of infinite may best be defined without words, as a picture or a vision. The image would be limitless outer space, of expanded size that is impossible to measure, filled with shapes of light and matter, beyond reach or calculation.

Simply stated, the infinite is the unknown.

Yahweh is the God of the infinite, the unknown or unmeasurable.

God is exceedingly great! His power is unmeasurable and unlimited. The meaning of infinity is to be uncountable, or to be expanded without limits or border. Although Yahweh is great and the heavens cannot contain him, he is not to be described as a great unbounded expanse. He is the beauty and wonder of all of existence.

The infinite cannot be completely explained. All we can do is to stand in awe of the majesty of the unknown and wonder what might be there. The beauty and wonder of the infinite nature of Yahweh is that we know that he is there. He is light and love. We have heard him say, "I Am."

Although we are unable to see or understand the infinite nature of deity, the infinite One has, as an act of love and grace, revealed himself by and through Immanuel, Yahweh with us. (John 14:9)

# 36
# Invisible

Love is the evidence of the existence of Deity. Like love, no one has seen God at any time. If we love one another, his love dwells in us. The way that we know that we dwell in him and he in us is because he has given us of his invisible Spirit. (1 John 4:12-13)

To be invisible is to be unnoticeable, undetectable, unperceivable, or even without form or void, but existing and present in a state of reality.

Any form or substance that is nonexistent would be invisible. However, a state of invisibility does not establish a state of nonexistence. The concept of being invisible implies that something exists or is present that cannot be seen.

An invisible object or subject can be physically described with non-visible attributes. What is invisible, although beyond sight or perception, may also be sensed through feeling or perception, or by an unknown or undescribed psychological understanding. Awareness cannot be used as proof of the existence of the invisible; however, in contrast to that which is merely hidden from sight, the presence and existence of the Holy Spirit is evident by the actions of the Spirit. The Holy Spirit is like the wind that, although invisible, can be experienced as a gentle breeze.

YHWH may be present as invisible Spirit; however, he is also more than invisible spirit. Job, the man of honor, understood that although God is invisible, God is always present. (Job 9:11) The apostle Paul identified Jesus, the first born of all creation, as the image of the invisible God. (Colossians 1:13-15)

The apostle Paul also gave a beautiful description of the invisible nature of Deity. The apostle called God the King eternal, immortal, invisible, the One to whom everlasting honor and glory should be given. (1 Timothy 1:17) (Hebrews 11:27)

The apostle John also understood that no man has seen God at any time. (1 John 4:12)

Although Yahweh is invisible, he is always present to watch over the earth.

(Proverbs 15:3) He humbles himself to observe the things that are in heaven and in the earth, to watch over the poor or those in need of acts of charity. (Psalm 113:4-6)

Yahweh is invisible; but has always been evident. To be evident is to exist, to be distinctly and unmistakably present. (Psalm 104:2-3) Yahweh is clearly seen in the beauty of the universe and the earth and in the magnificent wonder of creation. (Romans 1:20)

Yahweh is unseen; but always present. He has always been revealed. (Jeremiah 23:23-24)

This fact is an amazing, almost indescribable aspect of Yahweh. Although he is unseen, he is love that is not far from us. The apostle Paul attempted to explain this situation to the Athenians. The apostle Paul told the Athenians that Yahweh is the God that made the world and all things within it. Although Yahweh is Lord of heaven and earth, and although He does not dwell in temples, he is one that can be seen or known if one searches for him. (Acts 17:22-29)

The invisible Almighty One has been revealed by the One called Emmanuel, God with us. The apostle Paul offered a beautiful description of our invisible God of love. (1 Timothy 6:16-17)

The One who is the revelation of God is also the only One who has seen the Father, for he is the only One which is of God. (John 6:46) The One who is the image of the invisible God is also the One in whom mankind has been offered the forgiveness of sin. (Colossians 1:14-15)

Jesus is the only One through whom the invisible Yahweh can be seen. He is the light that takes away the darkness. (John 14:6-7)

Yahweh did not instruct us to look among the stars, or to search the Temple to find him, he has said, "Be still and know that I am God." (Psalm 46:10-11)

# 37
## Jealousy

The children of Israel were not allowed to worship false gods. Several reasons for this restriction have been given. One reason is that the Lord their God is a jealous God. (Exodus 34:14)

Jealously is commonly defined as a negative emotional feeling associated with insecurity or negative emotions such as anger or resentment. Although jealousy may be related to envy, jealousy may also be a positive aspect related to acts of protection.

The jealousy expressed by the statement that the Lord is a jealous God is completely contrary to a common definition of the word jealousy. The statement that Yahweh is a jealous God does not make Yahweh a God of jealousy. Yahweh is a God of righteousness.

For Yahweh, a state of jealousy is not a state of envy. His righteous jealousy is a righteous desire to protect something of great personal value. To say that God can be jealous or that he experiences jealousy would imply that God is provoked to anger when proper respect or honor is not given. This description is not accurate. Yahweh is a God of loving-kindness; therefore, his jealousy may best be described as righteous protection.

The Apostle Paul expressed God's righteous protection. (2 Corinthians 11:2) Yahweh is prepared to righteously protect Israel and those who have professed faith in him.

The jealousy expressed by Yahweh is directly related to Israel's unfaithfulness in worshiping other gods. Although unfaithful actions of Israel stirred up righteous anger, Yahweh was moved to protect his children.

The children of Israel, while camped near the land of Moab, began to commit unethical acts with the daughters of Moab. This was prohibited by specific instructions from Yahweh, not for the purpose of racial or ethnic separation but with a stated purpose of protecting the nation of Israel from the evil of false religion. God was very angry, but his anger was diverted by the actions of righteous priest. (Numbers 25:1-18) The Levite was given specific mention in scripture. Because Phinehas, the son of Eleazar, was zealous with the jealousy of God, Yahweh turned from his wrath against the Israelites. (Numbers 25:11)

Moses warned the people of Israel concerning Yahweh's righteous protection concerning other gods or graven images. Moses described God as a consuming fire. (Deuteronomy 4:23-24)

Moses also warned the people in a song, given by the Spirit of God. (Deuteronomy 31:22) Nevertheless, because the Israelites were often unfaithful, Yahweh was moved to jealousy. Yahweh was angry because of their vanities. Therefore, He decided to cause Israel to be jealous with those that were not the chosen children of Abraham. God had decided to provoke the Israelites to anger with a foolish nation. (Deuteronomy 32:21-22)

The explanation of this prophecy was offered by Jesus as an admonishment to a small group of Jewish elders. (Matthew 21:27–22:14) This passage must not be used to declare that salvation has been taken away from Israel, or that the covenant of Abraham and Moses has been annulled.

The kingdom of heaven or the kingdom of God is the present age, the times of the Gentiles, a time of salvation for a people that are to produce fruits of righteousness, if indeed foolish believers are capable of honoring God, if they are wearing wedding clothes.

As well, although Israel has not been wise enough to come to the King's marriage feast for his son, Yahweh has not rejected Israel. The apostle Paul called this decision a mystery of which all should be clearly informed. We must not be wise in our own estimation, for only a partial hardening has happened to Israel, until the fullness of the Gentiles is completed. "So, all Israel will be saved, for the deliverer shall turn away ungodliness from Jacob." (Romans 11:25-26)

YHWH is a God of righteousness who loves Israel with an everlasting jealous love.

## 38
## Joyful

Several emotional responses to the presence of God are expressed in the words of the Psalms. Amazement, fear, honor, and wonder are beautifully expressed; however, joy is the most precious. Joy is an expression of thankfulness, assurance, comfort, and peace that is felt deep withing the heart.

Joy is an emotional response to express happiness, delight, pleasure, and gladness. Joy may be expressed with tears or singing. Joy may be an overwhelming sense of peace that is present when sorrow and sadness has been taken away. Joy may be expressed with laughter, leaping and dancing, and even with shouts of praise.

Joy is a beautiful gift of blessing from Yahweh.
The Father of Heaven and Earth is a God of amazing, wonderful joy and celebration. Yahweh's gift to the world is to take away sorrow and sadness and pain and give unspeakable joy full of glory and peace and love. (John 3:16)
A promise of overwhelming joy was offered to Abram.
The promise to Abram from God for a covenant of friendship is an amazing choice by a God of love. (Genesis 17:2) When Abram was ninety years old, the Lord God Almighty appeared before Abram, to inform him that his wife Sarai would give birth to a son. Although the elderly Abram

laughed and expressed doubt, Yahweh did not directly respond. Instead, God told Abram that the name of the child would be Isaac. (Genesis 17:18-19) The meaning of this amazing name is one who shall laugh, or one who shall rejoice. Through the seed of Isaac (Romans 9:7) the gift of joy, that was given to Abraham and to Israel was to be shared with all of mankind. (Romans 11:26) To a woman of Samaria, Jesus affirmed this gift of love by telling her that salvation is of the Jews. (John 4:22)

As well, Yahweh offered a blessing of love for Ishmael. (Genesis 17:20) This blessing is also a prophecy of the joy that was to be offered to all of mankind. (John 3:16-17)

Because of the faith of Abraham, joy was given as a promise to the nation of Israel. Joyful celebration was promised to the children of Israel before the tribes entered the promised land of Canaan. (Deuteronomy 12: 7, 12)

As well, Israel celebrated their return to Jerusalem.

In Jerusalem the Israelites kept the feast of unleavened bread seven days with great gladness. Then, because they were so joyful, the people decided to celebrate an additional seven days. Since the time of king Solomon there had not been anything like this in Jerusalem. As stated in scripture, the sound of the celebration came up to the holy dwelling place of Yahweh, even unto heaven. (2 Chronicles 30:16-27)

Many of the Psalms are beautiful, amazing expressions of appreciation of joy and celebration.

Joy is expressed in dancing, singing, shouting and clapping of hands. Shouting with a "voice of triumph" would be a joyful shout of "freedom." (Psalm 47:1-2) The thought of being in the presence of Love is a joyful thought. (Psalm 95:1-11, 149:5, 150:1-6)

The joy of being free, alive in the Kingdom of Heaven, cannot be adequately or completely described. (Psalm 96:11-13)

Several prophecies for the nation of Israel are promises of joy. The prophet Zephaniah, offering a direct promise of joy, said that the Lord God will save Israel. Yahweh will rejoice over Israel with joy. He will rest in his love. He will joy over Israel with singing. (Zephaniah 3:17-20)

While speaking to the publicans and sinners, Jesus offered three parables as prophecy of celebration and joy for the children of Abraham. First, Jesus told the parable of the lost sheep, and the parable of the lost coin. (Luke 15:1-10) Then Jesus told a story of a certain man that had two sons. (Luke 15:11)

In this narrative, the two sons are used as lessons for the children of Israel. The first son, the prodigal son, dishonored his father by committing acts considered to be unforgivable. According to Hebrew law, when a son had dishonored his father, the father was allowed to disown the son, or even to take the life of the unfaithful son. However, in defiance of tradition, this father openly, before the entire community, forgave the repentant son. As a gift of forgiveness and grace, the son was restored to his position of honor. As well the father joyously celebrated with his son. (Luke 15:12-23) The service and honor offered by the second son was noted, appreciation was expressed, and opportunity of joyful celebration was offered to both Hebrew sons, to all of Israel. In this account, the prophecy of forgiveness offered by Zephaniah is vividly portrayed. (Zephaniah 3:18-20)

The apostle Paul clearly understood the joy promised to Israel. The following passage of scripture should be carefully read and studied, for the apostle Paul is teaching several lessons of theology; however, the joy of redemption has been clearly expressed.

(Romans 11:25-32) The fulfillment of the promises of God will be a time of rejoicing, for the descendants of the one named Israel. (Genesis 17:19) The gift promised to the house of Israel, the one who struggles but is protected, is a promise from the Father of Heaven and earth.

Jehovah is a God of joy for he appreciates joy and celebration. The words of the angels, "Joy to the world, peace, and good will" are words of joyful celebration. The joy of eternal life is a precious treasure, a blessing from Yahweh, to be cherished and appreciated.

The citizens of Jerusalem were given a brief time of joyful hope and celebration for the promises of Yahweh's gift of grace. As Jesus entered the city, the multitude that followed him shouted, "Hosanna to the Son of David. Blessed is he that comes in the name of the Lord. Hosanna in the highest." (Matthew 21:9) This brief account of celebration is also a prophecy of the future time of joy promised to the children of Abraham.

The people recognized the promised Messiah, and the joy and excitement of the event was expressed by the children with joyful shouts of hope and freedom.

Nevertheless, the chief priests and scribes were not celebrating. (Matthew 21:15)

Yahweh is indeed the God of joy and life and freedom, treasures offered as a gift of grace through his precious Son, Jesus Christ. Jesus submitted himself as a gift of love, to die on the cross, for the joy set before him. (Hebrews 12:2)

Those who believed that Jesus is the Messiah were joyful. The disciples of Jesus returned to Jerusalem, praising and blessing God. (Luke 24:52-53)

Yahweh has offered the fullness of joy through faith in Jesus Christ. (Psalm 16:7-11) The gift of salvation, offered by a God of love, includes the greatest gift of joy that will ever be offered. (Hebrews 12:2) The joy of God is expressed in the story of the shepherd and his lost sheep (Luke 15:4-6) the account of the lost coin (Luke 8-10) and in the story of the wayward son. (Luke 15:11-32) There will be joy in the kingdom of Heaven over all the lost that are found. In the same way, there is joy in the presence of the angels of God over one sinner that repents. (Luke 15:10)

Joy is an amazing gift of salvation. (1 John 3:1) As an act of faith we can rejoice in our salvation. (1 Peter 1:8) Our time of travail in this life will not be taken away, but joy is a promise from God. (John 16:20)

Because joy has been offered as a blessing, believers are encouraged to be joyful in all circumstances. (Philippians 4:4-7) Although we may not understand, strength is offered with joy; therefore, we have been instructed to pray, so that our joy may be full. (John 16:24) Joy is included among the gifts of the Spirit. The Holy Spirit offers love, peace, longsuffering, gentleness, goodness, faith, meekness, self-control, and joy. (Galatians 5:22-23) This is the fullness of joy that has been promised by God. (Psalm 16:11) The joy of the Lord is your strength. (Nehemiah 8:10)

Would it be reasonable to assume that because Yahweh is an almighty God that he would be unable to experience joy in the same way that we express joy. Surely, because he is love, he must experience joy. He is a God of love. He must be a God of joyfulness. He has commanded us to rejoice. He must consider joy to be a blessing. (Luke 10:42) He has experienced grieve. (John 11:35) Surely, he should be able to rejoice. (Genesis 6:5-7)

Although we know that we shall suffer trials and hardships, we are to rejoice, for when his glory is revealed, we will be joyful with exceeding joy. (1 Peter 4:13) (Acts 13:52) (Philippians 4:4)

Everlasting joy is a promise of love from a faithful Father of life and existence. (Psalm 30:5)

## 39
## Judgment

God did not send the Son to condemn the world; he sent his only Son as a gift of love and forgiveness. (John 3:17)

As an act of wisdom, judgment is the ability to make a logical or sensible decision or to take acceptable action. To make a judgment is to state an opinion or to take proper action. Judgment is also the authority of a judge to make a legal ruling. A judicial judgment is a decision of a court or a judge that is intended to be a ruling of truth and justice. An act of justice is a judgment that is true, accurate and fair. Judgment should not be defined as condemnation.

Judgment may be incorrectly defined as punishment, retribution, or penalty for a misjudgment or unacceptable behavior. Judgment is not necessarily punishment or correction. Judgment and justice are equal requirements of a legal ruling that should never be separated. For this reason, judgment may be a positive blessing.

As well, judgment is both simple and complex. For example, a beautiful fruit tree may be judged to be unworthy if unable to produce fruit. (Luke 3:9)

Yahweh is not a God of judgment. He is a God of justice.

Mercy and truth are expressions of God's love. (Psalm 89:14) The power and authority of mercy and truth, judgment and justice has been given to the Son of God. (Matthew 16:27)

The judgment of God is based upon the wisdom of God, and the wisdom and knowledge of God is unsearchable, and always true. (Romans 11:33)

As a God of justice, Yahweh must have the right of judgment. (Ecclesiastes 3:17) Without the right of judgment, justice would not be possible. Without judgment or justice, rewards could not be offered. (Hebrews 10:30-31) (2 Corinthians 5:12-13) (2 Peter 2:4-9) Without judgment, misjudgments or errors could not be corrected.

Justice depends upon the availability of truth and upon the honor of the judge and his ability to award justice. Yahweh is the only righteous judge. His right to judge and the justice of his judgment should not be questioned. (Psalm 7:11-16)

For Yahweh, the authority of judgment is a natural consequence of holiness or righteousness. (Psalm 34:16). For this reason, the judgment of Yahweh is never restricted. (Luke 19:27) The positive aspect of this fact is that justice is always present. (Luke 10:10-16) The judgment for the children of Abraham has been explained in a parable. (Mark 12:1-11) Judgment was required because the corner stone of the temple of the Kingdom of Heaven was rejected. Jesus was not recognized and accepted as the Messiah. (Mark 12:10) (Matthew 12:36-37) (Luke 19:11-27) (Matthew 11:20-24)

Concerning the judgment of mankind, Yahweh has made a choice concerning justice. He has given the final act of justice to his only son, Jesus Christ. (John 5:19-29)

Because Yahweh is a God of judgment, he did not send his Son to judge the world. Jesus offered a complete explanation of the judgment and justice of the acceptance or rejection of Truth. (John 12:46-49)

Jesus Christ came to provide justice for the world, not judgment. Jesus warned the religious leaders of the judgment of God. In response to their statements, Jesus said, "I honor my Father, and you dishonor me. I do not seek my own glory. There is only One that seek and judges." (John 8:49-50) This fact is true, simply because the world has already been judged. Judgment has been established for mankind; and Yahweh has reserved the right of final justice for himself. The gospel as an act of grace removes judgment, but justice is required. (Luke 12:49)

The truth, according to the words of scripture is that the Father sent the Son, to offer salvation through Jesus Christ. Justice has been foreordained as a matter of choice. The one that believes in Jesus is not judged; and the one that does not believe has been judged already, because he has not believed in the name of the only begotten Son of God. The truth that requires justice is that the light of life, which is Jesus Christ, has come into the world, and judgment is present for those who choose the darkness of separation from God and not the light of life that has been offered as a gift of love. (John 3:17-19)

Yahweh is indeed a God of justice. (Exodus 34:6-7)

The conclusion, when all has been heard, is that we must fear God and keep His commandments, because this applies to every person. Truly, Yahweh will bring every act to judgment, everything that is hidden, whether it is good or evil. (Ecclesiastes 12:13-14)

# 40
# Justice

With the warnings concerning judgment, the loving concern of God is always expressed. Because God is love, he will judge the world in righteousness. Justice will always be provided. As an act of justice, those who trust God will not be forsaken. (Psalm 9:7-10)

Justice is the positive aspect of judgment. Justice is fair treatment based upon respect, honor, equality, soundness, correctness, or impartial selection. Justice is a correct judgement achieved by action that is worthy, practical, logical, and fair.

The subject of justice is a primary theme among the words of scripture written by the prophets of Israel. Their words of poetry and prophecy are amazing words of truth. (Amos 5:24)

Yahweh is truly a God of Justice. Justice and righteousness are always obtained by the decisions of Yahweh. Judgment may be delayed, altered, or completely changed as a direct consequence of God's compassion, but his decisions and judgments are always acts of justice.

Eliphaz the Temanite experienced a vision. A form appeared. There was silence and then the form spoke, "Can mankind be just before God? Can a man be pure before his Maker?" (Job 4:12-21) Note that the evil one called Satan is most likely involved in this situation. We should assume that the form that appeared to Eliphaz may have been sent by Satan, to offer half-truths about the character of God. In this passage, a statement of truth concerning judgment is used incorrectly without any regard for the relationship of judgment and justice. The one of evil is always anxious to cause doubt concerning the judgment and justice of God.

Regardless of what is said by Job or his associates or anyone, Yahweh's right to judge, and the purity of his justice, is always the same. Because his actions are just, his judgment should never be questioned. He is always compassionate and understanding. He offers righteous justice with every judgment.

We may question or doubt the possibility of life after death, but we know that we shall surely die. However, we believe that because God is Love we have been offered, as an act of grace, the gift of eternal life and joy and peace and blessings. Jesus, by taking the judgment or condemnation that we deserve has set us free from the law of sin and death. (Romans 8:1)

There is only one righteous judge for mankind, the Lord God Almighty. No one other than YHWH has the right to judge; and there is no other One able to establish justice. As an act of grace, he has chosen to offer the choice of being set free, to have life instead of death.

Job clearly understood that we are all depend upon the loving mercy of a God of justice and righteousness. (Job 9:30-33)

A reward for faithfulness and honor has been offered to the nation of Israel. This promise is offered by an almighty God whose word is the same yesterday, today and forever. Because this is a choice made by God himself, the judgment is an act of justice. (Mark 12:9-11) This judgment is not a reward for righteousness. The judgment is a blessing to Abraham. This judgment is an act of grace. The judgment of God is an act of love.

The word of God, through Moses, offered words of prophecy for Israel concerning the latter days, a time of tribulation. When Israel seeks the Lord their God, they will find him. When all these things come upon them, if they turn to the Lord and are obedient unto his voice, he will reward them. The nation of Israel will receive mercy. (Deuteronomy 4:29-31)

Yahweh, the supreme Judge of life and justice, has chosen to give mankind free choice concerning eternal life. Because of Yahweh's choice, a complicated situation of self-condemnation has been established. Because eternal life on earth is not possible, the judgment of death is evident. All of mankind is condemned or judged. For life on earth, the existence of organic human life depends upon reproduction, and the order and stability of our organic environment.

In the same manner that organic life depends upon light, spiritual life or existence is sustained by spiritual light. A restriction of light intensity would be a severe judgment for a plant that is dependent upon sunlight.

When a plant that is dependent upon sunlight is placed in darkness, the photosynthetic process is restricted, and the plant will eventually shrivel and die. A plant cannot choose its location; however, we have freedom of choice. We can choose to place judgment upon ourselves by living in spiritual darkness. This is an act of self-judgment or condemnation.

In the same way that mercy, not judgment, has been given to Israel, a gift of grace has been offered to all mankind. Jesus is the light of the world, yet anyone can choose darkness. The precious gift of eternal life has been offered as a gift of love to anyone who will choose to believe that God is love. This gift of everlasting life was offered by Jesus, the One who is the Messiah. (John 3:16-20)

Jesus does not judge of condemn anyone. He does not judge the one who is unable to believe. Jesus did come to judge; he came to give eternal life. Jesus came as light into the world, so that everyone that believes in him will not remain in the darkness of separation from God. (John 12:46-50) (Psalm 98:9) (John 3:18)

## 41
## Kindness

Yahweh is a God of kindness. (Psalm 147:11)

Kindness is to be compassionate, generous, and agreeable. Kindness may be an act of respect or honor. Kindness is easily offered by those who are humble or merciful; for the gentleness of love is expressed in kindness.

An act of kindness, offered by God, is described as loving-kindness.

Several accounts of acts of kindness that were offered by Yahweh have been recorded in scripture. (Psalm 13:5-6)

The reason for the blessing of loving-kindness offered to Abraham has only been partially explained. This act of kindness was God's choice; and evidently Abraham proved to be worthy of God's attention. (Genesis 22:1-18)

And when Abraham was old, the Lord had blessed Abraham in all things. And Abraham's servant said, "Blessed be the Lord, the God of my master Abraham, who has not forsaken his loving kindness and his truth toward my master." (Genesis 24:1 & 27)

Loving kindness was offered to Leah, Jacob's first wife. God saw that Leah was unloved. God allowed Leah to conceived, and Leah gave birth to a son. She named the son Reuben, because she recognized that God had decided to offer her kindness. (Genesis 29:31-32) God also offered kindness to Rachael. God allowed Rachael to give birth to a son, and Rachael named the child Joseph. (Genesis 30:22-24)

God's purpose in offering kindness is often misunderstood. Neither Leah nor Rachel expressed sincere appreciation or understanding of what God had done for them. (Genesis 30:1-24)

The need for an act of loving kindness is expressed in an account when Yahweh became frustrated because of the lack of faith of the sons of Israel.

The account was recorded in the book of Numbers. God spoke to Moses and instructed him to send a small group, selected from every tribe, to search the land of Canaan. And Moses sent the men into Canaan, with instructions to spy out the land. (Numbers 13:1-16). The men returned from the search after forty days. (Numbers 13:17-25) Moses and the Israelites did were not aware that they were being tested by God.

Caleb and his friends gave a positive report, but those who did not have faith gave a false report. The false account caused a considerable amount of confusion. As a result, many of the Israelites were greatly disturbed, and began to complain against Moses and Aaron. (Numbers 14:1-4)

Moses and Aaron, Caleb and Joshua desperately reasoned with the people and advised them to not rebel against Yahweh. Moses and Aaron even humbled themselves before the assembly of the congregation of the children of Israel to plead with them. When the people decided to stone Moses and Aaron, the glory of the Lord appeared in the tabernacle. God informed Moses that He had decided to disinherit the Israelites, and through Moses, make a greater nation to take their place. (Numbers 14:5-12)

Thankfully, for the children of Israel, Moses was able to intercede. Evidently Moses had learned to appreciate the loving-kindness of Yahweh. First, Moses used an argument of honor and then he used God's own words concerning loving kindness as a reason for forgiveness. (Numbers 14:13-19)

Because Yahweh truly is a God of loving-kindness, he accepted the request. Yahweh was persuaded to pardon the children of Abraham, according to the request made by Moses. Words of prophecy were also given concerning a future time when the fulness of the kindness of Yahweh would be recognized. At a future time, not just the temple, but all the earth will be filled with the glory of the Lord. (Numbers 14:20-21) The fact that justice is not eliminated by God's acts of kindness should be recognized. (Numbers 14:22-45) The kindness of forgiveness was not offered because Moses had earned special consideration. Yahweh's loving-kindness was an act of grace. In the same way, attention or blessings from God cannot be obtained by acts of religious performance. Loving kindness is offered to us as a gift of grace.

Years later, king David and king Solomon had determined to build a house of worship and praise for the Lord, on the high place of Moriah, in Jerusalem. The people gave willingly and generously for the cost of the construction. When the construction of the temple had been completed and the house was to be dedicated, fire came down from heaven and the glory of the Lord filled the house. The response of the people was an expression of appreciation and praise for the loving kindness of their God.

Recognition of his kindness and mercy was recorded in scripture; however, a true recognition of the grace of God was evidently not understood. (2 Chronicles 7:3) The book of Jonah, recorded as a lesson concerning the kindness of Yahweh, illustrates the lack of understanding of the need for God's grace and forgiveness. Like Jonah, the nation of Israel should have been able to understand and to appreciate the loving kindness of Yahweh. Jonah did not approve of Yahweh's decision to have mercy on the people of Nineveh. Jonah knew that God is a gracious, merciful, slow to anger, and even offers kindness instead of judgment. (Jonah 4:2)

If Israel had listened to the words of the prophets, if they had not become religious and legalistic, they would have been blessed by the kindness of Yahweh. The Father of Israel has always been prepared to bless the nation of Israel. (Joel 2:13)

When the disciples of Jesus expressed a lack of understanding concerning loving kindness, Jesus quickly rebuked the apostles. Jesus did not come to judge of condemn or to destroy men's lives. Jesus came as an act of love and kindness to offer the gift of eternal life. (Luke 9:52-56)

Yahweh has offered love and kindness to the entire world. Nevertheless, because Yahweh is a God of justice, his offer of grace must also be an act of justice. Although God is rich in kindness and forbearance and patience, his kindness can only lead to repentance. The choice to accept his gift of love remains a choice of faith. (Romans 2:4)

Yahweh has offered his one and only son by placing him on a cross as a gift of love, as a supreme act of divine loving kindness that has risen forth from his desire to offer love to the entire world. Acceptance of this gift of love requires a personal individual choice, as an act of repentance, acceptance, and faith.

Acceptance of God's grace also requires loving kindness, living in the light of love, and not in the darkness of this world. (1 John 1:7-8) As a natural response of appreciation, those who have professed faith in Jesus Christ and have received his gift of grace should be able to be loving and kind. All who have accepted his grace should express kindness, in the same manner that the gift of reconciliation has been offered.

Just as love and kindness are primary characteristics of our God of love, kindness must be a primary characteristic of those who choose to be disciples of Jesus. (Colossians 3:8-17)

The greatest requirement of living as a Christ-one is to offer fervent charity to others. Acts of charity keeps us close to God. (1 Peter 4:8)

# 42
# Knowledge

The knowledge, awareness, and wisdom of Yahweh has been beautifully expressed in scripture. (Psalm 147:4-9)

Knowledge is defined as understanding, comprehension, or mastery of facts, information, or skills. Knowledge may be a state of awareness, consciousness, realization, or recognition. Knowledge may be obtained through education or practical experience.

Yahweh is truly a God of knowledge and understanding. The knowledge of God is infinite. Yahweh has unlimited knowledge and understanding. (Romans 11:33) The book of Job as been offered as an explanation and description of the knowledge and awareness of God. (Job 42:1-2)

A description of his nature and understanding has been offered by the prophets of Israel who have recorded accounts of his involvement with mankind. (Isaiah 40:28)

For Yahweh, knowledge is more than simple understanding, a mastery of science, or a state of awareness or realization. Knowledge possessed by Yahweh is the power and authority of life. His knowledge and understanding includes awareness and understanding of love. The knowledge of love allows Yahweh to be Love.

Knowledge is Yahweh's inherent gift of love to mankind. Knowledge and understanding are gifts of life, offered to mankind by an almighty creator. Knowledge is part of the gift of the likeness of God. Knowledge makes mankind human.

Wisdom is a gift of knowledge and understanding. The value of knowledge and wisdom is more valuable than having wealth or material possessions. (Proverbs 3:13-18)

Knowledge and understanding are absolute requirements of human life; for understanding and awareness provide meaning to life and existence. All of existence and all of life depends upon knowledge and understanding. (Proverbs 4:1-9) Knowledge and love are both beautiful, amazing, wonderful, and completely necessary, for life. Without knowledge we would not be able to comprehend the meaning and necessity of love.

As the sun sets over the open sea, a shimmering path of sparkling light that stretches from the horizon to the seaside, may be visible. Knowledge is a special gift from God that is much the same. The source of the shimmering light of understanding is the light of God's love. If we were able to see the mind of a child, to see the shimmering beauty of understanding, we would see sparkling jewels and diamonds and golden glitter of possibilities and wonder and imagination. Knowledge is indeed a precious gift from a gracious almighty God.

For the present time, in this life, spiritual knowledge is obscured. However, in Christ Jesus, the knowledge of love and truth has been revealed. The apostle Paul described our awareness of spiritual truth as though we are looking through a glass that distorts vision; however, when we are with Jesus, we shall have full knowledge of the grace of God. (1 Corinthians 13:12)

Someday, everyone will know and understand the value of having been created in the image of Yahweh. Someday, we will understanding the true meaning of love. We shall experience the joy and peace of the awareness, consciousness, realization, or recognition of the presence of Yahweh. Someday we will know the true meaning and purpose of knowledge, of wisdom and understanding.

This full awareness of understanding was described by Isaiah. The prophet Isaiah prophesied of one who would come, as a branch out of the stem or roots of Jesse. Isaiah said that the spirit of wisdom and understanding will rest upon him, and the earth will be full of the knowledge of the Lord. (Isaiah 11:1-10)

A basic truth concerning existence and knowledge is that both are worthless without love. The apostle Paul said that even if we were to have the gift of prophecy, and could understand mysteries, and have complete knowledge, or charity, or faith, we would still be worthless without charity. (1 Corinthians 13:2) A time has been predicted when this situation of knowledge without love will prove to be harmful to mankind. According to his prophecy, in a future unidentified time many things will be happening, and knowledge will be increased. (Daniel 12:4)

Jesus explained this problem of knowledge being available, without understanding, to the Jewish religious leaders. The religious leaders searched scripture, to answer questions concerning eternal life. They had decided that if eternal life was possible, everlasting life would need to be earned by fulfilling the works of the Laws of Moses. Jesus approved of their search for knowledge, but he also judged them for failure to understand that the words of scripture include a testimony of the fact that Jesus is the Messiah. (John 5:39,19-45) The Jews had the scripture, the story of God's love, but because they were like Jonah, who failed to understand the lovingkindness of Yahweh. They did not recognize that Jesus is the Messiah.

This truth is based upon the fact that Yahweh is the existence that gives meaning to knowledge and truth. The knowledge of God is more than an enormous collection of scientific facts, or a massive arrangement of material objects in space. Yahweh is more than mere physical observable existence. Yahweh is the I Am. Yahweh is love.

The apostle Paul offered a prayer of blessing for both love and understanding.

This beautiful prayer deserves to be read and memorized, and kept in a place of hope, within our heart and mind. (Ephesians 3:17-19)

We must always be thankful that Yahweh gives knowledge and understanding, and wisdom, that allows us to understand that God is love. (Proverbs 2:6)

# 43
# Liberty

Jesus, the Son of man, is the sovereign ruler of Heaven and earth. He is the Lord of the Sabbath Day. (Matthew 12:5-8)

Liberty is a state of freedom from oppressive restrictions that may be imposed on political, economic, or civil actions.

Liberty and freedom are often considered to be basically synonymous; however, liberty is in essence the fulfillment of freedom. Freedom is easily defined as a state of being set free from bondage or restriction. Liberty is defined as a state of having freedom of life, liberty, and pursuit of happiness.

Liberty and freedom are also aspects of life and civil arrangements that may be misunderstood and undervalued. As well, although civil liberty may be defined and explained, spiritual liberty is difficult to explain or appreciate.

Yahweh is a God of freedom. Yahweh is also a God of liberty.

The Almighty is completely free from any restriction or any limitation. He exists in a complete state of eternal life and liberty. He lives in the liberty of love, righteousness, holiness, and freedom from any form of evil or harm. Because he resides in a unified state of liberty, he has chosen to offer the same for the world.

Yahweh is truly a God of liberty. He has chosen to offer freedom to all of mankind. Spiritual freedom is to know the truth. The truth of existence, that Yahweh is the One who is love, must be understood and accepted.

Acceptance of the truth, that Jesus is the Messiah, the son of the One who is Love, will set us free. (John 8:32)

Perhaps because Yahweh exists in liberty, and understands the benefits of liberty, he has chosen to offer spiritual liberty as a blessing to mankind. The apostle Paul stated that if we understand the law of liberty, and choose to abide by it, not living as a forgetful hearer but as an effectual doer, we shall be blessed by God. (James 1:25) As previously stated, although the purpose and blessings of the law of liberty has been clearly explained in scripture, the purpose or reason for spiritual freedom may be misunderstood.

The law of liberty is a state of spiritual righteousness that enables the believer to be set free, truly free. This freedom from the law of sin and death, gives the believer the spiritual right of life, liberty, and pursuit of happiness. Liberty is a gift of freedom from the requirements and condemnation of the laws of righteousness. The fulfillment of the requirements of the law is accomplished by the engrafted word of Christ, which is the Holy Spirit working within us so that we will be able to obey the law from the heart, to lay aside all filthiness and worthlessness and lack of honor for others. (James 2:1-9) (James 1:20-21) The believer that follows the perfect law of liberty will be free to be a joyful doer of the word, and not a hearer only. (James 1:23)

The disciples of Christ, that live by the law of liberty, will be characterized by faith and by Christ-like characteristics, virtue, knowledge and temperance, patience and godliness, brotherly kindness, and charity. They will be free, within the liberty of faith, to be used in God's hands as an instrument of love. (2 Peter 1:6-8) These Christ-ones will be free from self-centered desires; and will be easily identified by deeds of humility and loving-kindness. They will be free to resist the legalistic requirements and expectations of religious performance that may be offered by others.

This truth of our state of liberty, or dependence upon the power of the Holy Spirit has been described by the apostle Paul. The apostle Paul clearly stated that we are not adequate in ourselves, to consider anything of goodness or worth as coming from our own thoughts or actions. Our adequacy is from God who also made us adequate as servants of a new covenant, that is not of the law but of the Spirit. The law of Moses offers only death, but the Spirit gives life. If the agency of death, letters of the law engraved on stones, came with glory, how shall the ministry of the Spirit fail to be even more with glory? Liberty has been offered by the gift of the Holy Spirit. Therefore, because the Lord is the Spirit, where the Spirit of the Lord is there is liberty. (2 Corinthians 3:5-17)

The gift of liberty is to be free from the penalty for failure to keep the Law; for keeping the law is an impossible task that no man can accomplish. The Law was a law of sin and death simply because no man was able to keep the requirements of the law (Romans 7:1-25) Even if we attempt to keep the law, and yet are an offender in one point, we are guilty of all. Therefore, the only way to keep the commandments of God is abide by the law of liberty. (James 2:10-12)

The Law of Moses was in essence, a curse; however, the law was also a blessing. The law was given as a capable instructor or tutor to teach a valuable lesson of truth. The law was given by a compassionate heavenly Father to teach the Israelites their need of forgiveness and grace. Jesus, by offering his life, set the prisoners of the law free from the captivity of sin. Liberty was announced with the words, "it is finished." (John 19:30)

Liberty is offered to the gentiles by a simple statement by the apostle John. The accounts of the gospel have been written, so that we may believe that Jesus is the Christ, the Son of God. And that believing, we may have life in his name. (John 20:31)

Yahweh is a God of freedom and liberty because he offers freedom as a gift of love or aloha. The believer, by faith in Jesus Christ, has been set free from the Law, and has been placed in a natural state of freedom, of choice and action. The believer resides on an island of liberty, free from any form of religious requirements or expectations. The believer is no longer restricted by the law or forced to obey legal rules. The believer has been reborn or born again, into a life of liberty.

The believer is free from the condemnation of the law; but remains bound to the law through love; for the law is truth. Truth and love are one. The believer is free, to live a life of love, to live by the spirit, not after the flesh.

The actual situation is that the Law, and the requirements of the law have been fulfilled in Christ. This theological concept is not easily understood and has therefore been misrepresented due to lack of understanding of the meaning of fulfillment. A rose bush does not immediately produce a flower. The branch first produces a bud, that grows tightly, covered, protected but restricted. Gradually, the flower breaks forth and the petals of the flower are spread. The rose flower is the fulfillment of the entire process. The bush and the rose bud still exist, in fulfillment, and in beauty and majesty. The rose is now in a state of fulfillment; and is free to be what a rose was intended to be.

We, who are in Christ Jesus, live by the power of the Holy Spirit, and the Law of Liberty has made us free from the law of sin and death. (Romans 8:1-16)

The security of liberty is like the position of the prodigal son after having been accepted by a forgiving father. (Luke 15:11-32) This beautiful story of a loving father was told by Jesus for the nation of Israel. The characters are used to teach Israel a lesson of redemption. However, the account can also be used as a basic understanding of faith and freedom. The relationship of liberty and faith is of extreme importance. Although righteousness is no longer by or through the law, being placed in a state of liberty does not eliminate a need to maintain a relationship with the One who has offered the gift of liberty. The basic requirement of the believer's relationship of trust and faith with Yahweh is referred to as works of faith. (James 1:22)

This concept of freedom is also illustrated by the account of a rich young ruler of Israel. This young man had lived a life of goodness; but he knew that a life of religious performance, or works, was not enough. Jesus said to the youth, the law is required, but the law cannot give eternal life. You will never be perfect. Stop trying to be righteous. Come, follow me. (Matthew 19:21)

Jesus did not say that to be righteous or good we must follow him. Faith in Jesus Christ offers eternal life, not goodness. Our religious effort to be good must be given away, as a past, present, and future gift of love to others. Righteousness or goodness must not be a purpose in life.

Following Jesus is a simple task. Our good deeds are not performed for recognition or for blessings here on earth. Our works are not deeds of righteousness or works to obtain sanctification. (Matthew 19:21) Although we are expected to be like Jesus, our primary task is to love others as Jesus loves others. We have been set free to love others in the name of Jesus. This is the state of knowing the Truth, which is Jesus Christ, so that we can be free, free indeed. (John 8:32)

Because Yahweh is a God of liberty, he has chosen to set us free, to live in the liberty of love, righteousness, holiness, and freedom from any form of evil or harm. Our task is to trust in the Lord, commit our way unto the Lord, rest and wait patiently for judgment. (Psalm 37:1-16)

The glorious liberty of Jesus Christ has set us free from condemnation. (Romans 8:1, 21) We live in hope, protected by the love of Yahweh. (Romans 8:38-39)

Yahweh is a God of Liberty! Hallelujah! (Matthew 11:28-30)

# 44
# Life

Yahweh, the Father of heaven and earth, is divine life.

Life is defined as a state of living. An adequate definition of life is not available.

The existence of life is a gift from God. The evidence of the creation of live is obvious and undeniable. The soul of every living thing and the breath of all mankind are sustained by God. (Job 12:9-10)

The presence of eternal life is a gift of God. The gift of everlasting life is a gift of the living Word of Life. (1 John 1:1-2)

Life is a gift of love that gives meaning and purpose to existence. Without life, the universe would be a massive expanse of light and darkness, power and motion, and sound and silence, that would exist in eternity as an unknown existence.

Life is a state of awareness of existence of light, substance, energy, motion, and thought. Life is a state of being I am.

Any substance of matter or state of matter with empirical reality is in a state of existence. According to this definition, although not synonymous, life and existence are interrelated and dependent. Existence is a state of presence; therefore, life may be defined as the reality or awareness of existence. In essence, the presence of life defines human existence and our state of being.

Biological life is a condition identified as being organic or consisting of organic matter. Organic life is identified by the existence of a process of growth, a state of defense and protection, a process of reproduction, and functional ability to sustain life.

The meaning of human life includes an understanding of the significance of life, related to an understanding of pragmatic facts about the universe or of exploring the purpose of physical existence.

Yahweh is a God of existence and life.

Elohim is the creator of life. He is the one who sustains life. He is the one who understands the significance of life. He is also the One who gives eternal life.

Scientifically speaking, the existence of life on earth must be classified as an unknown; for the origin of organic life is scientifically undetermined. Although we know that all living organisms are basically composed of chemical matter, the dust of the earth, we are presently unable to determine the events that provided the transition from a dead-rock chemical state to the existence of living organic matter. As well, life on earth is unsustainable, except through reproduction. Simply stated, the possibility or probability for any one individual to have eternal life, to live forever, is non-existent.

Because the origin or beginning of the existence of life is unknown, belief in the statements of scripture, that the Almighty Deity who is YHWH created the universe and all biological life on earth, must be accepted by faith rather than by knowledge or scientific fact. Because Yahweh is the creator of human life and existence, we must assume that both are of extreme value. Although a specific statement that human life is sacred has not been recorded in scripture, evidence to prove that human life is of extreme value is available. (Exodus 9:6, 20:13, 21:22-23) Obviously, the laws of Moses, given by Yahweh, require that human life should be protected and defended.

Just as time is different for the Lord, existence must also be different. The apostle Peter said that we should "not be ignorant of this one thing, that one day is with the Lord as a thousand years, and a thousand years as one day." (2 Peter 3:8) Every man is aware of the difference of the state of life and death. Every reasonable man loves life and is aware of the need to sustain life; however, we are unable to understand the existence of eternal or spiritual life.

In scripture, although spiritual life and light are not synonymous, light and life are equated. Yahweh is a God of light and life. Yahweh is a God of eternal enduring life.

Yahweh is eternal, immortal, and invincible with glory and honor forever. (1 Timothy 1:17) Job said that if God were to gather his spirit to himself, all of mankind would perish, and man would return to dust. (Job 34:13-15)

King David, who has been given credit for many of the Psalms, stated a firm belief that Yahweh is a God of spiritual eternal life. (Psalm 27:4) The king understood that for Yahweh to be a defender of life, he must also have power over death. Through the prophet Nathan, Yahweh informed the king that for the defense of the nation of Israel. the life of the child born by Bathsheba would be required. For seven days, the king lay on the ground and prayed for mercy; but when the child died, the king arose and worshiped the Lord. (2 Samuel 12:21-23)

Yahweh's promise of eternal life has been revealed by his son, Jesus the Messiah. Jesus has promised the gift of abundant life. (John 10:10, 3:16 & 35-36) This gift of life may be obtained by a simple act of faith and trust. (John 4:13-14)

For Yahweh, life is precious state of existence. The wise woman from Tekoa, of whom Joab sought assistance, said that life for mankind is like water spilled on the ground that cannot be gathered up again. (2 Samuel 14:14) God does not desire to take life, for life is precious, and he plans ways to prevent us from being cast out from him.

The word resurrection is a common word used to describe a renewal of life, to be raised from the dead. (1 Corinthians 6:14) Eternal life is resurrection to life in Christ. (John 12:25)

Many in Israel did not believe in eternal life. The Sadducees, who taught that there is no resurrection, came to Jesus to debate with him about resurrection. Jesus assured them of the existence of eternal by saying that according to the words of scripture, God is the father of the living and not of the dead. (Matthew 22:29-32)

Jesus offered teachings, instructions, and parables, to explain the kingdom of heaven. Jesus explained that he was the one sent from God. He explained what he would eventually accomplish. (John 4:13-14) He performed miracles and quoted words of prophecy; but even his disciples did not understand that he is "the bread of life." He had come to offer eternal life to mankind. He warned about the false teachings of the religious rulers. (Mark 8:15) He admonished the disciples because they did not understand. He reminded them of the miracles of feeding the thousands. (Mark 8:28-21) He admonished the disciples for having a hardened heart, or lack of spiritual awareness, with eyes that do not see, and ears that do not hear. The disciples were not able to understand that Jesus was telling them, with words and miracles, that he was sent from heaven to meet the spiritual needs of the world, to offer eternal life to a lost world.

Jesus preformed miracles and brought a young girl back to life, to prove that he had the power to restore life. (Luke 9:52-55)

Jesus raised Lazarus from the grave to prove that, as One with God, he has the authority to give eternal life. This is the glory of God. Jesus said to Martha, "I am the resurrection and the life. He who believes in me, though he were dead, yet shall he live. And everyone who lives and believes in me shall never die." (John 11:23-26)

Jesus, standing before the tomb in which his friend Lazarus was placed, groaned in his spirit and was troubled. Jesus wept. The ones watching understood that he loved Lazarus. (John 11:33-46) Jesus asked for the stone to be removed. He called to Lazarus; and Lazarus came forth, alive. We are all as Lazarus. Our only hope of eternal life is to receive the gift of grace offered by Jesus. Jesus was deeply troubled; and he wept. He suffered because he understood what was required, for eternal life to be provided for mankind. His tears were an expression of love and understanding of the debt to be paid. While observing the feast of the Passover Jesus said to the disciples, "Do you understand what I have done to you?" (John 13:12)

Jesus gave bread, the bread of life, to the multitudes. The meal would have been worthless if the people had not eaten, but they did eat and were satisfied. (Mark 8:8) (John 6:46-58) Jesus offered the water of eternal life. (John 4:13-14) Even after his crucifixion, Jesus attempted to explain eternal life. (Luke 24:27-31)

God has so ordained that eternal life requires a choice of faith. (John 5:24)

Life eternal requires a state of spiritual existence where one day with the Lord is as a thousand years, and a thousand years as one day. (2 Peter 3:8) Eternal life requires a state of spiritual existence. (John 3:5)

Spiritually speaking, light and life are united. Yahweh said, "Let there be light, and there was light!" Yahweh is not a God of the dead, but of the living. In Him things all are alive. (Luke 20:38) When Jesus swallows up death in victory, God will wipe away tears from off all faces, and the disgrace of his people will be taken away from off the earth. The Lord has promised. (Isaiah 25:8)

How will this be possible? How will God give life, eternal life, to man? With man it is impossible, but not with God. All things are possible with God. (Mark 10:25-27)

Jesus Christ is the resurrection and eternal life. (1 Corinthians 15:20-22) He is the Prince of Life. (Acts 3:15) Jehovah has given us eternal life. Eternal life is through his Son Jesus Christ. (John 13:8) (1 John 5:11-14) (Romans 6:4-8)

This eternal life is like new wine. This new life requires a fresh wineskin, a body different than what we currently possess. And no one puts new wine into old wineskins; otherwise, the wine will burst the skins and the wine is lost, and the skins are ruined as well. New wine must be put into fresh wineskins, so that both are preserved. (Mark 2:22) A spiritual body is required; therefore, those who believe shall be born again, as a spiritual eternal being.

As previously stated, we believe in the miracle of existence, of love and eternal life. We are Christ-ones. When we consider the majesty and holiness of Deity, we are reminded of our humble state of humanity. However, when we understand what has been given to us, as a gift of love from the Father of life, we realize that we are more than what we were. We have been set free from death. We live in in a state of pure liberty of life. By an act of love and grace we have been given precious life, abundant, supreme, and everlasting. (John 10:10-12) This truth has been clearly stated in the words, "And you shall know the truth, and the truth shall make you free. If the Jesus has set us free, we shall be free indeed." (John 8:32-36) In essence, with the presence of life that is everlasting, we have been rewarded or blessed with a state of friendship or unity with God. (Galatians 3:28)

The joy and peace and excitement of life can be appreciated at any state of existence; however, we have been given the greatest gift that could ever be given. We have eternal existence. (1 Timothy 1: 9-10) We have been given the precious gift of everlasting life. We shall live and love and enjoy life forever.

Yahweh is a God of life, in the past, the present, and in the future. He is the God of the living. (Luke 20:38) He is the God of the unborn child and of the newborn child. He is the Creator of life and light on earth and in heaven. Yehoshua the Christ is alive. He is the resurrected life. He is alive because Yahweh is life.

We are abundantly alive because Yehoshua has given us eternal life. We shall not perish. We will have everlasting life. (John 1:4, 3:15)

# 45
# Light

God is clothed with splendor and majesty, with light as with a covering. (Psalm 104:1-2)

Light is electromagnetic radiation that can be seen or detected by the human eye. Light is the source of illumination; light makes vision possible. The existence of organic life is not possible without light.

If it cannot be measured, it does not exist. If it exists, it can be measured. This axiom is an accepted principal of science and physics. This implies that visibility or lack of visibility does not determine existence. All matter or energy is empirical or measurable. An object, substance or property may either be in a vacuum, hidden behind another object, immovable and camouflaged, in complete darkness or microscopic and beyond the visual scale of the human eye. As well, a substance could exist even if a means to measure its existence has yet to be discovered or determined. Simply stated, although light reveals existence, the presence of existence does not depend upon light. In contrast, darkness depends upon the absence of light.

According to the laws of physics, light is a substance that can be, at low frequencies, a wave and at increased frequencies, a particle. Although light has not been absolutely defined or explained, one obvious fact is that light is present. Light can be felt and seen and measured. The effect of solar energy can be measured or studied. For example, we know that all organic life on earth depends upon solar energy. The universe is revealed by the presence of light and energy.

In scripture, the first mention of light is found in the creation story in the book of Genesis. This historical account was recorded by prophets and historians of the nation of Israel. The purpose or intent of the chronicle account was not specifically stated; however, according to several passages of scripture, Moses was instructed by God to write about the judgment for Amelek, about the journey in the desert, songs for the nation, and other legal instructions. As well, although we may assume that Moses or Aaron or a contemporary scribe was the authors or editors, the authorship of the book of Genesis has not been determined. Nevertheless, the writings of the Old Testament are accepted as authentic historical records for the nation of Israel and are applicable for Jewish faith.

According to the words of Hebrew scripture, light is the glory of God. The presence of light was spoken into existence. Yahweh spoke and the glory of Deity was present. This light, or life-giving presence, existed before the sun and moon were put in place. As the Spirit of God was moving over the surface of the water, over the formless and void, and darkness of the surface of the earth, YHWH spoke and said, "Let there be light." and there was light. (Genesis 1:3) God saw that this light was good and separated it from darkness.

The light brought forth life; and the awareness of earthly existence was established by the presence of life and light.

Light is also the glory and presence of God. (Luke 2:9) (2 Corinthians 4:6)

Yahweh appeared before the children of Abraham. His appearance was demonstrated as clouds and fire and light. However, although God spoke from the midst of the fire, no form was visible. Therefore, the children of Israel were instructed to not make any graven images, or to look to the heavens and worship the created rather than the creator. (Deuteronomy 4:10-19)

Because God was in the light, present without revealed form, does not mean that Deity is formless or void or simple pure light. Evidently, God does not need to reveal himself in an identifiable form. The apostle John emphasized the fact that no man has seen God, at any time; however, the only begotten Deity, who is with the Father, has explained or has revealed Him. (John 1:18) According to the words of scripture, Yahweh lives or exists in unapproachable light. He is the One who alone possesses immortality and dwells in unapproachable light, that no man has seen or can see. (I Timothy 6:16)

Jesus Christ is described as the One who brings the light of Deity, to make all things visible, when exposed by the light. The light of Deity is life. (Ephesians 5:13-14)

Attempting to explain this aspect of deity may be compared to trying to explain that zero, while being non-existent, must be in practical use, the beginning and end of any identifiable number. The fact remains that Yahweh does not choose to be identified with, or even associated with any visible form, on earth or in the heavens or in the universe. This does not imply that deity is some form of quasi-particle, anti-matter or any other unidentifiable substance that will remain unidentifiable. Perhaps because light is visible and measurable, light is an entity that is acceptable to be used for a limited description of a finite, transcendent, unexplained, or non-described deity that is the creator and sustainer of life on earth.

Because light and life are equated, and since life is basically an invisible existence, light is used to describe the revelation and presence of this invisible deity. Evidently the purity of light represents the very character, or the oneness of righteousness, of our Heavenly Father. However, there may be more substance or measurable meanings of deity than we are able to understand or comprehend. We should remember that the expression of light in a rainbow is viewed in brilliant color instead of clear light.

There are several accounts in scripture of the appearance of light, other than in the description of the creation of the world. Evidently, a small portion of the light was revealed to Moses. Moses made a request to God, for a blessing of seeing God's glory. Yahweh told Moses, that because he had found favor, he would make all his goodness pass before Moses. As an act of compassion, Yahweh proclaim the name of the Lord before Moses, but he did not reveal himself; for, no man can see God and live. The complete account of this amazing even has been recorded in the book of Exodus. (Exodus 33:18-23)

Light is clearly an expression of the beauty and majesty of the Almighty. Moses went up to Mount Sinai, the glory of God passed before him; and Moses bowed down to worship. He received the commandments and came down from the mountain, but Moses was not aware that the skin of his face shone because he had been in the presence of the holiness of God. (Exodus 34:1-35)

Light also distinctly reveals the righteousness of Yahweh. In a song of triumph about his life and the nation of Israel, king David uses a description of light to describe the wonder of Yahweh. King David said that the Spirit of the Lord spoke, and his word was in his mouth. The Rock of Israel spoke to him. (2 Samuel 23:2-4)

However, to say that God dwells only in righteousness would not be accurate. Light is more than a symbol of righteousness. Light is as well a symbol of beauty and majesty. The emphasis in the statement that God is light and in him there is no darkness at all is a definite reference to righteousness; however, light is also the divine presence of God. (1 John 1:5) Light brings life and godliness into the presence of man, and the absence of darkness or evil; for, the light of deity is perfect and pure and beautiful. (James 1:17)

At the birth of Jesus, the light of God was present. The angel of the Lord stood before the shepherds, and the glory of the Lord was around them. (Luke 2:9) Jesus is described as the Sunrise from on high, to shine upon those who sit in darkness and the shadow of death. (Luke 1:77-79) This light is the light of the glory of Christ, who is the image of God. (2 Corinthians 4:4) For God is the One who has shone in our hearts to give the light of the knowledge of the glory of God in the face of Christ. (2 Corinthians 4:6)

Light is also an expression of goodness or charity. (Luke 11:35-36)

Spiritual light and love and righteousness are essentially the same. The statement of living in the light, as Jesus is in the light, is a poetic description of sharing the light and love of God. Anyone that says that he is in the light, able to share the love of God, and yet hates his brother is in the darkness until now. The one who loves his brother abides in the light, and lives as a Christ-one. (1 John 2:9-11)

The spiritual light and life that was brought by Christ, in the beginning as the creator and later as Emmanuel, is the light of God. The one Deity, that is YHWH the Father of Abraham, Isaac and Jacob, and the Son are together as One. (John 1:1-3)

Jesus, the Messiah, was present as One to bring light and life into the world. The one who is identified as the Word said, "Let there be light!" As well, John offers an additional explanation of the unity of One. (John 1:4-5)

God, who is One is light, and dwells in incomprehensible light. (I Timothy 6:16) No man has seen God at any time; however, the only begotten Deity, who is in the bosom of the Father, he has explained him.

(John 2:18) He has revealed Deity by giving up his light of righteousness, by becoming flesh, to dwell among man, to be God with us, with the glory of the only begotten from the Father, full of grace and truth. (John 1:14) As Esaias the prophet said, "The people who were sitting in darkness saw a great light; to those who were in the land of shadow of death. Upon them a light dawned." (Matthew 4:14-16)

Referring to this passage of prophecy, Jesus clearly identified himself as the light of Deity. (John 8:12, 12:35-36)

As clearly stated, walking or living in the light of Christ is also a description of Christian fellowship and love. (1 John 1:6 -10) The existence of light in the kingdom of heaven is also a description of the presence of Deity. (Revelation 22:5)

Because there is obvious symbolism in the book of Revelation, one would be wise to not accept every situation or description as a literal interpretation. Therefore, we must acknowledge that the statement that God is light may be interpreted as symbolism or as substance, or a combination of both. (I John 1:5) As well, we must remember that everything to be known about the light of Deity has not been explained or revealed.

In the New Testament story of the transfiguration, Jesus took Peter and James and John with him up to a high mountain, and light was present. This is an unexplained miracle. Jesus was transfigured before them. His face appeared like the sun and his garments became as white as light. (Matthew 17:12)

The apostle Paul shared an account of his amazing encounter with the light of Deity. The apostle said that he was traveling to Damascus at midday. Suddenly a very bright light appeared from heaven and spread around him. The apostle was not able to see because of the brightness of the light. He was blinded by the light and his companions had to lead him into the city of Damascus. (Acts 22:6-14) God sent a believer named Ananias to tell Paul that he had chosen him for a special purpose of service. For this reason, Paul had been allowed to see the righteous one, and to hear his words. (Acts 22:14)

The light of Deity is also associated with the gospel, and specifically with sharing or testifying concerning the good news. Paul and Barnabas, speaking to the Jews in Antioch, informed them that Paul had been chosen as a light for the Gentiles. (Isaiah 49:6) (Acts 13:46-47)

The relationship of light and love is clearly expressed by the words of the apostle Paul. Paul emphasized the fact that the gospel of Jesus Christ is a gift of love from God, and when he said that "the light of the glorious gospel shines out of darkness into our hearts," he was stating that God has sent his love to us through the gospel of Christ Jesus. The light of Christ is the light of the knowledge of the glory of God. (2 Corinthians 4:3-6)

If we say that we have fellowship with God, but live in darkness, without the light of Christ or the love of God, we are false witnesses of our relationship with God. (1 John 1:5-10) (1 Thessalonians 5:5) If the spiritual light that is in us is darkness, how great is the darkness. (Matthew 6:22-23)

As Christ-ones, we are to shine as lights of love, holding forth the word of life. (Philippians 2:15) (Ephesians 5:8-9) The blessing for us is that we have the privilege of living in the presence of this beautiful light of righteousness and love. (1 John 2:6-11)

The story of Stephen is a testimony of a disciple of Christ who personally experienced the presence of the light of righteousness and love. (Acts 6:8 – 7:60) When Stephen had finished speaking, all in the council saw his face, lighted like the face of an angel. (Acts 6:15) And being full of the Holy Spirit, Stephen saw the glory of God, and Jesus standing at the right hand of God. (Acts 7:55)

Through faith in Jesus Christ, the light of Yahweh's righteousness is shared with us. Because we are children of light, we are to allow our light of righteousness and love to shine, for others. (Matthew 5:16) This light is not our light. The light that has been given to us, is to be shared for the glory of God.

Light is truly the glory of God; and Jesus the Christ who was sent as the light of the world, is the glory of God. God's mystery, that is Christ himself, in whom are hidden all the treasures of wisdom and knowledge, is like a rainbow spread across the open sky, to reveal the radiant beauty of One. (Colossians 2:2) Jesus is the Emanuel, sent from the Father of light. (James 1:17) He has been sent into the world to be the light, and the power, beauty, glory, righteous, presence of the Father, and life for the world. (John 8:12) Jesus came into our existence, to reveal the primary colors of faith, hope and love, of the one true God, and to offer the light of eternal life from One that dwells in inapproachable light. (I Timothy 6:16) (John 3:19)

## 46
## Love

Yahweh is One of existence. Yahweh is love. The first two commands for life are commandments of love. There are no commandments greater than these commandments of love. (Mark 12:28-31)

Love would not be an essential part of our biological existence without the presence of a Creator. A logical scientific reason for the existence of love does not exist. Love is not a chemical reaction or evolutionary development of a non-created world. Love is not a natural consequence of a process of evolution. A logical explanation for the existence of a biological or mental need of reproduction and preservation, that exist for every lifeform in our present world, cannot be found in a scientific journal.

Love is the evidence of creation.

The ultimate statement in scripture is that God is Love.

Every word, story, psalm, or statement in scripture declares the truth that YHWH is love. The ultimate truth, of life and existence, is that God is love.

Love is also the primary essence of humanity. We have been created in the image of God. The value of love is unmeasurable and beyond our human ability to understand.

The treasure of life, the value, purpose and meaning of life is that Yahweh loves us. (Romans 8:37-39)

The gospel is a supreme act of love that cannot be fully appreciated unless we understand that God is love. (Romans 5:8) (John 3:16)

The life of his precious son, the radiance of his glory and power, was offered as a sacrifice so anyone might have eternal life. (Hebrews 1:3) (Romans 10:13)

This sacrifice was not offered so that Yahweh might demonstrate majesty, righteousness, authority, or any supreme characteristic. As well, we who are believers have not been redeemed and sanctified so that we might express righteousness or perform religious acts of moral goodness. Our duty of love for Yahweh is to love others as Jesus loved us. (John 13:34-35) (Luke 6:27-38)

Yahweh's love is a natural love that resides within his very being. Yahweh is Love. In like manner, love that a Christ-one offers must be a natural love, given without design, intent, purpose, or expectation of reward. Acts of love must be offered from the heart, freely given, without expectation of response or appreciation. Love for others is the essence of worshiping God "in spirit and in truth." (John 4:24)

In two commandments, our primary purpose of life has been clearly established. (Matthew 22:37-40)

Our duty of honor and love is to love as Jesus loved. (Romans 13:10) We are to be disciples of love. (Romans 12:20-21) (1 John 4:21) Our duty of honor is to tell the world that God exist, and that He is love. (John 17:26) (1 Peter 5:20)

Our gift of love is to tell the world that Yahweh is willing to give an amazing gift of love to those who seek him. (Hebrews 11:6)

YHWH is Love. He is the one and only God of love.

# 47
# Majesty and Glory

The majesty and glory of God has been proclaimed in many of the psalms and words of the prophets of Israel. The glory and majesty of Yahweh is described as awesome and everlasting. (Psalm 93:1)

Majesty is defined as splendor, dignity, worth, and exalted value. Majesty is a description of the supreme power of sovereignty and greatness. To be majestic is to be beautiful and magnificent. To be majestic is to be amazingly remarkable and awe inspiring.

Yahweh, the King of kings and Lord of lords, is magnificent, brilliant, and beautiful in life and light and glory. As well, the majesty of God can be felt within the heart, not just seen or experienced. To experience the majesty of God is like looking at a beautiful sunrise and feeling the warmth of the radiant light.

Elihu, one of the friends of Job, who thought that Job was justifying himself instead of God, was anxious to speak on God's behalf or to defend God. Elihu said that man should stand and consider the wonders of God.

(Job 37:14) This is an interesting thought. However, the splendor and glory of an almighty Deity is difficult to adequately described or explained.

In accounts of scripture, the glory of God has been revealed or presented, but only as a dim reflection. (1 Corinthians 13:12) The splendor of Yahweh is amazingly remarkable and wonderful. The words of God are truth. The earth is full of the goodness of God. (Psalm 33:3-8)

Ezekiel experienced the glory of the Lord in a vision. Ezekiel described the appearance of the Lord as a rainbow of color within brilliant light. A voice spoke from the light. (Ezekiel 1:28)

Several of the Psalms offer poetic descriptions of the majestic splendor of God. (Psalm 148:13) The psalmist says that God is clothed with light or walks upon the wing of the wind. (Psalm 104:1-4) Yahweh is the King of glory. (Psalm 24:7-10)

The glory of Yahweh is also described by the prophet Isaiah. (Isaiah 6:1-4, 19-21) The splendor or God is expressed in power, and strength, and in love. (Psalm 33:8)

The tabernacle described in the book of Exodus was to be a reflection or representation of the glory and majesty of Yahweh. (Exodus 25:1 – 31:11 & 35:1 – 40:37) The tabernacle was not for the physical presence of God but would be a consecrated place where Yahweh would meet with the sons of Israel. (Exodus 29:43-46, 40:38)

The heavens and all of creation declare that God is awesome in power and might and splendor. (Job 26:6-14) To be in the presence of deity, in the presence of perfection and authority would be overwhelming. (Job 40:10) To stand in the presence of splendor and majesty would be breathtaking, astounding, and frightening. (Deuteronomy 10:17) Moses was commanded to not allow the people to come near to Yahweh. (Exodus 19:24) When the people saw the thundering and lightning, the noise of the trumpets, and the mountain smoking they backed away and stood at a safe distance. (Exodus 20:18)

Thankfully, his power is moderated by the presence of love.

Love is the true aspect of the splendid nature of God. To stand in the presence of love is to experience the amazing presence of joy and peace that takes away fear. Joy is the blessing of the good news of the gospel. (Philippians 4:4) At the birth of Jesus, the glory and splendor of the Lord appeared as light, and angels declared the glory of God. (Luke 2:9-11)

The shepherds stood in the awesome presence of the light and glory of an amazingly beautiful Deity, and a message of joy was given to them.

The evidence of Yahweh's glory is evident in all that has been created in our world and universe. Nevertheless, although we live in an amazing world, only a limited amount of the splendor of Yahweh has been revealed. For now, we see his glory as though looking through a distorted glass.

God is awesome in presence and authority; and the splendor of his spirit is amazing. In like manner, the awesome presence of the Father is openly expressed by Jesus; for Yahweh is One. The author of the book of Hebrews explained the presence of the love of God. Jesus is described as the brightness of the glory of God, the exact image of his person. Jesus is the awesome word of God. (Hebrews 1:1-3)

As believers, we stand in amazement of the power and majesty of the Almighty. We stand in reverence of his amazing love, mercy and grace that has been offered through Jesus Christ. We stand in awe and offer joyful praise for his gift of grace, liberty, and eternal life.

The splendor of deity is expressed as the majesty of One. In Heaven, the majesty of One is present as the Father, the Word, and the Holy Spirit. As well, there are three that bear witness in earth, the spirit and the water, and the blood. And these three agree in One. (1 John 5:7-8) Perhaps we may assume that these words are only poetic descriptions of Deity, nevertheless the fact that Deity is One has been clearly stated.

Amazingly, the majesty of the Father has been presented, in the past and present and future; however, because Jesus gave up his glory to be Emmanuel or God with us, his glory was not recognized; however, the beauty and majesty of the Son, the bright and morning star, has always been present with the Father.

Jesus has plainly said that he is the Messiah, the one who is to be the glory of God. (Revelation 22:13, 16) The apostle Paul and all the disciples of Jesus have testified that Jesus is the One that is the brightness of his glory and the exact image of his person. (Hebrews 1:1-3)

Matthew recorded the account of the transfiguration of Jesus. Matthew, Peter, James, and John, said that his face was enlightened, and his raiment was as white as the light. (Matthew 17:2) The brilliance and beauty of majesty of Jesus cannot be completely described or explained. The apostle Paul admonished the children of Israel for not "removing the veil" to see the glorious beauty of Jesus. The apostle Paul also said that we can see only a limited amount of the glory of the Lord. (2 Corinthians 3:14-18) (Exodus 34:29)

Although the majesty of One is evident, Yahweh does not openly demonstrate his majesty. As well, Jesus did not express a need to demonstrate majesty. Jesus came as the lamb of God and as the Prince of Peace, and not as a God of judgment. (John 12:15)

The presence of majesty must be accepted by faith. The evidence of Deity has been declared by the presence of the earth and the universe, but the evidence of the existence of Love has been declared by Jesus. (John 1:18)

The majesty of God is awesome and powerful and too great to be seen directly. (Exodus 33:17-33) The majesty of Yahweh must be seen and experience through the power of the Holy Spirit. (Acts 7:55)

After they had eaten the Passover meal, Jesus and the disciples departed. It was night, but the glory of God was present. (John 13:31-32) Someday, the glory of God will be present everywhere. (Revelation 21: 23-25)

Holy, Holy, Holy is God Almighty!

# 48
## Mediator/Messiah

According to the words of the apostle Paul, written as the inspired words of God, there is only one God, and one mediator between God and mankind. The mediator is Christ Jesus. Jesus is the lamb of God who gave himself as a ransom for all of us. (1 Timothy 2:5-6)

Mediation is intervention or intercession in a dispute or disagreement to resolve the conflict. A mediator is one who assist in the establishment of an agreement between two parties. A mediator is not a judge. (John 3:17) The mediator is one who has been chosen, selected, or appointed as an intercessor.

Yahweh is a supreme, sovereign, and unapproachable Deity. (Exodus 19:12)
As well, no man or woman is righteous. (Romans 3:10) For this reason, a mediator between God and mankind is required.

The New Testament authors clearly state that Jesus is the mediator between Yahweh and mankind. Jesus Christ is not only the mediator, the one who explains, he is the mediation, the one who acts. This relationship is not easily explained. (1 Timothy 6:12-16)

The Messiah is the only mediator between God and mankind. The Messiah, the promised one, is the only one with the power and authority to establish peace and agreement between God and mankind. He is the only one who can explain the fact that Yahweh is the God of existence and love. (John 1:18)

Simon Peter understood that Jesus was the Holy One of God, sent to us with the words of life. (John 6:69) Jesus was the fulfillment of all the words of prophecy that were recorded the laws of Moses, in the Psalms and by the prophets of Israel.

Jesus is the one who was identified by the apostles and disciples who followed him. (John 1:34-36) The followers of Jesus witnessed the words spoken and the miracles performed by Jesus. (Mark 9:7)

The apostles and disciples recorded the words of Jesus. They understood that the words of Jesus must be presented to the world, so that anyone who believes that Jesus offered the words of life can have eternal life. (John 3:13-16)

Jesus identified John the Baptist as the prophet that was promised by prophecy. (Matthew 11:14) However, even this chosen prophet did not completely understand the presence and purpose of the "son of man." John, the one who baptized Jesus, was in prison. He sent two of his disciples to ask Jesus, "Are you the One who is to come, or should we look for another?" (Matthew 11:2-4)

In a conversation with a Samaritan woman, Jesus clearly identifying himself as the promised Messiah. (John 4:25-26)

When reading in the Synagogue, Jesus used the prophetic words of the prophet Isaiah to testify that he was and is the Messiah. Jesus clearly stated that the prophecy had been fulfilled in their presence. (Isaiah 61:1) (Luke 4:18-21)

When challenged by the religious leaders of Israel, Jesus did not deny that he is the Messiah and the mediator between God and mankind. (Luke 22:67-71)

At his trial, standing before the Roman governor, Jesus answered the question, "Are you the king of the Jews?" Jesus answered, "It is as you say." (Mark 15:2-4, 17-18 & 26)

Pilate and the Jews expected Jesus to be an earthly ruler; however, Jesus did not come to establish a kingdom on earth. He came as the lamb of God to offer the gift of eternal life, in the Kingdom of Heaven. (John 18:36)

Jesus Christ is one who has been chosen by Yahweh as a peace maker or mediator between God and mankind. (1 Timothy 2:4-6)

Before this verse, or any statement of scripture, is used to attempt to prove that Christ Jesus and God are not One together, the reason why a righteous mediator was required for salvation through grace, rather than by the law or by acts of good works, should be carefully evaluated. We must understand why grace is necessary and why the righteousness of the Messiah is required for this gift of grace. We must also consider why the righteousness of Deity is the only righteousness that is sufficient.

A complete explanation of this fact has been offered in scripture; however, a comprehensive discussion would require an extensive review of the existence of Deity and of the nurture and transgressions of mankind and of the failure of Israel to abide by the laws of Moses. (Galatians 3:19-21)

A simple explanation is to state that the mediator was necessary, not because Deity is not One, but because the law was inadequate as a means of giving the promise of eternal life that was given to Abraham and to his descendants, and to mankind. The requirements of the law established a state of separation between God and man. The purity of Deity is the only thing that can wash away sin.

Jesus is the Mediator, but he is also the answer of mediation and the act of mediation. He is the High Priest, the Lamb of God, and the salvation of God. (Hebrews 2:1-18) Jesus the Christ, the Messiah or the anointed one, is not only the mediator he is also the revelation. He is the one who will reveal to everyone the blessed and only Sovereign. (1 Timothy 6:15-16)

In one account of the New Testament, the evil spirits recognized the deity of Christ. (Mark 5:1-8 This is an amazing account of redemption. (Mark 5:1-20) Evil spirits recognized Christ; but the religious leaders were blinded.

The words "Jesus, the Nazarene, The King of the Jews" were placed on the cross. (John 19:19-20) Everything about God's plan of salvation has been freely offered; nothing has been hidden. The words have been recorded, for anyone to read, and for any individual to choose to believe or to reject. (John 20:30) (1 John 5:1-13)

The apostle John has spoken for all of us. We believe that the Son of God has come, and has given us an understanding, that we may know him, the one true God. (1 John 5:20-21) This truth is available to anyone who is willing to confess with their mouth and believe in their heart that Jesus Christ gave his life as a ransom for those who are separated from the Father.

A new relationship between God and mankind was introduced by Yehoshua. In scripture the event is called the kingdom of Heaven or the kingdom of God. Jesus came to bring forth this new kingdom, a spiritual state of existence that establishes peace between mankind and God. The new Kingdom was introduced with the event that is called the transfiguration of Jesus. (Mark 9:1-13)

Without question, the mystery of the existence of Deity is difficult to explain or understand. (1 Timothy 3:16) An explanation of the mystery of godliness has been given by the Apostle Paul. This brief letter of exhortation includes an extensive description of what Jesus has done for us, and of what he has promised for the entire world. (Hebrews 1:1 - 13:22)

The truth, offered by the inspired words of life, is that the Father and the Son are One. (2 John 1:9-10) Jesus is the Messiah. (John 3:13)

## 49
## Meekness

Jesus came to be the Prince of Peace. He has been given all power and authority, but he is gentle and lowly in heart. Our task of being his disciples is not difficult, for being loving and kind is not work or labor. Jesus has said that the work that we have been given can be accomplished as acts of meekness. (Matthew 11:29-30)

Meekness is to be humble, submissive, gentle, modest, or lowly. As a negative trait, meekness is associated with being fearful, timid, or weak.

Humility and meekness are not character qualities that would be expected of a King, a Lord of lords, or a mighty one. Therefore, the characteristic of being gentle and lowly in heart must be carefully defined.

We would assume that only gentle and modest actions could possibly be applied to an almighty Deity. This seems to be correct, until we considered that Yehoshua, our Lord and Savior, humbly endured abuse from religious leaders and meekly placed his body on the cross, as an act of mercy for all of us.

However, this action of grace should not be used to incorrectly imply that Yahweh is a god of meekness. Any form of weakness or any characteristic related to submission would not be a characteristic of an almighty Deity.

Speaking to the multitudes, Jesus offered a blessing for the meek. Those who are meek will inherit the earth. (Matthew 5:5)

The words of prophecy of the coming Messiah include a description of a King that is meek, who comes sitting on the colt of a donkey. The king does not come riding a stallion in front of a mighty army (Matthew 21:1-9) Jesus did not entered the city of Jerusalem to be a reigning king of Israel.

The action of Jesus seems to create a theological problem. Many theologians have attempted to solve the problem by referring to meekness as strength under control. An assumption is made that, for those who are spiritually strong, meekness should be expressed as righteous actions, by being teachable, patient while suffering, or willing to submit to injustice without resentment. In other words, one should assume that meekness is to be expressed in noble actions, as a virtue of submission to God's will. This assumption appears to be contrary to the teachings of the prophets of Israel and of the apostles of Jesus.

A certain strength of character is indeed required for meekness. Mental and emotional strength is required to resist frustration, bitterness, or angry. A certain strength of character is required to be patient or gentle or humble; therefore, an act of meekness may require mental and emotional control or righteous action.

Regardless of how meekness or humility is defined or how a disciple of Christ responds, any definition or interpretation does not make Yahweh a God of meekness. The requirement of being gentle and lowly in heart only makes meekness an approved trait for the disciples of Christ.

Yahweh is a God of loving kindness. Acts of kindness may at times require an act of meekness; however, common acts of kindness should not be defined as acts of meekness. As well, acts of submission will not identify Christ-ones as those who are noble or patient. In essence, meekness must be an expression of love, for love is the primary requirements of being a disciple of Christ.

Jesus sent the disciples out for ministry, to be like sheep among wolves. They were to be as shrewd as serpents, and innocent as doves. (Matthew 10:16-19) To be shrewd and innocent seems to be contrasting traits, and the willingness to be scourged certainly surpasses a requirement of meekness.

We have been instructed to love our enemies, and to not mistreat those who hate us. We are to bless those that curse us and pray for those who offer disrespect. (Luke 6:27-35) Evidently, acts of meekness are beneficial for establishing a possibility of peace. Yahweh is merciful; and Yahweh is a prince of Peace.

Although we are unable to state that Almighty God is a God of meekness, we can at least say that Yahweh approves of humility or meekness; for he openly accepts the meek. For example, although Moses was meek, Yahweh selected Moses as a leader and prophet of the nation of Israel. According to the words of scripture, Moses was very meek, more than all the men who were on the face of the earth. (Numbers 12:3) Yahweh also defended Moses when this chosen one was unwilling to judge Miriam and Aaron. (Numbers 12:1-15)

And in the same way that Moses was protected, Yahweh offers special care and protection for the meek. Words of blessing for those who are meek are included in several of the words of prophecy and hymns of Israel. (Psalm 37:11 & 149:4)

Considering that man has been created in the image of God, and as well that Yahweh often expresses human-like characteristics, or that man has been given deity-like characteristics, meekness or humility must be determined to be a positive human characteristic, given by God, so that man would be able to live in love and unity and peace.

Even the gifts of love and eternal life offered by Yahweh should be received with meekness. (James 1:21) As well our service and love for others, especially for the children of God, should be acts of meekness. This example of meekness has been given to us by Jesus. (John 13:14-15)

Perhaps, meekness should be defined as a simple uncomplicated characteristic. Possibly, meekness is a character quality that guards against pride or self-centered selfish actions. (2 Timothy 3:2) Perhaps meekness is a simple choice of avoiding harmful or hateful actions. (Ephesians 6:10)

Possibly, as king David said, "Thy servant slew both the lion and the bear, and this Philistine shall be as one of them, seeing that he has defied the living God," meekness is a simple trust in the strength of the Holy Spirit. (1 Samuel 17:36) Perhaps, meekness is the true spiritual power of God. (Ephesians 6:10-18) Meekness may be a simple choice to be a Christ-one. (Philippians 1:21) (2 Peter 1:5-7)

Perhaps meekness should be defined as love that is strong enough to forgive others, or as faith that accepts the grace and forgiveness of a loving God. (Matthew 5:5)

# 50
# Merciful

Merciful kindness is a blessing from the One who is Love. (Lamentations 3:31-33)

Mercy is compassion or forgiveness offered to someone who deserves correction or punishment.

An act of mercy is to repeal, annul or delay judgment or punishment, even when the guilty one does not deserve lenient treatment or forgiveness. Mercy may involve being compassionate, lenient, sympathetic, forgiving, gracious, understanding, and benevolent. Yahweh is a God of unmerited and undeserved mercy and grace. (Psalm 145:8-9)

As a supreme sovereign deity Yahweh is not required to offer mercy to anyone. However, he is allowed to offer mercy at any time, for any reason, according to his divine will. (Romans 9:15)

Yahweh has chosen to offer unmerited favor and mercy to Israel. (Luke 1:54-55) He is described as a father who has mercy on his children. (Psalm 103:13) His goodness and mercy are everlasting. (Psalm 100:5, 145:8-9) The Lord opens the eyes of the blind, raises up those who are suffering, protects the strangers, and supports the fatherless and the widow. (Psalm 146:8-9) (1 Chronicles 16:34) (Psalm 119:64)

As well, his gift of eternal life, forgiveness, sanctification, redemption, and salvation through faith in Jesus Christ, is a gift of unearned or unmerited mercy. (Romans 15:8-12) Yahweh's offer of eternal life is a gift of merciful forgiveness and a supreme act of love, offered through the merciful sacrifice of Jesus Christ. (John 3:16-17))

Because Yahweh has forgiven, he justly expects those who have been forgiven to offer forgiveness to others, even to one's enemies. (Matthew 5:7) As well, if we do not shown mercy, we will receive judgment. (James 2:12-13)

Those who are Christ-ones are required to be known for acts of mercy and forgiveness. (Luke 10:37) We are to love our enemies, do good and lend and expect nothing in return. Just as Jesus was kind to ungrateful and evil men, we are to be merciful. If we condemn, we will be condemned. When we pardon, we will be pardoned. When we are merciful and kind, our reward will be great. For whatever we give to others, the same will be given to us in return. (Matthew 6:35-38) (Luke 6:36-38)

We who have been given eternal life have received a blessing of mercy that we do not deserve. We have been saved by an act of unmerited grace, not by our own deeds of righteousness. We have not earned and have not been granted the right of judgment.

Because we have received mercy, we are required to offer forgiveness and mercy to others. We must not be ungrateful unforgiving servants. (Matthew 18:23-27)

The gift of salvation and eternal life is a gift of love and mercy and grace. We have been given life in the Kingdom of Heaven. This is an everlasting gift of mercy. (Ephesians 2:4-7)

We should hold on to our faith, pray in the Holy Spirit, keep ourselves in the love of God, and depend upon the mercy of Jesus Christ for eternal life. (Jude 1:21)

## 51
## Miracles

The miracle of existence and the knowledge and awareness of existence is the story of creation that has been recorded in the Words of Life.

Miracles are events that are not explained by natural laws or scientific theories. Miracles may also be apparent violations of natural laws and physical and chemical laws of science. In essence, miracles are unexplained events that are beyond the realm of magic or deception or understanding.

Yahweh is a God of wonderous miracles.

Several miracles recorded in scripture are apparently simple acts of an almighty God. God dried up the waters of the Jordan until the tribes of Israel had passed over, so that the Israelites and all the people of the earth might know that God is mighty. (Joshua 4:23-24)

If miracles are discounted, biblical accounts will be difficult to believe. The actual problem of acceptance is that the existence of miracles is directly related to the existence of Deity, for miracles are indeed the witness of the existence of Deity. (John 10:25)

Yahweh is a God of unexplained miracles. Anything that is unexplained or not understood is difficult to accept. (Luke 1:20) Although Jesus performed miracles and fulfilled prophecy to testify that he was the one sent from Yahweh the religious leaders did not believe. (John 10:34-38, 15:24)

The purpose, intent, or specific reason for many miracles has not been explained in scripture. As a result, miracles may be easily discounted or considered to be unacceptable. Although Jesus performed miracles, many of the religious leaders and others did not believe that he is the Messiah. (John 12:37)

Jesus acknowledged this fact by telling the story about a certain rich man and Lazarus, the poor man. The wealthy man wanted Abraham to send Lazarus to his family, for he believed that if someone came to them from the dead, they would repent. But Abraham told him that if anyone does not accept the words of scriptures they will not be persuaded even if they witness a miracle. (Luke 16:17-31) Miracles can always be discredited or rejected.

To be able to accept the statement of existence, "Let there be light and there was light," a choice to accept miracles must be made. (Genesis 1:3) Therefore, concerning the existence of Deity, one alternative exists. The choice is to reject miracles and the existence of Deity or to accept the scriptural accounts and the existence of God.

Interestingly, many individuals attempt to find an alternative way of dealing with the requirement of acceptance. One way is to accept only a select number of miracles, and to reject those considered to be exaggerations or miss-interpretations. Accordingly, a few accounts of miracles may be accepted if a logical scientific explanation, or possibility of being an expected event is identified. For example, one might reason that because floods are natural events, the writer may have exaggerated a physical event. This person may believe that God created the heavens and the earth, but not that the task was accomplished in six literal days.

Another way to consider miracles is to scientifically reject the miracles; but consider the accounts to be worthy as myths or as an historical teaching. In other words, one may assume that the accounts of miracles should not be literally interpreted, for such exaggerations are merely a technique used by historians to assure the preservation of the account. The symbolic interpretation of the book of Jonah is a prime example of this method of limited or justified acceptance. Other miracles may be rejected because the events are extremely difficult to explain and may be easily misinterpreted; therefore, the description or explanation of the event may not be accurately recorded. The account offered by Joshua, when the sun and moon stood still and did not go down about a whole day is a prime example of this situation. (Joshua 10:12-13)

The biblical miracles are amazing events, but one of the most astonishing is the miracle of the shadow on the sundial, or on the steps of the stairway. King Hezekiah had prayed and had pleaded with God that he would be healed and not die. The prophet returned and told the king that the Lord had decided to grant his wish. The king wanted reassurance that this would indeed happen; therefore, he asked for a sign of confirmation.

Isaiah asked the king to make a choice to have the shadow on the sundial move forward ten degrees or back ten degrees. Hezekiah chose what he thought would the most difficult to accomplish. Isaiah prayed to the Lord, and God brought the shadow backward on ten steps of the stairway of Ahaz. (2 Kings 20:8-11)

The primary consideration, concerning miracles, is not to clearly explain miracles, or to study every miracle, to be in awe of the astounding events, or even to establish an acceptable process of interpretation. Our primary need is to understand why miracles are performed.

Perhaps, the performance of miracles is a natural response to a natural world. Perhaps, every miracle was an absolute necessity, to overcome a fault or malfunction of nature. Perhaps Yahweh performs miracles merely to demonstrate his power. This is an absolute fact concerning several of the miracles; for Yahweh is almighty. For nothing will be impossible for God. (Luke 1:37) As well, a purpose and intent for every miracle could be stated, for Yahweh is a God of purpose.

The miracles recorded by the prophet Elijah the Tishbite are worthy of consideration. A drought for three years was placed upon Israel. Ravens brought meat and bread to Elijah. A bowl of flower and a flask of oil did not become empty. A young child was brought back to life. Fire fell from the sky and consumed the burnt offering and the wood and stone and all the water in the trench around the altar. (1 Kings 17:1 -18:46) And for what reason were these miracles performed? When the people of Israel saw the miracle, they humbled themselves to worship and declared that the Lord is God. (1 Kings 18:39)

Perhaps Elijah and Elisha and Isaiah should be classified as the prophets of miracles. These noted prophets most likely witnessed more miracles than any in Israel; however, the greatest miracle witnessed is the appearance of the living God.

The Almighty One told Elijah to go forth to mount Horeb, the mount of God. Elijah went to the mountain and entered a cave. A strong wind raked across the mountain, an earthquake shook the mountain, and a fire raged across the landscape, but God was not in the wind, earthquake, or fire. When Elijah heard a soft voice, he went out to the entrance of the cave, and God spoke. (1 Kings 19:11-13)

Perhaps this miracle was given as a prophesy, so that we could understand that God speaks to us, by the power of the Holy Spirit, with a still small voice, to ask us if we love him or understand what he has done for us?

Many of the recorded miracles were acts of faith. The apostle Paul, as a brief review of acts of faith, said that some had subdued kingdoms, stopped the mouth of lions, quenched the violence of fire, escaped the edge of the sword, received their dead back to life again. (Hebrews 11:33-35)

Obviously, many accounts of miracles have been recorded as testimonies of the presence and existence of Yahweh. However, regardless of how miracles are interpreted, all miracles would be useless without the miracle of Jonah. This is the miracle of the death, burial and resurrection of Jesus Christ, and his miraculous gift of love to the world.

Yahweh, our God of miracles, performed this miracle with a definite purpose, to let us know that he exists and that he loves us. Although signs and miracles prove his existence to those who are willing to accept the miracle or to understand that the miracle is from God, all miracles would be useless without the true miracle of the resurrection of Jesus Christ. (1 Corinthians 15:13-14) This miracle of love and life has been given for a clearly stated purpose and intent.

A Pharisee named Nicodemus, a ruler of the Jews, came in the night to question Jesus. Nicodemus understood the purpose of miracles; and he wanted to know by what power or authority Jesus was performing miracles. The true theological question was not about miracles but about the promise of a Messiah. As well, Jesus did not offer Nicodemus a lesson about miracles; and he did not directly tell Nicodemus that he was the Messiah. Jesus told Nicodemus about the Kingdom of God. Jesus explained to Nicodemus that God is Love. (John 3:1-21)

For Yahweh so loved the world, he presented the miracle of the death, burial, and resurrection of his one and only son, not that his power and might should be demonstrated but so that those who believe in miracles may have eternal life.

The religious rulers asked Jesus to prove by a miraculous act that he is the Messiah. Jesus plainly stated that the only miracle that would be offered would be the sign or miracle of the prophet Jonah. And Jesus left them and departed. (Matthew 16:4)

Miracles show the majesty and wonder of an almighty God; however, miracles are of no value to those who choose to discount or discredit miracles. Once again, consider the words of Father Abraham, in the story of Lazarus and the rich man. "If they do not listen to Moses and the Prophets, or believe in miracles, neither will they be persuaded if someone rises from the dead." (Luke 16:26-31)

Jesus the Christ who is called Emmanuel or One-with us performed miracles, to prove that he is One with God; but many rejected the miracles. (John 8:45-52)

Jesus returned to Nazareth, where his parents and family lived. He entered the synagogue and stood up to read. When he had finished reading the prophetic words of Isaiah, he identified himself to be the Messiah. And the citizens of Nazareth took him to the brow of the hill on which their city had been built. They intended to throw him off the cliff, but Jesus passed through their midst and departed. (Luke 4:29-30)

Yahweh is a God of miracles; for he is the God of knowledge of the unknown.

Jesus spoke to a young ruler of Israel, who represents Israel. The young man wanted to know what good thing he could do to have eternal life. Jesus reminded him that only God is good or righteous, and that for anyone to receive eternal life by being holy or righteous would be impossible. (Luke 18:19, 27) However, because Yahweh is a God of miracles, the things that are impossible for man are possible with God.

Jesus died and was buried and was resurrected to life. This was a miracle that was only possible by the power and authority of Deity; however, this miracle was not performed to demonstrate that God is almighty. This was a miracle of grace and love offered by Yahweh, the God of miracles who offers eternal life to those who believe by faith in miracles.

The faith to believe in miracles is a gift from Yahweh. This gift must be accepted as a choice to believe in miracles. For the pragmatic humanist nothing can be a miracle. For us, everything in our beautiful, wonderful, amazing world is a miracle.

Although all the wonderous deeds of Jesus have not been recorded, the inspired words of God have been written so that we might believe that Jesus is the Christ, the Son of God, and that believing we might have life through his name. (John 20:30-31)

# 52
# Order

The prophets and scribes of Israel recorded observations concerning the order and stability of the earth and universe.

Order is a stable situation based upon sequence, alignment, arrangement, organization, distribution, or descending and ascending positions.

Mathematical computations are dependent upon a pre-determined order of operations. The functional value of a mechanical device, such as a watch, depends upon order and sequence. As well, the natural order of existence requires a mathematical stability of order and sequence. This system of physical order, established by a God of order, is functional and beneficial.

Civil order may be defined as a state of legal social and political relationships. Social order may be established by legal restrictions; however, the use of the word civil implies that order should rightly exist by establishing courteous agreements of well-mannered cooperation or acceptance.

Yahweh is a God of order and unity and logical function. Order eliminates chaos.

To not accept the existence of anything that cannot be seen, touched or sensed is a practical or pragmatic decision. To assume or believe that a state of order and intelligence evolved from a state of chaos or disorder is not practical or acceptable. The choice to accept or reject the scriptural account of creation is a decision that should not be made as a simple pragmatic choice. (Proverbs 16:25)

The fact that Yahweh is a God of order is not proven by biblical accounts or specific statements of scripture. The existence of order is proven by scientific facts and theories that have repeatedly stated that the earth and the universe and all that exist is maintained by a collective system of intricate order and dependence. A system of order is necessary for all of creation, not just for the religious practices of mankind.

Yahweh created everything. All that he has created is good. All of creation exist in a state of order, not chaos. The universe, arranged and organized, exists with purpose and order that did not evolve from a state of chaos.

The stars of the sky are visible expressions of the glory and majesty of God. They are evidence of his handiwork of order. (Psalm 19:1) As the Deity of order and the creator of existence, YHWH has absolute control, of everything. (Proverbs 16:4)

This world and all that exist belongs to the Creator. He allows both prosperity and adversity to exist; and because both are ordained by God with a purpose, all has been established in a state of order. Yahweh's choice for order is shown in the laws and social order that were established for the nation of Israel. Requirements for service in the tabernacle, and for the observance of the Passover and other religious practices for the tribes of Israel were included in the law. (Numbers 8:1-26) Religious order, to teach the necessity of sacrifice; and social order, to teach the necessity of honor or sanctification was instituted. Legal order to defend those who caused harm without criminal intent was written into law. Rules of inheritance and social order between male and female, and regulations to protect the alien and the bond slaves were included. (Numbers 34:1 - 36:13) Political and social order was established by allowing Moses to appoint elders of the twelve tribes as rulers and judges for the tribes. (Deuteronomy 1:13-18)

A state of order for the children of Abraham was secured under the prophets and under the kings of Israel. Twelve tribes, eleven with property inheritance and the tribe of Levi as priest, all of whom were of the sons of Jacob. Every individual within the nation had a position and a purpose, as officials of Israel, princes of the tribes, commanders of divisions of the army, owners of vineyards and flocks and field. Many served as overseers of property and livestock for the king. (1 Chronicles 24:1-27:34) The tribes of Israel were one extended family; and everything in the nation of Israel had order and purpose.

God has provided the fixed patterns of heaven and earth; and, as an act of creation God has numbered the stars and has recorded all their names. (Psalm 147:4) As well, the covenant that Yahweh has made with the children of Abraham has been established with the same order and endurance. (Jeremiah 33:25-26)

God has established order so that he will be in control, not man. Within this world of order, as individuals, we are given logical or orderly choices. We are allowed to be in control of our individual lives; however, individual control is possible only within the limits of divine order. All other choices concerning order or control are given as a gift of grace. (Acts 17:24-28) The One, the Lord of Heaven, has created this beautiful world of order that is our home, so that we might live and move and have our being. (Acts 17:28)

Because Yahweh is excellent, supreme, magnificent, unequaled, perfect, unlimited, uplifting, inspiring, and heavenly, his plans thoughts, and actions, are often amazingly complex; however, his actions may also be easily understood. (John 3:16)

God has not asked for approval of the order that has been established. He has not asked for approval of the plan for the gospel of grace. The apostle Paul, who was given the duty of explaining the mystery of the gospel to the gentiles, explained that even at the time of creation the gospel was present as a plan for our world, so that the wisdom of God might be revealed. The gospel is the plan of the eternal purpose of existence that has been carried out in Christ Jesus. (Ephesians 3:8-11)

God brought forth salvation, through grace, according to his plan, so that his wisdom would be revealed, for He is a God of order and unity.

The recorded accounts in the book of Acts are a record of the planned sharing of the Gospel. Jesus told the disciples to go into all the world and preach the good news to all nations. (Mark 16:15) Following the resurrection of Jesus, the disciples were in Jerusalem, gathering in small groups and praising God. As well, thousands were being baptized. And then, Stephen was stoned by a group of non-believers. And on that day a great persecution arose against the believers in Jerusalem. As a result, many of the followers of Jesus were scattered throughout the regions of Judea and Samaria. (Acts 8:2) All of the recorded events happened according to God's orderly plan.

Jesus Christ sent his Holy Spirit to the believers of the way, to the followers of a way of life. He did not send his Spirit to those who had formed a religion, or to priests of a religious order, but to ordinary saints. He sent his Spirit to allow his disciples to be unified in love and purpose, so that they might function as a family of equals. The Holy Spirit has been given to every individual believer as a gift of unity. The rule of unity was for all things to be done properly and in an orderly manner. (1 Corinthians 14:33, 40)

The mission and purpose of every believer is to be a disciple of Christ. This is according to God's plan of unity. We are to conduct yourselves in a manner worthy of the gospel of Christ; for Yahweh is not a God of confusion or disorder. (Philippians 1:27)

We are designed to function together in sequence, alignment, arrangement, organization, and distribution, but not in ascending or descending positions. The first century church of faithful believers was a simple organization of brethren of equal status that were assisted by overseers and deacons. The chosen and anointed leaders were servants who were given the obligation of tending to the physical and spiritual needs of the common individual believers who are called saints. (Philippians 1:1-2)

The body of Christ is to be an expression of the unity of one. God is not the author of confusion or disorder. He is the God of peace. (1 Corinthians 14:33) (Matthew 13:41-43)

The conclusion is that because we are unable to discover the work that has been done under the sun, we must trust the logical wisdom of Almighty God; for Yahweh is a God of wisdom and order.

## 53
## Patience

According to the apostle Peter, one day is with the Lord as a thousand years, and a thousand years as one day. This statement is a description of patience. (2 Peter 3:8)

Patience is the capacity or ability to accept or tolerate any kind of provocation such as interference, delay, disappointment, annoyance, suffering, or pain without being upset, expressing angry or offering complaint. Forbearance, tolerance, and control are synonymous terms.

Patience is not a natural characteristic of most children or youth or adults. As well, because there are many accounts in scripture when Yahweh was provoked, disappointed, and angry, we may assume that Yahweh is not a God of patience; however, the actual truth is that patience may be a quality of character that is possible only for Yahweh. (Psalm 9:17-20)

For the Israelites who called for swift punishment against the wicked, Jesus offered a parable, to remind them of how patient Yahweh had been with the children of Abraham. The parable was about a certain man who had a fig tree that was planted in his vineyard. The owner of the vineyard came to find fruit on the tree and did not find any fruit. (Luke 13:6-9)

When God is patient, when he does not act, an assumption should not be made that he is limited in power or authority. Several of the psalmist were concerned about the delayed judgment of their enemies. Why should the wicked be allowed to boast and the greedy man to not be judged. (Psalm 10:1-3)

When dishonorable ones are blessed, and tragedy befalls the faithful, the patience of Yahweh should not be judged. Patience is not lack of strength or resolve. Yahweh stands prepared with power and might to offer justice. At all times in every circumstance, Yahweh is in control of everything. (Ecclesiastes 8:11-12)

The patience of Yahweh is evident in his choice of Israel. (Romans 10:21) The patience of God is also demonstrated in the redemption of Israel. At the appointed time, the deliverer shall come out of Zion and will turn away ungodliness from Jacob. This is the covenant of God, to take away their sins. (Isaiah 59:20-21) (Romans 11:25-32)

The patience of Yahweh is evident in his gift of salvation. (2 Peter 3:9 -10)

The Lord is not slack concerning his promise. God is not willing that any should perish. His desire is that all should have eternal life. Patience was demonstrated in the life of the apostle Paul, for mercy and patience was given to him as an example for those who would believe in Jesus for eternal life. (1 Timothy 1:16) The writer of the book of James, also offered a statement concerning honor, and humility and patience. (James 5:8-10)

Patience expressed as compassionate love, is beneficial for all of mankind. For believers, patience is especially beneficial. We accept tribulations, for we know that tribulation produces patience, and patience experience, and experience hope. (Romans 5:3-4)

In certain situations when defense or relief is not offered by God, a delay of justice is not necessarily an act of patience. His delay of judgment during difficult times may be a choice of love. (2 Peter 3:8-10) In a certain time, the last days of perilous times, judgment by God will be delayed. However, the time before "the last days" is not necessarily a time of patience. The "time of waiting" is God's choice of love and grace. (2 Timothy 3:1-5)

Yahweh is a patient Father (Romans 15:5) however, there will be a time when everyone, the entire world and the house of Israel, will know that his patience has been expended, consumed by the requirements of justice.

A time will come when all in the city of Jerusalem will say, "Blessed is the One who comes in the name of the Lord!" (Luke 13:34-35)

## 54
## Peace

The promise of peace to the house of Israel is a promised gift of love. (Nahum 1:15) The promise of peace to mankind is a gift of eternal life. (Luke 2:14)

Peace is defined as freedom from disturbance or fear. Peace is a state of tranquility, a time when the existence or possibility of war or conflict has been eliminated. Peace is a time to be thankful and to enjoy comfort and the absence of conflict or harm.

Yahweh is a God of peace. The reason given to Noah for the destruction of the earth was that the earth was filled with violence and lack of peace. (Genesis 6:13)

Yahweh honors peace on earth in several special ways. For example, wisdom is a gift from God that includes a gift of peace. (Proverbs 15:1-2) Peace may be a simple blessing of life. (Proverbs 17:1) Spiritual peace is a gift of the Holy Spirit, for "the peacemakers shall be called the children of God." (Matthew 5:9) Jesus, the son of the God of Peace, instructed his disciples to offer the traditional greeting and blessing of peace to those that gave protection and care to the disciples. (Matthew 10:11-13)

However, the special blessing of everlasting peace, a future time of peace for mankind, will be brought forth through one called the Prince of Peace.

The Lord God of Israel intended for the descendants of Abraham to live in peace in a land that had been promised as an inheritance; however, because they were unable to remain faithful, Yahweh removed peace from them. This historical situation was revealed to Moses by prophecy. (Deuteronomy 31:1 -52) For most of the times of the kings of Israel the kingdoms of Israel and Judah were at war with surrounding nations, as well as with Egypt and the kingdoms of Mesopotamia. Naturally, the Israelites longed for peace, and traditionally greeted others with words of peace. (Isaiah 2:1-5)

A standard Hebrew greeting is Shalom Aleichem, "Peace be upon you." The response to the greeting is Aleichem shalom, "Unto you, peace." As well a full response may include the words, "and the mercy of Yahweh and his blessings." Considering the wars and conflicts throughout all generations, a state of peace would be a cherished blessing for the Hebrew descendants, and for the world. (Micah 5:2-5)

In ever age of stress, defeat or trouble, the prophets prophesied of the eventual peace for the nation of Israel. (Haggai 2:5-9) (Zechariah 12:10) Because God is compassionate, he has chosen to have mercy upon the earth and mankind. He established a covenant with Noah, as an act of compassion and mercy, and offered a future hope for peace to the children of Abraham. (Genesis 6:18) For the nation of Israel, peace is a promise from Yahweh, to be offered through the One called the Messiah. This will be a universal peace that will be brought forth with everlasting freedom and liberty. (Romans 11:25-33) As well, by the grace of God, peace and unity has been established between the children of Israel and the children of other nations. This situation of unity was explained by the apostle Paul. (Ephesians 2:11-19)

Jesus, the Prince of peace, entered Jerusalem, the city of peace, sitting on a beast of burden that is a symbol of peace. (Matthew 21:5) (John 12:13-16) However, the people did not recognize this One of peace. (John 12:16)

Everlasting peace and liberty, a time of rest, has been offered to the world as a blessing from God. A time of peace was established as a Seventh Day rest and is fulfilled as a special gift that is offered to anyone who is willing to accept his gift of eternal life. (Hebrews 4:1-10) Jesus, the Messiah, also offered the gift of spiritual peace to those who have chosen to follow him. (Romans 8:6) Righteousness and peace and joy in the Holy Spirit are gifts of love. (Romans 14:17) (Philippians 4:7) (John 14:27) We know that in this life we will encounter hardships, but we can live in spiritual peace; for Jesus has overcome the world. (John 16:33)

Jesus told the disciples to go forth and make disciples, and he promised that his gift of peace would be with them. (Matthew 28:20) Yahweh desires unity and peace for everyone. For this reason, he instructed his disciples to follow his example by striving to be peacemakers. (Hebrews 12:14) A simple promise from God is that peacemakers will be blessed and will be called the children of God. (Matthew 5:9) (Colossians 3:15)

However, although Yahweh is a God of peace, Jesus did not come to bring peace on the earth. (Matthew 10:34-37) (Luke 12:51) His warning to his disciples is not a blessing of peace. The disciples were told that many would hate them. (Matthew 10:22)

For every believer, peace is a present reality of spiritual assurance; however, just as peace is a future event for the nation of Israel, peace on the earth for all of mankind is a future event. (Matthew 10:34-42)

Nevertheless, in everything, we should rejoice. We should be like-minded, live in peace, and allow our God of love and peace to comfort us. (2 Corinthians 13:11-12) (1 Thessalonians 5:14-15, 23) In the name of Jesus, we should joyfully offer peace to others.

Shalom, Peace be upon you, and the mercy of God and His blessing.

# 55
# Perfection

The words and laws of God are perfect, beautiful, and true. (Psalm 19:7-9)

Perfection is a state and quality of being free from flaws or defects. Perfection is to be classified as excellent, magnificent, faultless, or immaculate. Perfection is to have obtained the highest possible position of excellence or worth. Perfection is the quality of being complete in every possible way, in the past, present and in the future. Perfection is a state of pure righteousness.

The very essence of Deity is perfection. (Psalm 19:7-11)

Truth is a state of perfection, for perfection is an absolute requirement for the existence of truth. As an example, a straight line must not have variations of degrees, at any point on the path of the line. The line must not be misaligned at any location. For the words of scripture, "we shall know the truth, and the truth shall set us free," the word perfection could justifiable be substituted for the word truth. (John 8:32)

God is the only One who is perfectly righteous. This state of perfection or holiness makes God unapproachable. This simple truth places the world and mankind in a state of condemnation. Because Yahweh is also perfect in love, he has chosen to offer grace instead of condemnation.

A man or woman of perfection has never lived or existed. A perfect human being will never exist. Even Adam sinned. Indeed, there is not a righteous man on earth who continually does good and who never sins. (Ecclesiastes 7:20) As human beings we are like a wooden ball, crafted by hand without use of a lathe, as an interesting object of imperfection. This does not imply that God is incapable of creating perfection; he has simply not chosen to create a perfect human being.

The almighty I Am is the only righteous One who exist in perfection. His actions are touched or influenced by his own perfection. By his choice or will, he is able to do anything, that is complete and perfect, such as the act of grace offered through his son, Jesus Christ. We should be constantly aware that God is perfect, and that we are not perfect or righteous. (Philippians 3:15)

The perfection in Christ that is given to believers is described by the word, righteousness; however, no one is perfect or righteous, except the Almighty. The righteousness of Jesus Christ, that is referred to as sanctification, has been given as a spiritual gift to believers; however, this state of righteousness has not been earned by deeds or works of perfection. Righteousness in Christ is not inherent perfection like the righteousness or perfection of deity. Spiritual sanctification is a covering of holiness or righteousness that has been given as a gift of grace and love. (1 Corinthians 6:11)

This imputed righteousness is obtained only by an act of faith and a statement of belief and a willingness to trust Christ and to live as a disciple of Christ. A status of deity has not been established. Yahweh is the only One that is a righteous deity; and Jesus Christ is the only righteous son, who is One with the Father. (Hebrews 5:8-9)

We are required to make a verbal confession and believe in our heart that Jesus has been raised from the dead, that Jesus is alive. Belief in the heart offers righteousness, and a confession offers salvation. (Romans 10:8-10)

## 56
## Personal

A bright light suddenly shined around Saul, and he heard a voice. Saul did not know who was speaking. Then he heard the words "I am the One called Yehoshua whom you are persecuting." (Acts 9:3-5)

To be a person is to be an identifiable one, with distinguishable characteristics and identifiable appearance or description.

The personal presence of Yahweh is undeniable.

The story of creation is an account of an encounter with a supreme Deity. The story is an account of a personal encounter between mankind and the Heavenly Father, the identifiable personal One known as YHWH, I am that I am.

There are many accounts in the Bible of personal encounters with Yahweh.

Adam and Eve (Genesis 3:8-19) Cain (Genesis 4:6-15) Noah (Genesis 6:13-22, 9:3-17) Abraham (Genesis 12:1-4, 15:1-6) Isaac (Genesis 26:2-5, 24) and Jacob (Genesis 32:24-30) had a personal encounter with God.

When Jacob encountered the personal presence of God, he named the place Peniel, for he had seen God face to face, and his life had not been taken. (Genesis 32:30, 48:3)

Several encounters with Moses (Exodus 3:1-22-24) and with Joshua (Joshua 6:1-2, 10:8-15) are recorded. In this event the presence of God was with power. There was no day like that day, before or after, when the Lord listened to the voice of a man and fought for Israel.

Appearances were made with judges and kings including Gideon (Judges 6:11-18) the prophet Samuel (1 Samuel 3:1-18) and King Solomon. (2 Chronicles 7:12)

One of the most dramatic personal encounters was with Job. Job stated that he had known God only by what he had read or heard, but being in the actual presence of God was frightening and humbling. (Job 42:5-6)

A few supernatural encounters were also recorded. (Genesis 18:1-33) This appearance to Abraham is also a testimony of Jehovah's honor and mercy and love, and judgment.

Yahweh appeared again when Abraham was ninety-nine years old. (Genesis 17:1-22) And when God had finished talking to Abraham, God departed. He appeared again to announce the birth of Isaac. (Genesis 18:1-17) The Lord watched over Abraham for his entire life. Abraham lived for many years, and the Lord God was with Abraham to bless him in every way. (Genesis 24:1)

The personal relationship that Yahweh has with Abraham should never be discounted or transferred to another. With authority, Yahweh confirmed this covenant relationship with Isaac's son Jacob; and changed Jacob's name to Israel. (Genesis 32:28) As well, Yahweh demonstrated his power and authority to the people of Israel. (Exodus 20:22) Yahweh appeared to Moses in a pillar of cloud at the entrance of the tent of meeting and spoke to Moses face to face, just as a man speaks to his friend. (Exodus 33:11)

Although a personal conversation with God was possible, an actual visible encounter was not possible. Moses was allowed to see the back of Yahweh as he passed by, but to see His face was not allowed. (Exodus 33:18-23) Obviously, Yahweh chose to have a special relationship with

Moses. He spoke to Miriam and Aaron, not to defend Moses or his own actions, but to declare the righteousness of this relationship. (Numbers 12:5-9) When the people complained because of lack of water, "the glory of the Lord" appeared to Moses and Aaron, and "the Lord" spoke to Moses to give specific instructions concerning the problem. (Numbers 20:6-8)

The prophet Isaiah delivered personal messages from Jehovah to the children of Abraham. (Isaiah 1:1) Isaiah's words of prophecy were given only to Israel, at a specific time of history. (Isaiah 1:16-20) This is a personal message, by a specific prophet, to a specific people, during a specific time, and should not be taken out of context, to be used by any other nation or by any individual for a moral or religious purpose.

However, because the words of Isaiah are scripture, the words can be used to explain the character and purpose of our loving Father, for the Lord is the same yesterday, today and forever. (Hebrews 13:8) Yahweh is Deity and he does not change. (Malachi 3:6) Obviously, we can assume that Yahweh is not pleased with insincere religious performance, or when one fails to love and honor others. As well, although a direct application should be made only to Israel, we may consider the fact that Abraham and the nation of Israel and their covenant relationship to Yahweh is a type or an example to all people. Therefore, the words of Isaiah can be used for the purpose of understanding the character of almighty God.

The special relationship between Yahweh and Israel is emphasized in the appearance to the unknown prophet Balaam. (Numbers 22:9-12)

The personal presence of Yahweh has also been encountered through visions and dreams. The prophet Ezekiel testified that the heavens were opened, and he saw visions of God. The word of God came expressly to Ezekiel the priest, son of Buzi. (Ezekiel 1:3)

The importance of not taking personal statements or events out of context or of making a general non-personal teaching concerning the statement or event should be stressed. For example, when Yahweh spoke through the words of King David to his son Solomon the words were personal, given only for the king. (1 Chronicles 28:9)

This passage of scripture should not be used to teach that any individual could be cast off forever for not serving with a perfect heart. However, the passage does illustrate Yahweh's personal presence and understanding of every individual.

The Apostle Paul of Tarsus had a life changing personal encounter with the living Christ. (Acts 9:1-20) In a similar way, we who believe in Christ have a personal encounter, by the power of the Holy Spirit, with the Almighty God. Jesus has told us that he is with us, even to the end of time. The reason given is that he jealously desires the Spirit which he has made to dwell in us. (James 4:5) Jesus is with us, all of us, because in Christ there is neither Jew nor Greek, slave nor free, male nor female, for we are all the same in Christ Jesus. (Galatians 3:28)

The accounts of the apostles and disciples of Jesus are testimonies concerning Yahweh's personal involvement in the affairs of mankind. Most importantly, his presence is evident in the One called Emanuel, Yahweh with us. The personal presence of Yahweh with us, after his death, burial, and resurrection, is recorded in New Testament scripture.

Simon Peter had informed the other disciples that he intended to go fishing. The other disciples agreed to go with him. If Jesus were not a personal Deity, this recorded account would have been the end of the story; however, Jesus was alive. He met the disciples in Galilee at the sea of Tiberias, where he had told them that he would appear. (Matthew 26:32 & 28:7, 16) He ate with the disciples, talked to the disciples, and met their individual needs. (John 21:1-25) Yahweh was present and aware of the needs of Adam and Eve, Noah, Abraham, Moses and of all the prophets and heroes of Israel. Jesus was present and aware of the needs of the disciples.

By the power of the Holy Spirit Yahweh continued to be personally involved in the affairs of mankind. Yahweh saw an Ethiopian diplomat and sent Philip to answer his theological questions. (Acts 8:38) He heard the prayers of Cornelius and sent the apostle Peter as a witness. In the city of Philippi, the apostle Paul was placed in prison so that a personal contact could be made with a jailor and his family. (Acts 16:25-34)

The Holy Spirit of One is present today. All who have accepted God's gift of grace have a personal relationship through Jesus Christ. An understanding of this relationship is of extreme importance, for knowledge or understanding of Love will directly influence our religious and social character. If we are unable to understand our personal, spiritual relationship we will be unable to know the Truth. Jesus admonished Philip for not being aware of the personal presence of God. Jesus told Philip that anyone who has seen Jesus as seen the Father. (John 14:9)

As well, although we are separate individuals, we are together as a spiritual unity with the One who is the King of kings and Lord of lords. We are spiritually united in Christ to our loving Father. This is indeed an indescribable personal relationship. (2 Corinthians 19:7)

The apostle Paul said that God does not show favoritism, for in every nation, anyone who fears him and is righteous or honorable is accepted by him. (Acts 17:26) After all, because Jehovah has made all nations of men that dwell on the face of the earth, we are all the same, and we all live on the same earth. God makes the sun to rise on the evil and on the good and sends rain on the just and on the unjust. (Matthew 5:45)

Yahweh is your personal God. He sees our heart. He reads the thoughts of our mind. He does not consider our outward appearance; he looks on our heart. (1 Samuel 16:7) (Psalm 8:3-5) He knows everything about us. (Matthew 10:39)

The twenty-third psalm is a praise for the fact that God is a personal God. The valley of shadows is life here on earth. He is with us, and he comforts us. Our days of life are like shadows that are fading, and we live in a land of darkness and death. (Job 8:9, 10:21) (Isaiah 9:2) Psalm twenty-three should be joyfully read as a shout of victory. The Lord is like a faithful shepherd. We can joyfully proclaim that goodness and love and kindness will follow us all the days of our life, and we will dwell in the house of the Lord forever. Yes, Jehovah is a wonderful caring personal Father. (Proverbs 3:32) The prayer of the upright is His delight. (Proverbs 15:8)

Yahweh is present with every man, and he is spiritually present with those who have faith in him. (Proverbs 15:29) (John 9:31)

The personal relationship that a Christian has with God cannot be explained or described in simple terms. Our relationship is like friendship, for we live according to the Spirit. We keep our mind in agreement with the Spirit, for the Spirit dwells within us. (Romans 8:5-9) Our relationship is like the unity or bond of love between a parent and child. (Romans 8:11) This relationship is like a son to a father. (Romans 8:15-16) The relationship is one of trust, like sheep that remain close to the good shepherd. For all who are being led by the Spirit are sons of God. (Romans 8:14) Our relationship is a relationship of unity and love. We are Christ-ones together with the Father. Our personal relationship is like soldiers that depend upon each other in times of conflict. The Holy Spirit is God's gift of love that offers faith, hope, and love. (Romans 8:22-26)

Our personal relationship with our almighty Father has not been given through an apostle, a priest, or any religious organization. (Acts 10:44) This friendship with God has not been given because we perform acts of love or honor or faithfulness. Our relationship is physical and mental and spiritual; but the connection is within the heart of every believer, for we believe in our heart, that God raised Jesus from the dead. (Romans 10:9) We have not been given a list of works to accomplish. We do not need to get closer to God. We have been set free to live in the presence of his love.

The greatest blessing of the Holy Spirit is that the Spirit personally intercedes for us with our Almighty unapproachable God. The Holy Spirit is our mediator, our gift from our Messiah. And the Spirit gives us assurance within our hearts. (Romans 8:27-28)

Our personal connection with the Holy Spirit is a relationship of sincere faith and love. Our personal unity is a relationship of hope and assurance. (Romans 8:33-39)

We have the honor of praying a simple yet profound prayer to a Father in heaven. (Luke 11:2-4) As well, we can pray a personal prayer with confidence, with assurance that our prayer will be answered. (Luke 11:9-10) We stand on truth; and truth is a firm foundation.

Our relationship with Yahweh is love; and love is always personal.

## 57
## Power and Might

Whatever the Lord wishes to do, he does, in heaven and on earth, or in the universe. (Psalm 135:5-6) (Isaiah 40:25-26)

As a principle of physics, power is defined as the rate at which energy is transferred by movement of mass, heat, or conversion of energy or substance. A common social definition of power is that power is control, authority, or influence. Power may also be strength and ability to change a state of existence or circumstances. Power may be used or expended as a positive or negative force, to create or to destroy.

The absolute power of Deity includes the positive authority of creation of life and substance, and the power and authority to sustain life. The absolute power of deity is also seen in truth, righteousness, mercy, justice and especially in love.

Although Yahweh is an almighty Deity with unequaled and unlimited power, in the accounts of scripture he is often identified in simple terms as the Almighty. Although his kingdom is not of this world, he rules over the earth as the almighty King of the universe. (Psalm 47:8)

Yahweh has often used power and might to demonstrate his presence and his love; however, he has not chosen to eliminate the evil that exist in the world. Jesus gave a partial answer for this choice. Jesus said that if his kingdom were an earthly kingdom, his servants would defend him from the Jews who intended to crucify him. (John 18:36)

Yahweh has demonstrated his power and might by using kings, prophets, and warriors as defenders and protectors of the nation of Israel. Joshua and Gideon, king David and his mighty warriors, Samson and Daniel, Elijah and Elisha were, by the power of God, strong and mighty defenders of the children of God.

The demonstrations of God's power and might are often recorded as personal appearances and revelations, or as miracles. He brought up quail from the sea to feed thousands, and like a father, he admonished Israel for questioning his faithfulness. (Numbers 11:31 -34)

God gave a song about the rock of Israel to Moses and instructed Moses to teach the song to the people of Israel. The song includes expressive descriptions of the greatness, strength, truth, righteousness, and justice of the almighty God of Israel. (Deuteronomy. 32:31&37)

God's protection, by power and might, was given to Joshua and the people of Israel. The Israelites were instructed to be strong and courageous, to not tremble or be dismayed, for God had promised to be with them wherever they might go. (Joshua 1:6-9)

The story of Samson and the records of the mighty men of the armies of Israel are accounts that illustrate the use of power and might by the God of Israel. The names of the mighty warriors in the army of David, thirty-seven in all, were known to all in Israel. (2 Samuel 23:8-39)

Although Yahweh has specifically demonstrated his authority to the children of Israel by acting as a strong and mighty father of Israel, the people of Israel often failed to remember that Yahweh is always in control. To remind the Israelites of his faithfulness, Yahweh directing Gideon to limit the number of armed soldiers, from thirty-two thousand to three hundred. Three hundred trumpets were sounded, and the Lord set the sword one against another throughout the army of the enemy, and the soldiers fled as far as Beth-shittah in Zererath. (Judges 7:22) With power and wisdom, and only three hundred warriors, Yahweh destroyed an entire army. (Judges 8:13-29)

The Lord God of Israel has often chosen to use his power to defend the nation of Israel in battle against their adversaries. In one account, as Samuel was offering a burnt offering, the Philistines drew near for battle against Israel; but a loud thunder sent from God confused the Philistines, so that they were routed before Israel. (1 Samuel 7:9-11)

The power and strength of God has also been demonstrated by the power of the Holy Spirit. For strength and protection, the Holy Spirit was given as an anointing to king David. Samuel took the horn of oil, and anointed David; and the Spirit of the Lord came upon David from that day forward. (1 Samuel 16:13) (2 Samuel 22:31-33, 36 & 50-51)

The promises of God, for strength and protection, will never be taken away from the nation of Israel. The promises given through the prophet Ezekiel are worthy promises. The words written to the people called Gog should be considered as a warning to all who do not accept God's personal choice to protect Israel. (Ezekiel 39:1-29)

A complete description of the power and might of Deity has not been recorded in scripture. As well, a complete description of the oneness of deity, and the power and authority that Jesus shares with his Father has not been explained. Perhaps God assumes that we should understand the relationship, without explanation. The answer, "I Am" that was given to Moses seems to imply that Moses should already know the answer to his question concerning the existence of Deity.

The power and authority of Deity is shared with Jesus. Jesus is the one who has gone into heaven and is on the right hand of God, Angels and authorities and powers have been made subject unto him. (1 Peter 3:22)

Jesus demonstrated the power of Deity by performing miracles. (Mark 4:37-41) A certain woman, who was very ill, decided that if she could touch the clothing of Jesus, she would be healed. When able to push her way through the crowd, she reached out and touched his clothes. She was immediately healed. Jesus, aware that power or strength had been taken from him, wanted to know who in the crowd had touched him. After the woman reluctantly identified herself, Jesus told her that her faith had allowed her to be healed. (Mark 5:25-34)

Evidently, the power to perform miracles is directly related to the power of faith. (Mark 5:35-43) When Jesus was in Nazareth, he was only able to heal a few of the citizens of Nazareth. (Matthew 15:38) However, for those who had faith, the result was different. In the region of Gennesaret, whenever Jesus entered a city, or a village or country, the people laid the sick in the streets, and asked Jesus to heal them. All who touched him were healed. (Mark 6:56)

Finally, the time came for Deity to withhold power and might. As an act of love, God chose to withhold protection of his only son, and Jesus chose to withhold his power and might. Jesus could have prayed to his Father to give him twelve legions of angels; but he chose to offer his life so that we might have eternal life. (Matthew 26:53)

The most amazing fact concerning the power and might of Deity is that Jesus has the positive power of life. Death has no power over him. This fact must be accepted by an act of faith. (Acts 2:24) (Hebrews 2:14)

Jesus also has the right to share the power of faith in any way that he chooses, with anyone that has been chosen. Consider the story about Tabitha of Joppa. (Acts 9:36-43) Tabitha had died, but her friends sent for Peter. Peter sent everyone out of the room where Tabitha had been placed. He knelled down to prayed, and said, "Tabitha, arise." She opened her eyes and sat up, and Peter presented her alive.

The Apostle Paul joyously acknowledges the power and protection of Jesus. The challenge to rejoice is an amazing expression of thankfulness for the power and protection of a Father of love. (Philippians 4:4-7)

Because Yahweh is a God of strength and power, we have no reason to fear. We are protected by the power of the Almighty. (1 Peter 1:3-5) We do not need to plead for protection; we have received the Holy Spirit. (Psalm 140:6-7) Yahweh is strong and mighty, and the strength of his love is awesome or amazing. Because he so loved the world, he is willing and able to use his strength to defend those who are unable to defend themselves.

The meek and lowly are blessed, for they are protected by the power and might of the angels of God in Heaven. (Matthew 18:10) Although we are without strength, we are blessed. The will of our Father who is in heaven is that none of his children should perish. (Matthew 18:14)

# 58
# Praise

Praise is a natural response to a God of Love. (Psalm 145:1-3)

The meaning of praise is to openly offer approval and admiration, to laud, glorify, bless or to acclaim. Praise may be offered as a shout of admiration or by giving a gift of honor. Praise is to acknowledge worth and honor and love.

Yahweh is worthy of praise.

Praise to Yahweh is an expression of love. Praise to Yahweh should be a natural response of thankfulness for his gift of grace and love. Our praise can be offered as a joyful celebration. (Acts 3:6-8) Praise can also be offered as service and devotion. (Romans 12:1)

Praise and worship and love are often expressed in much the same way. (Psalm 96:1-13) However, praise is an expression of love and devotion that is expressed differently in attitude and action. The difference can easily be seen by reading the first few lines of the psalms that begin with words of praise. "Make a joyful noise unto God, all ye lands. Sing forth the honor of his name. Make his praise glorious." (Psalm 66:1-2) Obviously, praise is a joyful, lively expression of love and devotion.

When holiness is revealed, the presence of Deity demands acknowledgement of worth, and expressions of honor, praise, and love. Jehovah deserves praise and worship, but the royal law is a law of love. Yahweh does not interact with man or angels, so that he might be praised. He does not give, expecting to receive. He does not love, to be loved. He loves because he exists, as the I AM who is Love. He is not One because he wishes to be one; he is one because he is One. God did not create the world and the universe because we wanted to be known as the Creator. He is the Creator because he is the "I Am." This truth is the amazing awesome greatness of his being and existence as Deity. His love is perfect and righteous and holy, beautiful, and mighty. This truth establishes him as the One to be praised, or the one who must be praised.

Jesus, the Prince of Peace, entered the city of Jerusalem, riding on the colt of a donkey, and the people offered joyful shouts of praise to God, "Hosanna! Blessed is he that comes in the name of the Lord!" (Mark 11:9-10) The Pharisees within the multitude wanted Jesus to rebuke his disciples, and Jesus told them if the people did not praise him the stones would immediately shout praise. (Luke 19:39-40)

Yahweh is an Almighty King who is worthy of praise. He enjoys thanksgiving, joyful celebration and times of peace. Perhaps, instead of stating that Yahweh is a God of praise, we might rightfully say that Yahweh is a God of celebration. As a God of loving kindness, Yahweh enjoys joyful celebration. (Psalm 150:1-6)

Yahweh is also a God who offers praise to others. He offers praise for actions or deeds that he appreciates or wishes to recognize. (Matthew 5-13) His praise is offered to those who are humble and kind and loving. He gives love and honor and blessings, hope and freedom and life to those who are faithful.

Those who have professed faith in Jesus Christ have been justified, sanctified, redeemed, and given eternal life. (1 Corinthians 6:11) We live in the presence of Yahweh by the power of the Holy Spirit. We are free to offer praise and worship to YHWH. We are free to praise him for his loving grace. (Ephesians 1:3-14) Celebration and rejoicing is a proper way to offer praise to God. (Philippians 4:4)

Yahweh is worthy of praise! Yahweh will be praised, because he is worthy of praise. Praise is a natural response to his amazing Love. (Psalm 11:1-5, 147:1) "Praise the Lord. Shout joyfully unto God, all ye nations." (Psalm 66:1-3)

## 59
## Presence

Yahweh is the Father of Heaven. He is the father of the children of Abraham. He is our Father of Love. (2 Chronicles 16:9) (Psalm 33:13-19)

To be present is to exist in a state of reality. To be present implies existence and stability. A state of reality or presence may be a permanent state of existence or a temporary manifestation, like a rainbow that is visible for a temporary time. As well, a temporary manifestation may be present as an actual physical appearance, or as a vision.

The presence of Deity has been clearly revealed. The apostle Paul clearly stated that what may be known of God has been manifested into us. God has shown himself unto us. His existence has been known from the creation of the world. The evidence of his existence and love is clearly seen and understood by the things that have been created. (Romans 1:19-20)

To describe the presence of God as being invisible, yet present, is a state of reality that is not easily explained. The people of the nations of the Old Testament required visible objects to represent their deities. Many of the citizens of Israel were also attracted to objects of stone and metal and wood, made by human hands; however, physical representations of deity were rejected by Yahweh. The Lord of Israel did not even allow the children of Israel to construct altars or memorials with cut or carved stones. The Ark of the Covenant was constructed, but God was not in the ark. He allowed the nation of Israel to build a house of the Lord, but he did not reside in the house. The temple was too visible to contain "his presence." Yahweh was present in the holy of holies, only in spirit and majesty.

Yahweh's spiritual presence is described as "the presence of God with us." In the New Testament the presence of God is Emmanuel, God with us.

The presence of Deity is a state of omnipresence and omniscience, meaning that Yahweh is everywhere and is aware of everything. (Exodus 2:24-25) This description seems to make Yahweh distant or impersonal. Although God resides in a spiritual realm, he is a personal Father. His presence also seems to be threatening, for the presence of his holiness requires judgment. (Luke 5:8) However, the presence of Deity is not expressed as judgment or condemnation, but as loving kindness.

Several accounts have been recorded in Old Testament scripture concerning the presence or the appearance of the Almighty. For these appearances a phrase such as, "So, I have come down" is used to acknowledge the actual presence of God. However, Yahweh is always present and personal. (Exodus 3:8) He "looks down" or observes everything from Heaven. (Psalm 34:13)

Yahweh promised the blessing of his presence to Moses and the children of Israel. Yahweh told the Israelites that his presence would go with them, to give them rest or comfort. (Exodus 33:14) He was with the children of Israel to speak out of the midst of the fire, to give them the ten commands and the law, and to remind them that He is an awesome God and there is none else beside him. (Deuteronomy 5:22-24 & 4:33-37)

The presence of Yahweh is represented in the Ark of the Covenant. (1 Kings 8:1-18) The ark was to be an actual expression of the presence of Israel's loving Father. (1 Kings 8:22-23)

The Lord God, by the power of the Holy Spirit, was also present with the prophets, in defense of the people of Israel. He was also presented as the angel of the Lord. (Judges 5:4-5) Yahweh was nearby, at hand, or present to watch over the children of Israel. When they were unfaithful, their evil behavior always caused their transcendent God to come down to earth to deal with the situation.

As an example, when the sons of Israel did acts of evil in the sight of the Lord, God allowed the Midianites to rule over them for seven years. Then God sent the angel of the Lord to Gideon. Yahweh promised to be present with Gideon and the Israelites, to defeat the army of the Midianites. (Judges 6:6-12) After Gideon had prepared an offering, the angel gave Gideon a sign for confirmation. (Judges 6:21)

The Lord of Israel appeared to the wife of Manoah, the father of Samson. According to this biblical account, the wife of Manoah told her husband that a man of God had appeared. He looked like an angel of God. She did not ask him where he came from, and he did not tell her his name. (Judges 13:1-6)

Then Manoah prayed and asked God to send the angel a second time. When the angel appeared, Manoah did not know that this was the angel of the Lord, therefore he asked the angel to give his name. But the angel only said that his name is wonderful. As directed by the angel, Manoah prepared an offering for the Lord. When Manoah and his wife realized that they had seen the angel of the Lord, they were afraid that they would die. (Judges 13:9-23)

God was present and spoke to the young prophet Samuel. (1 Samuel 3:1-21)

Yahweh was often present to speak to king David or to admonish him for his actions; and God promised to be with Solomon, as he built the house of the Lord and as he ruled over the nation of Israel. (1 Chronicles 28:20)

After Solomon built a magnificent temple for the Lord, Yahweh was present in awesome power and glory. (1 Kings 6:1, 8:1-6) When the priests had come out of the holy place of the house of the Lord, a cloud with the glory of the Lord filled the house of the Lord. (1 Kings 8:10-13)

God was pleased that Solomon had constructed a temple, a place of prayer and worship; however, Solomon understood that although Yahweh may be present on earth, at any time, there is no specific location on earth that is a sufficient residence for an Almighty Deity. (1 Kings 8:27-29) (2 Chronicles 6:18) The king was only asking God to give this place of worship special attention, so that his eyes might be open toward this house to listen to the prayers of the people so that all the people of the earth may know that the Lord of Israel is God; and that there is no One else. (1 Kings 8:60) (2 Chronicles 6:40) When king Solomon finished his prayer, fire came down from heaven and consumed the burnt offering and the sacrifices, and the glory of the Lord filled the house of the Lord. (2 Chronicles 7:1)

Then God appeared to Solomon a second time. (1 Kings 9:1-3) The Lord offered a prediction as well as a blessing of his presence among the children of Israel. The Lord vowed that if the children of Israel were once again unfaithful, that tragedy would come upon this magnificent structure. (1 Kings 9:69)

The greatest story of the presence of Deity is the account of the birth of Jesus. (Matthew 1:18-2:23) (Luke 2:1-40) Jesus, the Messiah, is the presence of the light and love of God that came down from Heaven, to be present with mankind.

For everyone that was outside Israel, within the surrounding nations and in distant lands, the presence of God was also revealed. The gentiles were not forgotten. The Apostle Paul explained the situation to the citizens of Lystra. (Acts 14:8-18)

Jesus announced the presence of God in a different fashion, in a different way. This presence of God is called the kingdom of heaven or the kingdom of God. The birth of Jesus introduced the presence of the glory of God. (2 Corinthians 4:3-6)

When the Pharisees demanded that Jesus should tell them when the kingdom of God would come, Jesus told them that the kingdom of God cannot be observed, for the Kingdom of God was in their presence, with them. (Luke 17: 20-21)

Jesus was announcing the invisible presence of the salvation and redemption of the nation of Israel that can only be seen through the eyes of faith. He was in their midst. They only needed to believe. They should have been like the blind man who called out, "Son of David, have mercy on me!" They would have heard Jesus say, "Receive your sight; your faith has made you whole." (Luke 18:39-43)

When Jesus entered the city of Jerusalem, he announced the presence of the One true Deity, for Deity is present as the Messiah. Jesus was fulfilling the prophecy of the blessings of love that the Father of Israel had promised to Israel, and to a lost world. (Matthew 21:1-11) (Mark 11:1-10) The word of God and the presence of God was explained in several accounts of prophecy in the words and accounts of the Old Testament. (Psalm 22:11-18)

The almighty God, the Lord of heaven and earth, remains non-visible but never non-present. The apostle John said that grace and truth are realized through Jesus Christ. Although no one has seen God at any time, the only begotten God, who is in the bosom of the Father, has explained him. John is speaking of Jesus Christ. (John 1:17-18) God is not seen, but this does not mean that he is hidden. God has sent his son into the world, as a revelation, a revealing of himself, to express his love for the world. (John 3:16)

The historical records of the Hebrew people prove that the children of Israel had a difficult time accepting the non-visible presence of Deity. They continually chose to worship visible gods and failed to understand that God was present among them. Appearances of God or angels of God were accepted, but an awareness that God is always present seems to have not been acknowledged. Judgment of the children of Abraham has been reserved by Yahweh himself; therefore, we should judge not, lest we should be judged.

Even today, many biblical scholars seem to be unaware of the presence of God. Scripture passages are often interpreted as though the written accounts have only been recorded as accounts of the men or women that are involved. Obviously, this statement requires a proper explanation. One specific passage of scripture (Luke 7:36-50) is useful for an explanation.

One of the Pharisees invited Jesus into his home. A woman, a known sinner, heard that Jesus was eating a meal with the Pharisee. The woman brought a box of ointment and anointed the feet of Jesus. When Simon expressed objection, Jesus told a parable as a lesson of forgiveness and appreciation. (Luke 7:47)

This account of a sinful woman is an illustration of two differing attitudes of love or appreciation that are expressed by the children of

Israel. Normally, the emphasis of interpretation for this account is upon spiritual or moral expectations. The woman is praised. Simon is judged or condemned. Although this account may be useful for a moral teaching, the presence or actions of Yahweh must not be neglected. We should remember that Jesus was sent, by the Father, only to the children of Abraham. The two characters in this story both represent the people of Israel. Jesus is teaching that some in Israel will understand that he is the Messiah, and others who will "love less" will be concerned about religious service to God. They are those who will miss a blessing from God.

Now we must ask the important question, "In this account, where is Yahweh?" God is always present. (Psalm 33:13-19) Yahweh is present as Jesus teaches, the lessons that Israel should understand, that had been taught by the prophets of Israel. Yahweh is present, using a sinful woman, to anoint his only son, as a proper preparation for death and burial. (Luke 7:45) (Matthew 26:12) (Mark 14:8-9) Yahweh is present, with Jesus, to teach the important theological lesson of faith. The account is recorded to emphasize the fact that love and honor and appreciation for God are of extreme importance; however, the lesson of grace by faith is not neglected. (Ephesians 2:8) Notice, that Jesus did not say, "Simon, your lack of honor and love has condemned you." As well, Jesus did not say to the one who anointed him, "Go in peace, your love and honor has saved you." Jesus said to her, "Your sins are forgiven; faith has saved you; go and live in peace." (Luke 7:50) Yahweh was teaching that Jesus is his beloved son, in whom he is well pleased. We should listen to him. (Luke 9:35) Yahweh was also reminding us that, because of Abraham, a covenant of love was made with all of Israel, whether they are a Simon or a sinful woman. (Genesis 17:7) God was also teaching that our future relationship to him will be through his son Jesus. (Acts 17:29-31)

Yahweh was present as his only begotten son was offered as a sacrifice for sin. He was unseen but present with the One who was with him! He was with the Son who had always been with him. In the beginning was the word, and the word was with God and the word was God. (John 1:1)

The apostle Paul, who had been one who loved only a little, eventually became one who loved much. Yahweh appeared to the apostle and sent the Holy Spirit to teach Paul an understanding of love. (Acts 9:1-9) (Galatians 1:15-18)

The apostle Paul lived in the presence of the Holy Spirit. He listened to God's commandments and followed the directions of the Holy Spirit.

He did not question God's appearance or his presence. (Acts 23:11) The apostle never hesitated to be obedient; for God taught him to know him and to love the One God of Israel.

The Apostle Paul had a difficult time explaining the non-visible presence of God to those who lived in a world that had accepted many visible gods, with many understandable tasks. Paul stood in the center of the Areopagus and spoke to the men of Athens. He talked about an altar dedicated to an Unknown god and then told them about the true non-visible Deity. (Acts 17:22-34)

Today, Christians also have a difficult time explaining the presence of the Holy Spirit. The One who is "God with us" is revealed, by the Holy Spirit, to those who have faith; however, this presence may be felt or experienced differently. Awareness of the presence of the Holy Spirit depends directly upon child-like love, faith, and appreciation for God's gift of grace through Jesus Christ. (Luke 10:21-22)

Yahweh is omnipresent. God is everywhere, to observe the evil and good of mankind. (Proverbs 15:3) Almighty God is aware of everything. He knows every believer. He knows us. He loves us and wants to give eternal life to us. (Revelations 3:20) (Psalm 139:1 &13)

To know that God knows us, was with us before conception, in the womb, at birth, and knows us now, is an awesome realization. When we understand that Yahweh is present, full of compassion and love and understanding, how could we not accept his gift of love. (Mark 12:34) (Psalm 139:23-24)

Someday everyone will be aware of his presence and his love.

We should be still and sense the presence of God. (Psalm 46:10)

# 60
## Promise

The promises made by Yahweh to the children of Abraham are gifts of love.

A promise is a pledge, an oath, a vow, or a statement of agreement. A promise may be an offer of a gift, or an assurance of a future event or appearance. However, a true promise must be openly offered by statement and by commitment. A promise must be offered with assurance.

The value or worth of a promise is based upon the ability and authority of the one that has made the promise. The value of a promise also depends upon truth and honor.

A promise made by an omnipotent Deity reveals both his authority and will. The Father in Heaven has the power and authority to make any promise that he wishes to make. God has promised assurance, protection, and blessings to anyone who believes that he is I AM. As well, he is able and willing to reward those who trust in him. (Psalm 34:13-22)

Yahweh's promises of assurance and hope to Israel demonstrate his steadfast faithfulness to the entire world. His promise of love and protection was made to Abraham and offered to the children of Abraham many times within the recorded history of the nation of Israel. He has clearly said that he is prepared to hear and to answer their prayers. (2 Chronicles 7:13-14)

Moses reminded the children of Israel of the covenant promise that Yahweh had made with Abraham. (Genesis 17:1-8) (Deuteronomy 4:40) Moses offered words of prophecy to tell the Israelites that when they are in distress in the latter days, if they will return to the Lord their God and listen to his voice, God will not forget the covenant with their fathers that was swore to them. For the Lord their God is a compassionate God. (Deuteronomy 4:30-31)

The promise made to Abraham was extended to king David, the sovereign ruler of Israel. David informed the prophet Nathan that he wanted to build a house for the Lord, but that night God instructed Nathan to tell the king that a house was not necessary. However, the prophet was instructed to tell the king that God's loving kindness would not be taken away, that the throne of David would be established forever. (2 Samuel 7:1-17) King David responded to Yahweh with words of praise. (2 Samuel 7:22)

Interestingly, God made this promise, although he knew the king would commit an unfaithful act. (2 Samuel 11:1-27) Now, instead of a complete fulfillment of the promise, king David would receive judgment and justice. (2 Samuel 12:1-12) Even when the unfaithful children of Israel were exiled in the Chaldean kingdom of Babylon, Yahweh remained faithful. His willingness to bless Israel remained unaltered. (Jeremiah 29:11-14) (Proverbs 3:1-10)

The Biblical promises made directly to the children of Abraham have often been taken out of context and used as though they were written for all of mankind. One should not assume that what the Father of Israel has given to his children has been given to the entire world. Yahweh established a special relationship with one Chaldean named Abraham. He made specific promises only to Abraham and to his descendants, who through Isaac and Jacob are the Hebrew people of Israel. (Matthew 15:24)

However, we are all blessed because Abraham remained faithful. This fact has been clearly stated in scripture. Yahweh accepted the faith of Abraham as righteousness, but not for Abraham's benefit only. Through Abraham God has also granted to us the right to receive righteousness through faith in Jesus Christ. (John 4:22) (Romans 4:20-25) We have become adopted heirs of the promise. We have become children of Abraham through faith. (Romans 5:1) And if we are Christ-ones, then we are Abraham's heirs according to the promise. (Galatians 3:29)

Many of the Hebrew prophets offered prophecy concerning God's promises to the house of Israel. The prophet Ezekiel compared the nation to a valley of dry bones and prophesied that God would, at some time in the future, revive the nation to a state of prosperity and peace. This promise would be fulfilled, not because Israel deserves to be blessed, but will be accomplished for the sake of Yahweh's honor. (Ezekiel 37:1-14)

The prophet Amos gave prophecies of judgment for the nation of Israel, and he also gave promises of hope and blessings. (Amos 9:13-15) Ezekiel prophesied that a new heart and a new spirit would be given to Israel. God will take away their stony heart and give them a heart of flesh. (Ezekiel 36:22-38) And the nations will know that Yahweh is the Lord who sanctifies Israel. (Ezekiel 37:28) The prophet Joel also promised that Judah will be inhabited forever, and Jerusalem for all generations. (Joel 3:20)

John the Baptizer understood that God had made promises to the Israelites. He also knew that he was a chosen vessel to prepare the way for the promised Messiah. When John needed assurance, he sent disciples to Jesus. (Matthew 11:2-6) Jesus gave John assurance of the promise of a Messiah by saying, "To the poor, the gospel is preached. Blessed is he, whosoever shall not be offended in me." (Luke 7:22-23)

Jesus also knew that the disciple John would understand the promises of prophecy, "The stone that the builders rejected has become the chief cornerstone. This is the Lord's doing; it is marvelous in our eyes." (Psalm 118:22-23) Jesus offered the specific words of assurance that John would understand and accept. A false prophet, who was claiming to be the Messiah, would not have identified himself as the promised corner stone of Israel. (Isaiah 28:16)

The promise of protection and peace was also given to the children of Israel by the prophet Zechariah. (Zechariah 8:1-8) A complete explanation of this protection was offered by the Apostle Paul. (Romans 11:1-36) Paul said that only a partial hardening has happened to Israel until the fullness of the Gentiles had come; and thus, Israel would be saved. Of the gospel the Jews are enemies, but according to God's choice they are beloved for the sake of the fathers. The gifts and the calling of God, the promises made, are irrevocable. (Romans 11:25-28)

Nevertheless, the children of Israel should guard against pride, for being the chosen children of promise. For as the prophet John said, "God can raise up children unto Abraham, even from stones." (Matthew 3:7-9)

The greatest promise made to Israel is the promise of the Messiah, the king of Israel. This promise was confirmed by Jesus Christ. (Romans 15:8) (Acts 3:36-40)

The Jewish scholars of Israel were expecting a Messiah, a king of Israel, but none of the Pharisees or Sadducees were acknowledged as authorities on the subject; and many passages of scripture were not considered to be words of prophecy. However, all agreed that the Moshiach, the anointed one, would be the fulfillment of God's divine purpose. This king was to be a blessing for the Nation of Israel and as well for the entire world. The problem for the Hebrew scholars was that the concept of grace, or the good news of grace was an unidentified theological concept. (Acts 20:24) Therefore, the religious leaders in Jerusalem failed to recognize "the mercy and grace" that was offered through Jesus.

The Apostle Paul was a Jewish scholar who also did not recognize that Jesus was the promised Messiah. (Acts 22:4-8) After several years of instruction from the Holy Spirit, this apostle was able to give a concise account of the promise of the Messiah. (Acts 13:13-41)

Today, through faith, God is spiritually present with us by the Holy Spirit, as the promised presence of Yahweh. (Matthew 18:19-20) Yahweh is a father of promise to those who profess faith in Jesus Christ. The promise given to us is the promise of eternal life. (1 John 2:25) This promise, given through the King of Israel, is a prophesied and completed promise, for eternal life was promised before the world began. (Titus 1:1-2)

The Holy Spirit, given as a pledge of this promise, is a gift of protection, assurance, and salvation. (2 Corinthians 5:5) Yahweh will always remain faithful; he will not deny the promise of eternal life that has been given to the believer. This is the promise of hope that we have in Christ Jesus. The value and worth of this promise are based upon the firm foundation of love and the power and authority of Deity.

The faithfulness of Yahweh is the firm foundation of our hope and assurance. (2 Timothy 2:11-13) The promise, made to Israel, is now an assurance for us. (Jeremiah 28:11-13) The One who made this promise to the nation of Israel has made the same promise of love to those who have accepted his gift of grace. (1 John 3:23-24) This promise has been made through his son Yehoshua before the world began. (Titus 1:2) (2 Peter 1:2-4)

A promise from Yahweh is more than a promise. (Luke 7:48-50) His promise is an absolute assurance. His promise is founded upon an absolute commitment. All that he has promised is a reality that is already present or has already happened. His promise is real and true. His promise and his words are truth.

Because Yahweh is a faithful God of promise, we look for new heavens and a new earth, wherein righteousness dwells. (2 Peter 3:13)

# 61
# Prophecy

No words of prophecy have been written by men, for the true author of prophecy is the Holy Spirit. (2 Peter 1:20-21)

A prediction is a forecast concerning a future unknown or anticipated event. A prediction may be based upon inspiration, knowledge, experience, assumptions, or a combination of all aspects of awareness. A prediction may be accurate or inaccurate, partly accurate or inaccurate, and as well valuable or worthless. A true prophecy is a foretelling of a future unknown or anticipated event that is always accurate and always valuable.

Yahweh is a Deity of prophecy and revelation. Prophecy and miracles are gifts of love.

Scriptural prophecies are true statements that have been given with divine authority, by the power of the Holy Spirit. Biblical prophecy involves more than foretelling a future event. A biblical prophecy offers knowledge or information that God has revealed. The information may be revealed in a vision, a revelation or an actual appearance and voice of Deity. A verbal revelation by a prophet is called an oracle, but prophecy may be received as an answer for a problem, a foretelling or a revelation, or advice concerning a future event in several different ways.

The one restriction of a biblical prophecy is that prophecies offered by Yahweh must be true and accurate. Future events are not altered or changed, to fulfill the statements of prophecies. The fulfillment of a prophecy occurs when the predicted or expected event happens. To assume that events are manipulated or changed so that the prophecy may be fulfilled would be an incorrect assumption. Prophecies are nothing more than revelations of future events that have been intended by God. Simply stated, God is transcendent; he knows what will happen, and through prophets and words of prophecy he has chosen to reveal future events.

According to the words of scripture, no true prophecy was ever made by an act of human determination. As well, all prophecies given by God are accurate and true. Prophecies made by diviners or spiritualist, or by human or demonic means, whether true or false, must not be accepted as the word of God.

Although Jewish scholars have interpreted prophecies differently than Christian theologians, God has obviously used prophecy to guide the children of Abraham, and to offer future blessings. The Hebrew people clearly understood that all words of prophecy are from God, given by prophets that were moved by the power of Spirit of God.

Prophecies were given by God in many places during extended periods of time and were given for different reasons. Prophecies have been given as warnings of destruction or as cautions concerning discipline. Revelations of future events were also used for encouragement and for protection.

Although biblical prophecy, especially prophecy that is offered in poetry, may be difficult to accurately interpret, there is only one true interpretation, that which is true and is what the Lord God of Israel intended to be prophesied.

Prophecies in scripture may be complicated or simple, non-revealed or openly presented. For example, several prophecies for the children of Abraham are simple historical accounts. Yahweh changed the name and identity of Jacob. (Genesis 32:28) The meaning of Jacob is deceiver or non-wielding one. The name Yis-ra-el is one who contended with God, who saw and knew God, who will triumph, have power over life, and prevail with El or God. Prophecies concerning the Messiah, the anointed one, are scattered throughout scripture and have been offered in many periods of time.

The Hebrew disciples who recorded the letters of the New Testament have provided several interpretations concerning the prophecies of the Messiah as well as many other events of prophecy. They believe that Yehoshua has fulfilled the prophecy of the Old Testament concerning the coming of the Messiah.

Without the scriptural interpretations offered by the Apostles, contemporary scholars should not take credit for interpretations of prophecies. Any apparent words of prophecy within the writings of the Old Testament that are not noted by the Apostles should not be used to teach theology or to predict what God will accomplish.

For example, when we read the words "My God, my God, why have you forsaken me" the speaker or the voice of the words must first be identified. (Psalm 22:1-31) This psalm is written for King David; therefore, the one speaking could be the king. Because many of the psalms are about the entire nation, with the king included, the words could be offered by a spokesman for the nation of Israel. Many of the words are obviously associated with Israel. Yahweh did forsake Israel, for a brief period. He allowed the nation to be taken to exile in Babylon. Other sentences are personal or individual and would not be used for an entire nation. Some of the words do not directly apply to king David. The hands and feet of king David were never pierced, even with a sword. He was never looked upon with pity. No one ever cast lots for his clothing. (Psalm 22:13-18)

The words of this psalm have been identified as prophecy concerning the suffering Christ and his crucifixion. However, because this passage of scripture was not identified by the authors of the New Testament as prophecy concerning the Messiah, the words should not be directly used to teach theology.

On the other hand, the New Testament authors did refer to the fulfillment of several Old Testament prophecies. One example is a passage of scripture that was identified by Matthew as words of prophecy. (Matthew 1:22-23) Matthew is referring to an account in the book of Isaiah, concerning king Ahaz. In this account God spoke directly to Ahaz through the prophet. First Isaiah told Ahaz that God wanted the king to ask for a sign or confirmation for the instructions of war that had been given. Ahaz refused to honor the request, and God himself gave a sign, a prophecy of protection and blessing for the nation of Israel. Speaking for Yahweh, the prophet Isaiah prophesied that a virgin would conceive and bear a son. His name would be Immanuel. (Isaiah 7:14)

Other passages of scripture may be logically accepted as prophecy. (Psalm 110:1-5) What earthly king is righteous enough to deserve to sit beside God Almighty? What human individual would be qualified to receive a blessing of special priesthood?

There is also a prophecy for future worship to the Lord. (Psalm 22:27-31)

There are more words of prophecy, concerning future events, in the book of Isaiah and Ezekiel than any of the other Hebrew writings. Except for the last chapter of the book, the prophecies of Ezekiel are clearly presented. Several of the prophecies given through Isaiah were offered for past events, but others are for the distant future, during a time of judgment or reckoning when the Lord God of Israel will arise to make the earth tremble. (Isaiah 2:21)

Several passages of Isaiah, that appear to be prophetic words, are difficult to understand or interpret. (Isaiah 4:1-6) The prophecies of Ezekiel concerning the temple, in chapters forty through forty-eight are also difficult to interpret.

Several of the prophecies are given in the form of parables, which the prophet Isaiah clearly interprets. The prophet said that the "vineyard of the Lord of hosts" is the house of Israel, and the "delightful plant" is a description of the men of Judah. (Isaiah 5:7)

Prophecies have been given for several different reasons.

The prophecy given to king Ahaz was even given as an admonishment. (Isaiah 7:10-14) (Matthew 1:23)

Prophecies or revelations given to several early Christians, who were blessed with the gift of prophecy or interpretation of prophecy, were used to protect the early Christians. (Acts 11:27-29)

The prophet Daniel has also given prophecies for the end times. The prophecies are difficult to interpret; and Daniel even expressed caution concerning certain prophecies. The prophet stated that the prophecies concerning events for many days in the future should not be openly revealed. (Daniel 8:26)

Clearly God is motivated to offer prophecies as warnings or encouragement, (Luke 5:10) however, prophecies are also given as acts of compassion, discipline, empathy, honor, justice, or simply because God truly expects the children of Israel to have a willingness to repent. However, perhaps Yahweh is simply a God of prophecy because he is always aware of everything, past present or future, and has chosen to share a limited amount of awareness with mankind. Obviously, there is much about our Almighty God that has not been revealed, even to the prophets. Thankfully, Yahweh has allowed the Holy Spirit to assist in the task of interpretation of his messages and of the revelation of his personal character.

Concerning all prophecy, one would be wise to remember that most of the prophecy of scripture has been given directly to the Hebrew people and to the nation of Israel. (Luke 5:34-39) Prayerfully, the nation of Israel will accept the foretelling that Yahweh has offered.

According to the words of the disciples of Jesus, the Hebrew people are "the children of the prophets." Israel has been chosen by Yahweh for a special purpose. They are the children of the covenant that God made with their fathers, Abraham, Isaac, and Jacob. God promised that in the seed of Abraham, all the people of the earth would be blessed. God sent the redeemer first and only to Israel, as a blessing to Israel, and having raised up his son Jesus, sent him to bless the children of Abraham, to offer them the gift of eternal life. (Acts 3:24-25)

# 62
# Protection

Yahweh is a God of protection, comfort, and strength. (Isaiah 25:4)

God is our strength and protections, he is with us, even to the end of time. (Matthew 28:19-20)

Protection may be defined as safeguarding, providing a defense, or offering sanctuary, shelter, or immunity. Protection may provide defense against physical attack or legal harm. An act of protection may be a natural response or reaction, or a humanitarian act of kindness or love.

The Father of Heaven and earth is a defender and protector of his children.

Yahweh's protection was given to Adam and Eve, and to Noah. (Genesis 8:1) Protection, as a blessing of faith, was offered to Abram, the Chaldean sojourner. (Genesis 12:1-3) Yahweh protected Abram from the ruler of Egypt. (Genesis 12:17) This nomadic Hebrew was also protected in battle against an army in the land of Damascus. After the battle, Melchizedek who was the priest of the Highest God, offered a blessing for Abram and to God who had delivered his enemies into his hand. (Genesis 14:20)

By faith, Abram gained favor with the Almighty and was granted an everlasting covenant of protection and defense. And when Abram was ninety years old and nine, the Lord appeared to Abram and said unto him, "I am the Almighty God; walk before me and be thou perfect. I will make my covenant between me and thee; and will multiply thee exceedingly." (Genesis 17:1-2)

Several accounts that describe or explain Yahweh's protection of the descendants of Abraham are included in scripture. Defense and protection are acts of loving kindness. A place of refuge is a place of comfort and protection. Yahweh is also declared to be a defender of the oppressed, to be a refuge in times of trouble. (Psalm 9:9)

Yahweh protected Jacob from the deception of his father-in-law. (Genesis 31:2-3) During the night, God came to Laban the Syrian in a dream and told Laban to not do either good or evil to Jacob. (Genesis 31:24) Laban understood that Jacob's personal God was protecting him; therefore, his only request was that Jacob should return his idols.

Yahweh protected Joseph. Even while in a dangerous prison in Egypt, God used a chief jailer to protect Joseph. And whatever Joseph did, the Lord honored it. (Genesis 39:23) As well, through Joseph, Yahweh protected all the descendants of Abraham. (Genesis 41:1-57)

Moses was offered authority and protection as a sign that God had sent him to rescue the Hebrew tribes. (Exodus 4:1-9) However, Yahweh was not pleased when Moses expressed doubt about his promise of protection. (Exodus 4:14)

According to his sovereign choice, the Lord extended protection to the nation of Israel. (Exodus 23:20-22) Yahweh often protected Israel in times of war or conflict. If the Israelites went to war, all they needed to do was to sound an alarm with the trumpets, and God would save them from their enemies. (Numbers 10:9)

The Lord of Hosts gave attention to Israel during many years, from the reign of king Saul to king Zedekiah, to protect them from their own failures. The account of the miracles in the book of Daniel was most likely written to assure the children of Israel that Yahweh would always protect them. Although the task was not simple, Yahweh even used a powerful ruler for their benefit. (Daniel 2:1-4:37) Yahweh used Daniel to interpret the king's dreams. Yahweh also used an unusual method of persuasion, to help Nebuchadnezzar recognize that "the God of Israel" is a God of authority and protection. (Daniel 4:37)

The book of Esther is a detailed story, a testimony of the protection and encouragement of a loving Father for his children. This story is about Yahweh's intervention and his personal presence for those who have honored him.

After years of exile in Babylon, God allowed the children of Abraham to return to Jerusalem to reconstruct the house of the Lord that king Solomon had built many years before. When their enemies attempted to prevent the restoration of the city of Jerusalem, Yahweh protected them, even during a time of political change in the Persian kingdom. King Darius gave orders for a search to be made in the archives. When the original decree of King Cyrus was found, king Darius, whose heart had been turned by the God of Israel, sent word back to the protesting governor. The enemies of Israel were directed to keep away from Jerusalem, to not interfere with the reconstruction, and to let the elders of the Jews rebuild the house of God. As well, the full cost of construction was to be paid with local tax revenues. As well, king Darius added his own authority to the decree. (Ezra 5:11-12)

There are also prophecies of protection from God recorded by the prophets Ezekiel and Zechariah. These words of prophecy are powerful words of amazing protection. This will be a time when everyone will know that Yahweh is the Lord their God. (Ezekiel 28:24-26) (Zechariah 2:5-10) This will be a time when God will dwell in their midst. (Zechariah 2:10)

Yahweh's protection for the nation of Israel is not an act of racial preference. His requirements of separation have been offered for a greater purpose. The reason was that Yahweh is a jealous God who wishes to protect Israel from the deceptions of Satan. (Exodus 23:22, 32-33)

As well, although he has made special promises of peace and protection to the nation of Israel, God has used Israel to bless all nations. (Zechariah 2:11-12)

Yahweh also offers loving kindness and protection for all nations, for Yahweh has a special concern for the poor and neglected. (Psalm 10:31 & 102:17) As "those who are to be like him," Yahweh expects us to be defenders of those in need of protection. We are to be defenders and protectors of the poor and a helper of the fatherless. (Psalm 10:14)

God also offers protection for those who choose to honor him. (Psalm 34:15,17)

Although he has never promised to protect the disciples of Jesus from illness or physical harm, Yahweh has often intervened to defend the faithful. When the disciples were brought before the Jewish Council, they were set before the council and asked by what authority they were teaching in the Synagogue. They told the leaders that they were obeying the God of their fathers who raised up Jesus, the one that they had crucified. When the Jewish leaders heard this testimony, they were greatly offended. (Acts 5:29-33)

However, God had a plan of protection. A Pharisee, named Gamaliel, who was a doctor of the law with a noted reputation among all the people, gave advice to calm their fears. Gamaliel advised that the disciples should be released, for if the work of the disciples is ordained by God, they would not be able to overthrow their work. (Acts 38-39)

Nevertheless, divine protection is a choice made by God himself. Herod the King arrested several believers, intending to mistreat them. He had James the brother of John executed with a sword, and when he saw that this pleased the Jews, he also arrested Peter. Peter was kept in prison, but the other believers prayed fervently for him. In the night before he was to be brought out to king Herod to be executed, God delivered Peter. (Acts 12:1-17)

The apostle Paul was never allowed to know if God would protect him. Jews from Antioch and Iconium followed Paul to Lystra, where they convinced the people that Paul was a religious threat to the laws of

Israel. Paul was stoned and dragged out of the city and left for dead. But God allowed Paul to survive the stoning. The next day he traveled with Barnabas to Derbe. (Acts 14:19-20)

During another journey, instead of protecting Paul by preventing or delaying the sailing, Paul was almost lost at sea; however, after fourteen days in a storm God intervened. God told Paul that he would be protected, and that there would be no loss of life. (Acts 27:14-25)

As previously stated, God is also our protector. The Holy Spirit has been given to us for protection. (Jude 1:24) However, the Holy Spirit does not protect us from persecution, or trial or tribulations. This fact is clearly illustrated by Apostle Paul's description of his life as a humble disciple. (2 Corinthians 6:3-10)

If God is for us, who can be against us. (Romans 8:31) This is an absolute statement of spiritual protection; however, we must also remember that the apostle Paul said that everyone that chooses to live godly in Christ Jesus will suffer persecution. (2 Timothy 3:10-12) However, when difficult times are encountered, prayer for protection is available. (Ecclesiastes 9:12)

There is nothing that can separate us from the love of Christ. (Romans 8:35-39) The promises of scripture are abundant. The needy shall not always be forgotten, the expectation of the poor shall not perish forever. (Psalm 9:18, 31:23-24 & 84:11-12) (1Peter 1:3-6 & 5:7) We know that God is our refuge and strength. (Deuteronomy 33:27) He can preserve the souls of his saints and delivers them out of the hand of the wicked. (Psalm 97:10, 23:4-5, 27:1-3, 46:1-5, 91:4-6 & 118:6) (Luke 12:32) (Romans 8:15-17 & 37-39) He is our God of Love, and there is no fear in his love. (1 John 4:18)

We are chosen ones, "according to the foreknowledge of God the Father, through sanctification of the Spirit unto obedience and sprinkling of the blood of Jesus Christ." We are those "who are kept by the power of God through faith into salvation ready to be revealed in the last time." (1 Peter 1:2-5)

We are ambassadors for Christ. We are protected by an almighty King. We should remember that although we may suffer trials and temptations and persecutions and hardships of various kinds, we are encouraged to be at peace and to rejoice, for we are never separated from the protection of his love, or from the joy that we receive from being a Christ-one.

Read the words of the apostle Paul and rejoice. (Philippians 4:4-7)

# 63
# Purity

The purity of God cannot be adequately described, neither with words, physical objects or works of art. (Psalm 12:6)

Purity is a condition of being without stain or blemish, free from contamination, spotless and immaculate. Ethical purity is a state of being virtuous in mind and in action. Mental purity is to be free from thoughts of evil, depression, or fear.

Only God is pure in thought and actions. Yahweh is pure and righteous. His purity is like silver tried in a furnace, purified seven times. Every word of God is pure and true. (Proverbs 30:5-6) (Psalm 119:140-142)

Yahweh is pure in nature, thought and words. Every possible thought, attribute, or situation to be considered is pure. Light, life, and love are words used to express the essence of his character or being. No imperfection or lack of purity can be found in Yahweh.

Yahweh is allowed to bestow any attribute of his character upon another that he wishes. He can bestow authority, honor, love, and blessings in any manner or in any degree that he has chosen. Nevertheless, the attribute given to man is not the purity of deity; for only God is pure. Yahweh is the only one who has supreme authority or perfection of character. The sanctification given to followers of Christ is a blessing that is referred to as a divine nature but is not the purity of deity.

The attributes of purity that Peter refers to as divine nature are listed as moral excellence, knowledge, self-control, perseverance, godliness, brotherly kindness, and brotherly love. (2 Peter 1:4-7) The theological question of sanctification for the believer involves the following question. Have these qualities been granted to the believer by the power of the Holy Spirit, through the true knowledge of God, so that the one who follows Christ might have everything pertaining to life and godliness; or has only the possibility of having a divine nature been given?

The apostle Peter states that these qualities of sanctification are not given as a promise or as a possibility; they are complete and guaranteed with complete assurance.

The apostle Peter says that we have been given all things that pertain unto life and godliness. (2 Peter 1:3) The one who lacks these attributes has forgotten that he was purged from his old sins. (2 Peter 1:9) The apostle Paul agrees. (Romans 8:9-10) The believer is justified and glorified in the love of Christ. (Romans 8:30-39)

The reason that believers are free from religion performance is because something greater than the law is present. Our Sabbath or rest, the One who has fulfilled the requirements of the law, is present with us. (Hebrews 4:1-6) We live or exist in his grace and forgiveness. We have been justified and purified, not by works of the law but by an act of mercy. (Titus 3:5-6)

Because Yahweh is pure and holy, giving his Spirit, within or upon, an unclean vessel would not be possible. Although we remain as earthen vessels (2 Corinthians 4:7) we must be made holy, by being reborn as a new vessel, a new wine skin, to be qualified to receive the blessing of the Holy Spirit. (John 3:3-8) (Romans 6:4) (Luke 5:27-39) Simply started, the believer must be purified or sanctified to be able to receive and to hold the Holy Spirit. Although we are sanctified in Christ, called to be saints, we must remember that we have this treasure in earthen vessels, that the excellency of the power may be of God, and not of ourselves. (1 Corinthians 1:2) (2 Corinthians 4:7)

As representatives of God, we who follow Christ are expected to yield to the Holy Spirit so that we might be pure in thought and in action, because God is pure and holy. (2 Peter 1:9) However, this expectation of purity does not establish a requirement of moral activity or of religious duty of works and faith. The presence of the attributes of purity are a consequence of having received the Holy Spirit, to be washed clean or made pure by Christ's gift of grace.

Sharing words of encouragement to Timothy concerning the requirements of being Christ-like, the apostle Paul said that the law of Moses is worthy and useful if it is used lawfully, according to the law of liberty; however, the Law was established for the lawless and disobedient rather than for the righteous man. The law was not written as requirements of religious performance. (1 Timothy 1:8-9)

Therefore, because the believer has been given a divine nature through faith in Jesus Christ, the requirements of the law are fulfilled somewhat differently. (2 Peter 1:3) The fulfillment of the law is to be accomplished as a natural consequence of having been given a pure heart and divine nature. By the gift of grace, which includes sanctification, righteousness, and justification, we who profess faith in Jesus Christ have been washed clean or purified by the Holy Spirit; and the requirements of the law have been fulfilled for us by the sacrificial gift of Christ. The certificate of death that includes our sin and impurity has been nailed to the cross. The end or requirement of the commandment is charity out of a pure heart, and of a good conscience, and of faith unrestricted. (1 Timothy 1:5)

Therefore, we should be pure as he is pure, or perfect as he is perfect. These words of admonishment for us have been clearly recorded. (Ephesians 4:20-32 & 5:1-4)

The apostle Peter also states that a divine nature of love and honor is evidence of the believer's faith. (2 Peter 1:10-11) Yahweh, the One who is pure, offers "a washing of purity" as a gift of love. (Hebrews 10:22)

Purity as a robe of righteousness can be worn with honor within the court of the King of kings. (Revelation 3:5)

The response expected for this unearned and undeserved gift should not be to offer religious fervor or committed service, or even a gift of moral excellence, but a heart-felt response of rejoicing.

Rejoice in the Lord always. I say again, rejoice. (Philippians 4:4-8)

# 64
# Purpose

Yahweh is a God of purpose. For mankind, God has an unchangeable purpose that has been confirmed with a promise and an oath. (Hebrews 6:17) His purpose is to put his laws of love and honor into our hearts and in our minds, so that our sins and iniquities will not be remembered, so that we might receive the gift of eternal life. (Hebrews 10:16-22)

Purpose is the intent, objective, or reason for which something is achieved, accomplished, or created. Purpose implies that something is to be accomplished or obtained. A purpose of life may be defined as a goal, an ambition, a realization, or a search for knowledge, wealth, power, or honor.

Although the reason for existence may be undefined or unexplained, there is a purpose or reason for creation and existence. Anything accomplished without purpose is unintentional. According to several scientific theories, our universe and earth came into existence by a physical event of universal proportion, without an identifiable objective or reason for existence. Therefore, this unintentional accident or miracle would not have had an identifiable purpose. A non-created world would be a world without an objective intent or reason for existence. All of creation would exist in a state of chaos.

Yahweh is a deity of unchangeable purpose.

The bible includes the unalterable story of creation and of the existence of deity.

The written word of God is not a chronicle account of the kings or heroes or prophets of Israel. The bible is the story of the One who is deity. The purpose of the bible is not to provide a collection of lessons of morality for religious adherents. The purpose of the bible is to explain the existence and purpose of YHWH. The bible is an account that explains the purpose of existence. The bible is the written word of God that reveals and explains the living word of God. The purpose of the Bible is to explain that God is Love.

Through the prophets of Israel and through the one called Emanuel, the almighty deity known as YHWH has testified of himself saying, "I am that I am, and I will be what I shall be." As well, within the recorded words of scripture Jehovah has also revealed his purpose and plans for mankind. The Lord has made all things for himself. Yes, even the wicked for the day of evil has been made by him. (Proverbs 16:4)

Yahweh has a purpose for life and existence. He has a plan and purpose for this world. To everything there is a season, and a time to every purpose under the heaven. (Ecclesiastes 3:1-8) Although Jehovah has not completely explained the reason that he created man, we must clearly understand that this was and is for his chosen purpose. This purpose must not be challenged. (Isaiah 46:9-10)

Yahweh has a plan that was established before the creation of the world. This overarching plan, in which we are all included, is illustrated by Moses and the children of Israel. The purpose and meaning of Yahweh's plan of existence has been revealed, by the power of the Holy Spirit, as the good news, or the Gospel. (Luke 2:10-11) His plan is to redeem Israel and offer eternal life to mankind. (John 3:16-21)

The Gospel is not a system of religion. The good news is a simple way of finding purpose and meaning of life, of faith, and hope and love, in Jesus Christ. The gospel is the simple way of finding and accepting God's plan and purpose.

Everything that Jehovah does, and everything that He will do, is accomplished with a purpose or intent. King Solomon said that he knew that whatever God does, it will be forever. Nothing can be added to what God has done. Nothing can be taken from what has been accomplished. (Ecclesiastes 3:14)

YHWH is not a God of chaos. There is a reason or reasons why God created the world, that he created man, that he sustains the world, and that someday the world will be replaced. A limited understanding of his thoughts and designs have been revealed, but lack of revelation or understanding does not prevent having faith and trust his promises.

Mankind, having been created in the image of God, psychologically rejects chaos or disorder, for a state of chaos establishes a state of lack of purpose. For mankind, an understanding of purpose and order is necessary for comfort and hope. We are driven by the desire to avoid chaos and to establish purpose or meaning for life.

Scientific knowledge offers a sense of power or control. The knowledge of science offers psychological and emotional comfort, for knowledge and understanding allows one to discover the interrelated design of life and existence. Comfort can be found in the knowledge of science; for understanding removes disorder and gives meaning to existence. A scientific understanding of our world and universe allows one to see the beauty of existence. We are disturbed by that which cannot be explained or controlled; therefore, we search for something that offers trust. The study of science is a search for life and for the meaning and purpose of life. The knowledge of science allows man to establish a sense of purpose, to understand the design of creation, to hope for an understanding of existence.

The search for knowledge allows one to step out of darkness into the light of existence; however, the only knowledge that will provide the true meaning of life is an understanding of the light of Truth, which is the Gospel. Yahweh is a God of reason and knowledge and understanding. His designs and plans are perfect and complete. The true knowledge of the meaning and purpose for human existence can be found only by discovering the truth of the Gospel.

God looked at everything that he had made; and it was very good. (Genesis 1:31)

## 65
## Redemption

The satisfaction, or the mental and emotional responses of finding something of great value that was lost and then recovered cannot be adequately described or explained. (Isaiah 44:23) Job understood the joy of redemption. Job understood that his redeemer lives. (Job 19:25-26)

Redemption is regaining possession of something of value, in exchange of payment or action of clearing an obligation or debt.

Yahweh is a God of redemption for Israel, and for all of mankind. (Matthew 15:24-28) Spiritual redemption and the redemption of life, offered by Jesus Christ, is an act of grace given to those who are unable to repay the cost of redemption. (1 Peter 1:19) The requirement or need of redemption for Israel and for the world is difficult to explain. This book is not intended to be lessons of theology; therefore, only a brief discussion will be offered.

Because redemption may be accomplished for several different reasons, redemption is an action that is difficult to adequately explain. Redemption may be to regain or to recover something that has been lost, by payment of the required price of redemption. The redemption may be to purchase something previously sold or lost. An effort to recover a status of moral standing or a position of honor that has been lost or forfeited may also be redemption. Redemption may be atonement for guilt or an act of honor to fulfill an obligation.

The requirements of redemption may be accomplished by the one in need of redemption or by another as an act of grace. Redemption may also be given as a blessing by a sovereign power.

The biblical story of redemption can be found within the historical accounts of the children of Abraham and the New Testament account of the life, death, and resurrection of Jesus Christ. Because much of the story has been taught within biblical prophecy, the subject has often been discussed and debated by the theological scholars of Israel. Many questions were asked concerning the need for redemption, the payment of redemption, and especially concerning "who would be the redeemer of Israel."

According to the writers of the New Testament, redemption by Yahweh is an act of loving kindness, to be accomplished by the living Word of God, which is Christ Jesus. (Isaiah 55:11) (2 Corinthians 5:19-21)

The children of Abraham were used by Yahweh to teach a valuable lesson concerning the need of redemption for the world. Rules and requirements of social and financial redemption were part of the code of honor within the laws of Moses. The one who was a redeemer was respected and honored. For the Hebrew, the closest relative was the one who had the right of redemption for restoration of property or social status. The book of Ruth is a beautiful story of love and redemption. This story has been specifically recorded to teach that Jehovah is the Father of Israel and has claimed the right of redemption, for the children of Abraham.

Isaiah prophesied about a coming redeemer for the entire nation of Israel. (Isaiah 54:5, 7-8) A full account of the prophesies concerning this redemption and salvation has been offered by Isaiah.

Redemption is an act of honor and love. The required payment, the full cost for redemption, the atonement for guilt, the acts of purity and honor will be paid or accomplished by God himself. (Isaiah 59:15-21)

Redemption will be brought forth as good news, peace and happiness and comfort for the children of Abraham. (Isaiah 61:1-3) (Isaiah 52:7)

This redemption will be a fulfillment of the covenant that God made with Abraham, Isaac, and Jacob, and with king David and the children of Israel. Redemption will be a time of rejoicing for everyone. (Isaiah 62:1-5)

Yahweh's redemption, according to Hebrew scholars, is a future event to be delivered to Israel by the promise of the Messiah. The problem for Hebrew scholars is that the one who is to be the Messiah has not been identified or revealed. Perhaps when these scholars answer a theological question proposed by Jesus, they will be able to know the promised Messiah.

On a certain day, when the Pharisees, the lawyers of the Law, were together, Jesus asked the religious leaders a question. Jesus wanted to

ONE

know what they understood about the Messiah, the Christ. The lawyers stated that the Messiah would be the son of David. Then Jesus asked a complicated theological question concerning the relationship of David to the Messiah, for king David had called him Lord. Jesus was stating that the prophesied Messiah could not be simply a physical descendant of king David. (Psalm 110:1-7)

And none, of the Jewish scholars, were able to answer. And from that day, no one else asked him any more questions.

Jesus admonished the religious leaders for failure to recognize that Yahweh is a God of grace, forgiveness, and redemption. The Pharisees and Sadducees were so concerned with protecting moral and religious status that they became blind to the prophecy that would have revealed the true Messiah. While teaching the religious leaders, Jesus told the parable of the vineyard; and concluded by saying that the owner of the vineyard will come and destroy the unfaithful attendants and will give the vineyard to others. The scribes and the chief priest tried to arrest Jesus, for they understood that the parable was against them. (Luke 20:1- 19)

We have been redeemed with the precious blood or the sacrifice of Jesus. This was according to God's plan and purpose, before the creation of our world. (1 Peter 1:18-20)

## 66
## Resurrection

Jesus said, "I am the resurrection, and the life." (John 11:25-26)

The word resurrection may be defined or used in several different ways, with several differing meanings. An act of moral achievement may be called a revival, a resurgence, or an awakening. For a scientific or physical event, resurrection may be defined as a renewal after a long period of lack of function, or a spontaneous return of life, such as a sprout or a root that has grown from a plant that was assumed to be dead.

Yahweh is a God of resurrection.

The basic meaning of spiritual resurrection is the reappearance or renewal of life, after a state of death. The happening or the arrival is a rising from the dead and a return of life. The event may be described as a re-birth or a renewal of life; however, a true event of resurrection must be more than a spiritual renewal or revival, or more than one life that has replaced another. The event of resurrection must be an actual renewal or return of life to an actual mortal body that was previously physically dead.

No one has ever witnessed an actual event of resurrection. Lazarus came forth from the tomb, but no one was within the tomb to witness this renewal of life. (John 11:38-44) An actual resurrection would be an event like the arrival or appearance of a previously unknown object. However, because no one has ever witnessed such an arrival or event, any declared arrival must be accepted by faith, rather than by actual or scientific proof.

As clearly stated in scripture, Yahweh is a God of resurrection, and of faith.

Yahweh is not only a God of resurrection; he is the resurrection and life.

(John 11:25-26) This statement, a declared belief in resurrection, must be accepted by faith. The woman to whom Jesus offered the declaration, answered by expressing faith. Martha said that she believed that Jesus is the Christ, the Son of God. The question concerning resurrection must be answered by every man; for Yahweh, who is a God of resurrection, is also a God of faith.

The angels said that Jesus is alive. (Mark 16:6) Mary Magdalene said that Jesus is alive. (Mark 16:9) However, some doubted that he was alive. (Mark 16:11)

No one, except perhaps the angels of God, has ever witnessed an actual event of resurrection; however, many have testified of having seen the resurrected Christ.

The disciples saw Jesus depart to go to heaven. (Mark 16:19)

By faith we believe that Jesus is alive. (Romans 6:5-10)

Jesus said that he is the resurrection, and the life. (John 11:25)

Jesus also said that whosoever lives and believes in him shall never die. (John 11:26)

# 67
# Revelation

The actual revelation of Jesus Christ has been described as a presentation of majesty and glory. (John 1:51)

A revelation is a disclosure or announcement of an event, relating to existence or nonexistence. A divine revelation is a disclosure, presentation, or announcement of extreme spiritual importance.

Divine revelation is a gift of love from a Heavenly Father.

The Lord of Heaven and earth has spoken through prophets, signs, and miracles to make his presence known. As an almighty transcendent deity, Yahweh has the power and authority to come down to earth to defend his honor or to present his plan or purpose of life and existence.

By use of miracles and signs, and by personal appearances to certain chosen men and women, Yahweh openly presented himself to the children of Abraham. The light of his glory it was shown so that they might know that the Lord is God; and that there is no other Deity besides him. (Deuteronomy 4:31-38) These personal appearances were not special disclosures or presentations; for Yahweh's existence was known since the time of Adam and Eve. The Almighty simply appeared, with authority, as a supreme Deity to do his will. Although descriptive words such as disclosure, presentation, or announcement are used to describe these appearances, only a divine presentation of spiritual importance would be referred to as a revelation.

God appeared and spoke to Moses to say, "I will be to you a God. You shall know that I am the Lord your God." (Exodus 6:4-8)

Moses also went before God with Aaron, Nadab and Abihu, and seventy of the elders of Israel. They saw the presence of God, and they ate and drank. (Exodus 24:8-11)

On Mount Sinai, God appeared in a cloud of glory, like a consuming fire on the summit of the mountain. (Exodus 24:15-17)

Throughout the historical times of the Old Testament, prophecies have been recorded concerning a future personal appearance that would indeed be a revelation.

At various times and in several differing ways, the prophecy of a revelation of the Messiah, the true King of Israel, has been presented.

A prophesy of a future revelation was given through the unknown prophet Balaam. (Numbers 24:17) These words of prophesy, concerning a king of Israel, were recorded during a time when Israel did not have a sovereign king. The message was through a prophet that was not a descendant of Abraham. Balaam was the son of Beor of Pethor in Mesopotamia. (Deuteronomy 23:4-5) At this time in history, Israel was ruled and judged by Moses and Aaron and appointed elders of tribes that were specifically chosen by God. The point is that Yahweh does not always speak through the prophets of Israel; he is free to reveal his plans or to offer prophecies, in any way that he chooses.

Specific or special appearances are always with a purpose; however obvious general disclosure has been presented since the creation of the world. The wise men, the magi from the east who were perhaps from the same area of the prophet Balaam, clearly believed that the stars in heaven are revelations of God's handiwork. Yahweh gave these men knowledge concerning the alignment of stars, so that they were motivated to come to worship the newborn king of Israel.

Jesus offered prophecy of a special revelation to the children of Israel. The words that Jesus spoke are words of truth, "You shall not see me, until the time comes when you shall say, blessed is the One that cometh in the name of the Lord." (Luke 13:35)

Jesus also offered a prophecy of this revelation to his disciples. (Matthew 24:1-2) And later, the disciples asked Jesus to tell them when these events would happen, and what would be the sign of the end of the world. The words of Jesus, of the prophecy and revelations of God have been recorded in scripture. (Matthew 24:4-51) (Matthew 25:1-13)

The apostle Paul was given direct information by the Spirit of Christ. (Galatians 1:12) In much the same way, we who have been baptized by the Spirit of Christ, will receive information concerning Yahweh, from the Holy Spirit. (Luke 10:22)

The book of Revelation is a writing concerning special revelation. The revelation of Jesus Christ, which God gave unto him to show unto his servants, things which must shortly come to pass. (Revelation 1:1) Neither Jesus or any of the disciples offered interpretations for the words of

Revelation; therefore, cautious should be taken when making assumptions of interpretation, or to decide if the words are to be read as symbolic or literal. Nevertheless, the words of the book of Revelation are valuable. "Blessed are the ones who read and blessed are those who hear the words of prophecy and heed the things that are written in it; for the time is near." (Revelation 1:3)

At some point in the future, the time of general disclosure will end, and the promised revelation of Yahweh will be fulfilled; however, the privilege of knowing the times or the seasons, which God has put in his own power, has not been revealed to us. (Acts 1:7)

In scripture the revelation and understanding of his existence has been presented. The evidence of his existence is undeniable. His promise of eternal life is like a firm foundation and as pure as silver tried by fire. He has said that he is the resurrection and the life. His word is truth. He has promised that he will return. (Acts 1:10-11)

Yahweh's divine revelation of his son Jesus Christ (John 1:51) is of extreme spiritual importance, for through his son Yehoshua the Messiah, eternal life will be revealed. Through the son, the Father will be glorified. Yahweh has said, "I will magnify and sanctify myself. I will be known in the eyes of many nations. They will know that I am the Lord. (Ezekiel 38:23)

# 68
# Rewards

Gifts of appreciation, honor, and love are the true rewards offered by God. (Psalm 37:23-40)

A reward is a gift, an honor, or recognition given in recognition of service or achievement. The greatest gift offered to mankind is eternal life. Eternal life is not a reward; eternal life is a gift of grace.

Yahweh's gifts of love are beautiful and amazing. (1 Corinthians 2:9)

Yahweh openly rewards those who are humble, who are willing to submit to his perfect will. (James 4:6) As well, he rewards zealous action against dishonor to his name.

In the book of Numbers an account of a zealous priest was recorded. One of the Israelites brought a woman of Midian into his tent. This was a forbidden act. When Phinehas, the priest, saw it, he took a spear and went after the man into his tent and pierced the man of Israel and the woman. So, the plague of the sons of Israel was checked. (Numbers 25:1-18) Then the Lord told Moses that Phinehas had turned away his wrath from the sons of Israel. (Numbers 25:7-14)

Because Yahweh is a God of love his actions of protection, mercy, and grace may often appear to be a reward, blessing, or approval. A promise of protection and love has been offered to the nation of Israel. This special blessing is a gift of mercy and love; for God is the keeper of Israel, by a covenant relationship. (Psalm 121:1-8) Jesus also promised a special protection to his twelve disciples. (Matthew19:26-28)

Therefore, although Jesus has offered Yahweh's rewards to those who follow his teachings, we must be cautious when describing a blessing or gift as a reward. That which may be called a reward may in truth be a gift of mercy or grace which could never be earned.

We have been instructed to give, and by giving we will receive blessings. Blessings will be given for deeds of love, which we have been commanded to do, but not for religious or moral performance. (Luke 6:38 &17:9) Although we may suffer hardships or may be persecuted, our reward will be the joy and peace of doing the will of God. (1 John 2:15-17)

To be blessed, not to be rewarded, is the gift of love to those who are suffering. The reward for those who are persecuted is the gift of eternal life. Our reward is a gift of peace and joy, to rejoice and be glad, for great is our reward in heaven. (Matthew 5:4, 10-12) (Matthew 19:29) (Romans 6:18,22)

Eternal life in Heaven is the reward for faith in Jesus Christ (Revelation 121:1-8) This truth has been clearly stated in the words of scripture. The only foundation for eternal life is Jesus Christ. When we "build our lives" on this foundation, our work will be evident, and the works of love will remain, and the reward will be blessings. Whatever else may happen depends upon the gracious mercy and love of Yahweh. (1 Corinthians 3:11-17)

At some point in time, or in life, every man shall receive a reward. For according to the words of Matthew, Jesus will come in the glory of his

Father with his angels and shall reward every man according to his works of life. (Matthew 16:27)

The judgments and the rewards of Yahweh are righteous and true. This fact has been clearly and openly declared in the words of scripture. (Matthew 25:31-34)

# 69
## Righteous

Yahweh is righteous; he is the only One in all of existence that is righteous. (Psalm 53:1-3)

To be righteous is to be virtuous, morally right, or excellent in thought and conduct.

Righteousness is a state of perfection, purity, and holiness.

For the Lord is righteous. He loves righteousness. (Psalm 11:7) No evil dwells in him. (James 1:13) Yahweh is not a God that has pleasure in wickedness and no evil can be found in his presence. (Psalm 5:4) The righteousness of God is an everlasting state of perfection, purity, and holiness. The righteousness of God has been expressed in the laws of Heaven and as well have been included within the laws of Israel. (Psalm 119:140)

Yahweh is righteous, pure and justified in all his actions; for righteousness is his nature and he is pure in thoughts and actions. Yahweh has been described as one who loves righteousness. He is a God who is pleased with the upright, or those who strive to be morally and socially acceptable. (Psalm 11:4-7)

The fact that God loves righteousness is a problem for mankind; for no man is righteous.

The laws of righteousness were given to Moses; and the laws were recorded and given to the nation of Israel. However, because no man living is pure or holy, the laws of righteousness would be a curse and not a blessing. This truth is difficult to explain, for the requirements of righteousness that have been placed upon the children of Abraham have been both a blessing and a hardship. (Psalm 143:1-2)

The commandments of righteousness given to Israel by Moses were clearly stated. God told Moses to tell the people that they were required to be holy, for God their Father is holy. (Leviticus 19:2) This righteous expectation or moral requirement was clearly explained to Moses. The nation of Israel was to be different than the people of Egypt and Canaan. Moses told the Israelites that if they were able to follows the laws or statutes given by God that God would bless and protect them. (Leviticus 18:1-5) The Israelites were not to dishonor themselves by committing acts of evil. (Leviticus 18:24)

As the family of Jehovah, the nation of Israel was judged for unrighteousness. Each tribe or family was judged together as father and sons and daughters, until the age of the exile when God changed this relationship. The Israelites were told that this rule would be changed. (Ezekiel 18:1-4) The new rule was that if a man abided by the statutes and the ordinances of the law, to deal faithfully, he would be righteous, and his life would be protected. As well, if the man was unfaithful, and committed abominations, he would surely be put to death; his blood would be on his own head. (Ezekiel 18:9-32)

This requirement of righteousness has also been given to the disciples of Christ as a requirement of perfection. The apostle Matthew recorded the instructions of Jesus concerning righteousness or perfection. Jesus was instructing the disciples about the necessity of love and charity. One lesson was specifically about loving enemies. We must remember that God is not a respecter of persons; he loves and cares for everyone. To be children of God, we are required to bless those who curse us, do good to those who hate us or persecute us. Therefore, our attitude of love must be the same as the righteousness of God; we must be "perfect as he is perfect." (Matthew 5:43-48)

Simply stated, because Yahweh is righteous, he requires his children to also be righteous; however, because only God is righteous or good, purity or righteousness must be a gift of grace. (1 John 1:5-10) (Jude 1:1)

The early Christians lived in a social and religious world that was guided or restricted by the teachings and traditions of men. For centuries, religious performance had been a primary requirement of life for the Hebrew people. The first small gatherings of Hebrew believers were obviously concerned about maintaining their relationship of right standing with God. As well, these Christians resided in a time when every nation was identified by the religions that were observed or accepted. Obviously, these Christians were proud of the fact that they were zealous for God. (Acts 22:3) They were disciples of Christ. They considered themselves to be "the righteous ones." They understood that Jesus had been rewarded the throne of his Father, and a scepter of righteousness. (Hebrews 1:8-9)

A desperate need to be religious prevented many of the early Christians from enjoying the liberty offered by the act of grace given through the sacrifice of Christ. Several of the believers decided that religious requirements, to properly live this new life in the Kingdom of Heaven, should be identified. Many decided that all believers should still be circumcised. Others decided that the observance of the Sabbath restrictions should be maintained.

Priest or scribes or Pharisees or Sadducees or other religious leaders were no longer available to guide the followers of Christ concerning rules of law and strict traditions. (2 Timothy 4:14-15) The followers of Jesus that gathered in separate meetings only had older men, or elders, to help them understand the words of scripture. "And when they had appointed elders for them in every gathering, having prayed, with fasting, they commended them to the Lord." (Acts 14:23)

In this time of disagreement, some men came down from Judea and began teaching the brethren a false teaching, that salvation is not complete unless one is circumcised according to the custom or the laws of Moses. (Acts 15:1)

Thankfully, after much debate, and having listened to the Apostle Paul's strong argument, the believers decided that religious legal requirements could be set aside. They agreed to accept the fact that the grace of Christ is sufficient for righteousness and for salvation. (Acts 15:1-29) (2 Timothy 4:8) They all agreed to accept the truth that only God is righteous; and the only way to have a right standing with Yahweh is by accepting his gift of grace.

The apostle Paul during the extended time of his travels, writings, and ministry continued to firmly teach that the righteousness of God is obtained only by faith of Jesus Christ, for we have all sinned and have come short of the Glory of God. We can only be justified by grace through the redemption that has been provided by Christ Jesus. (Romans 3:21-15)

We have received the righteousness of Christ as an anointing by the Holy Spirit. (1 John 1:27) which gives us the right and power to live in the light of truth. (1 John 1:7) Love is the evidence of having been anointed, and of living in the light of Christ. (1 John 1:10 & 3:11)

The apostle John has said, "Let no man deceive you; the one that does righteousness is righteous, even as Christ is righteous." (1 John 3:7 & 5:1-2)

# 70
# Salvation

Salvation is a precious gift of eternal life, given by a God of love.

Salvation is an act of rescue from danger or harm, to be saved from loss of life by another who performs an act of rescue.

Salvation is the theme of the writings of the Old Testament and of the New Testament. The prophecies of scripture include promises of salvation, of peace and freedom and eternal life. The gospels of the New Testament and the writings of the disciples of Jesus have been written to explain and to offer the gift of salvation.

The amazing gift of eternal life has been offered to those who will choose to read the words of Jesus, for his words are truth and life. The teachings, instructions, and explanations of salvation have been presented in prophecy, parables, and with direct statements by Jesus and the apostles of Jesus. The New Testament is available, for anyone who chooses, to read and to understand "what Jesus has done for us." (John 13:12) (John 1:1)

The word "salvation" can be found in several Psalms and in the prophecy of the prophets of Israel. Many of the prophecies express a sense of expectation of redemption, of joy and rejoicing. The promise of a new King and a time of peace and prosperity are common themes of the prophecies of the Hebrew writings. (Psalm 14:7) The prophecy of Zechariah is one example. Zechariah said that Israel should rejoice greatly. A king would be coming. He would be just and would be bringing salvation. This king would be a prince of peace, riding of a colt of a lowly common animal. (Zechariah 9:9)

The gift of salvation is indeed a unique act of rescue for the nation of Israel; however, because prophecies are often difficult to understand, the scribes and teachers of Israel did not completely understand this promise. (Luke 2:11) The scribes and Pharisees understood that the fulfillment of the prophecies would be a unique blessing for the children of Abraham; however, the fact that the blessing would also be a gift of eternal life was not accepted by many of the scribes and teachers of Israel.

According to the authors of New Testament scripture, Jesus is the fulfillment of the Old Testament prophecies. Yahweh's gracious act of rescue for Israel and for "every nation on earth" has been fulfilled by Jesus Christ. The Gospel is the "good news of love" that God so loved the world that he gave the life of his only son that the world might be rescued from death and destruction. (John 3:16-17)

The prophet Isaiah prophesied that salvation, a promise of redemption, would be offered from the Almighty to the children of Abraham. (Isaiah 9:1-6) Salvation would also a time of judgment for Israel and for those who have failed to hear the words of God. (Malachi 4:5-6) (Luke 2:30-31) Jesus testified that he had come to fulfill the prophecies of Isaiah. (Matthew 4:17) The disciples of Jesus said that this salvation would also be given to the Gentiles. (John 4:22)

Salvation is an amazing gift that is difficult to explain. The gift of salvation includes an act of atonement, which is the life, sacrifice, death, burial and resurrection of Jesus. The gift of the life of Jesus was necessary because the evil of mankind has separated man from a righteous Deity.

The gift of salvation that has been offered to Israel and to the Gentiles is an unearned and an undeserved gift of grace. Salvation is not a reward. Salvation is not a statement of approval. The purpose of salvation was not to give righteousness to mankind, or to make man righteous before God; the purpose of salvation was to give life to mankind. Because salvation cannot be achieved by an act of righteousness, an act of mercy and forgiveness was required. (Luke18:19)

Salvation is offered as a blessing of eternal life. (Acts 26:18) However, this gift of life must be accepted. The acceptance of the gifts is dependent upon a choice of faith. Whosoever will confess faith in Jesus, before men, will be accepted before God. (Matthew 10:32-32) The gracious gift of salvation, that has been offered to Israel, is available to anyone who hears the "good news" and chooses to believe the words of Jesus. The gift of eternal life must be accepted with simple humility and gratitude. (Luke 18:17) Eternal life will be given to those who have faith. (Luke 18:42) (2 Thessalonians 2:11-14)

God has given to us eternal life. This life is in His son. The one that has the son has life. The one that does not have the Son of God does not have life. (1 John 5:11-13)

The one who believes will hear and understand the words of Jesus and will bear fruits of righteousness. (Matthew 13:23) Those with an honest and good heart, having believed the words of the gospel, will bring forth fruit with patience. (Luke 8:15) Those who believe will be faithful followers of Jesus Christ. (Matthew 15:6-9) Those who believe will have faith, like a small child. (Luke 18:17)

Salvation is a supreme gift of love, a unique blessing from God, that shall never be taken away. (Galatians 3:29) Salvation is a gift of everlasting peace and joy. (Isaiah 35:10) God's loving hope is that there will be many like the apostle Paul, who will accept the love of Christ. (1Timothy 1:15) Yahweh has chosen to rescue us from death and destruction. Jesus Christ is our redeemer, the one who rescues. Yahweh is our God of salvation. (John 3:17)

The apostle Paul understood the blessings of the "joy of salvation." We have been encouraged to rejoice always, in all circumstances. (Philippians 4:4) We were prisoner who have been set free. We can take the chains of sin off, we are free. We can shout, rejoice, sing, cry or dance, we are free. We can walk in the sunlight or beneath a beautiful rainbow, we will never be in darkness again. We can rest in peace, for we will never have anything to fear again. We can breathe deeply, we are alive; and we will life forever. We can rejoice, our life is a gift of love from Jesus. We can sing, "Hallelujah, blessed be the King that comes in the name of the Lord; peace in heaven and glory in the highest." (Luke 19:38)

Salvation is the greatest gift ever given, for Jesus gave his life that we might have eternal life. (Ephesians 5:1-2) As a praise for salvation, the apostle Paul prayed, "Now unto the King eternal, immortal, invisible, the only wise God, be honor and glory forever and ever. Amen." (1 Timothy 1:16-17)

# 71
# Sovereign

Yahweh is the sovereign ruler of existence. (Psalm 24:1-10)

Sovereignty is to have unlimited power and authority.

Yahweh is the sovereign King of every kingdom in Heaven and Earth.
Yahweh, the sovereign ruler of creation, reigns over the entire universe. (Psalms 135:6-7)

Within a political realm or kingdom, all sovereign political authority, to write the law, to rule on the justice of law, and to enforce the law belongs to the sovereign ruler. In a monarchy, one individual reigns as the sovereign ruler.

In a Democracy the sovereign power of government is invested with the individual citizen, within a sovereign union of equal status with other citizens. Sovereign authority to write laws, to rule on the justice of laws and to enforce laws, is equally shared through the rules and regulations of the Constitution. In essence the Constitution is the sovereign king and the servant of all citizens. All citizens pledge allegiance to the union of citizenship and to the rules of the Constitution.

In scripture, the title King of kings or Lord of lords is used to describe the absolute sovereign power of Yahweh and of his son Yehoshua, who is the sovereign ruler with him. (Isaiah 46:9-11) (Deuteronomy 10:17) The names or descriptions of sovereign power are often used as descriptions for Yahweh. (Isaiah 44:6-8)

Through Abraham, the father of the tribes of Israel, God has established a special relationship with the nation of Israel. (Genesis 12:1-4) Yahweh has chosen to be the sovereign ruler of the children of Abraham. He is the King of Israel. He has not relinquished this position of authority. Because of the hardness of heart and because of the failures of the prophets God allowed the nation of Israel to have earthly kings; however, this was not according to his perfect will. (1 Samuel 8:1-7 & 12:12)

Yahweh is the true God, the living God. He is the everlasting King of Israel. He will always be the sovereign ruler of Heaven and earth. (Jeremiah 10:10)

The book of Daniel is a demonstration of the sovereign authority of Yahweh. In this account the royal Chaldean ruler Nebuchadnezzar was given visions and miracles so that he might learn about the sovereignty of Yahweh. (Daniel 2:1-47, 3:1-30 & 4:1-37) Because he was filled with pride and unable to understand, king Nebuchadnezzar was required to learn the lesson through a process of discipline. God offered the king twelve months grace and then exercised his authority as the supreme ruler of heaven and earth. (Daniel 4:29-33 & 5:18-21) And at the end of the seven years of chastisement, when his sanity was restored, Nebuchadnezzar offered praise to the sovereign King of Israel. The words of the king are words of humility and honor and recognition of the power and authority of Deity. (Daniel 4:34-36)

After Nebuchadnezzar was restored to his position as the ruler in Babylon, he offered another testimony concerning Yahweh. (Daniel 4:37)

Yahweh is the King of the Universe. He is the only One deity, He is the only sovereign ruler who will reign over heaven and earth and all of creation. His kingdom is an everlasting kingdom. He is the King of Glory. (Psalm 24:1-10)

The kingdom of everlasting existence, the kingdom of God, was revealed. The glory of the Kingdom of Heaven was introduced as a display of glory. Peter and John and James saw the presence of glory. (Luke 9:27-36)

For Christ-ones, our sovereign ruler is the Word of God. Like the words of the Constitution, the word of God "the one" to whom all believers must pledge allegiance. (Matthew 28:18) (1 John 2:23) Yahweh has ordained an existence of order and unity, in which all believers are equal. (Matthew 23:8-12) We reside in a new kingdom of freedom and liberty. Jesus Christ, our sovereign Lord and master, is our King and our Truth; and truth has set us free. There is joy and freedom in the Kingdom of Heaven, for our sovereign ruler is Love.

Jesus is the King eternal, immortal, invisible, the only wise God. He is the one who deserves to receive honor and glory forever and ever. (1 Timothy 1:1

## 72
## Spirit

The spirit of God was with God, in the beginning when the heavens and earth were created. (Genesis 1:1-3)

Spirit is the nonphysical part of a living person.

The Holy Spirit is the spirit of YHWH. The Spirit is One. Since the beginning, the Spirit of Yahweh was with Yahweh and was Yahweh. The Holy Spirit is the invisible presence of God that is clearly seen by the things that have been created. (Romans 1:20)

Yahweh is Spirit. Those who worship him must worship him in spirit and in truth. (John 4:23-24)

Only a limited description of the holiness of Yahweh has been revealed. The spirit life of man is often referred to as our inner being or soul. Would it be possible to describe or explain the inner life of man? Consider, how much more knowledge or information would be required to describe or explain the life of deity.

Therefore, the best way to understand the Holy Spirit is to have a personal relationship through faith in Jesus Christ. When we know the truth of the Spirit, we are free to understand, all that we are required to understand. Even with assistance from the Holy Spirit, we will yet be "looking through a distorted glass."

Just as there are many invisible yet freely expressed spiritual or mental attributes of every man, there are many spiritual attributes of Yahweh. The relationship that Yahweh has with the life within, that is his Spirit, is unique in every possible way. The Spirit of Yahweh is the presence and the evidence of holiness and wonder and beauty and power and majesty and honor and faith and hope and love. The most amazing attribute of the Holy Spirit is Love. God is Love and is One with the Spirit. The Holy Spirit holds and protects the amazing power of love. The Holy Spirit is the amazing power of faith. In the same way that a smile on the face of a man may reveal thoughts, attitudes, or even character, the Holy Spirit is the presence and revelation of the beauty and majesty and glory of Deity.

A beautiful explanation of the unity of Spirit and Father has been offered by the apostle Paul. The apostle said that the Spirit of God is the only one that truly knows and understands Yahweh. (1 Corinthians 2:9-11)

The Spirit is related to the Father in a similar way that we are related to our own spirit; for we are created in the image of God. Therefore, because our individual spirit is not a second persons of our humanity, perhaps referring to the Holy Spirit as the second person of the Trinity is as well incorrect. However, because Yahweh has an entirely unique relationship to his Spirit, this comparison does not offer an adequate understanding of the Spirit of Deity. Our spirit offers us an awareness of life and existence and love, but the Spirit of God is the very power and beauty of the creation of life and existence.

Our spirit is simple; the Spirit of YHWH is awesome and almighty and indescribable. For example, a complete understanding of the power and majesty of the actions of the Spirit of God in the account of creation will not be possible. (Genesis 1:2-3)

Another simple truth concerning the Spirit was offered by Jesus. Jesus said that God is Spirit and must be worshiped in spirit and in truth. (John 4:22-23)

Like invisible wind, the presence of the Holy Spirit may be evident or even obvious. That which is invisible, although beyond sight or perception, may in essence be sensed through feeling or by an undescribed psychological understanding; however, this awareness cannot be used as proof of the existence of the invisible. In contrast, the power and actions of the Holy Spirit may be visible as light, action, or movement.

For the believer, the presence of the Holy Spirit is an "indwelling of the Spirit," the gift or blessing of the Spirit that has been given to everyone who has professed faith in Jesus Christ. The presence of the Holy Spirit is the presence of the Kingdom of God, for the kingdom of God is within us. (Luke 17:20-21) The Spirit, that is life, gives spiritual birth to those who believe, who are children of God in the Kingdom of Heaven.

To be able to understand the Holy Spirit, we would need to use each stated characteristic of the Almighty to explain how the Spirit of the living God interacts with the Father to save us, to bless us, and to use us for his glory and honor and love. We would need to offer examples and teachings from scripture, of men like Ezekiel and Daniel, and the Apostle Paul, and many others who were blessed and strengthened by the Holy Spirit. However, we do not need to accomplish this task; for all that must be accomplished is to read the Bible. As we read, we can ask the Holy Spirit to speak to our heart; and we will understand. As we read, we can ask the Holy Spirit to teach us about the character of Yahweh. As we read, we can ask to be taught how to love God with all our heart, soul, and mind. (Romans 8:11)

The gift of the Holy Spirit is the invisible presence of the gift of eternal life. (John 3:5-6)

God uses His Spirit as a personal encounter with those that are chosen. The Holy Spirit is not the spirit of the world but is the spirit of love. The Spirit of God has been given to us so that we might know the things that have been given to us by God. The Spirit has been given so that we might understand instructions that are offered from God. (1 Corinthians 2:12-16)

Many of the "characters of the Bible" were directly anointed or influenced by the Holy Spirit. For example, Yahweh interacted with king Saul and king David and with other kings of Israel in unique ways and at differing times. (1 Samuel 10:3-6 &16:13) As well, other non-Hebrew rulers were influenced by the Holy Spirit.

A devout citizen of Jerusalem named Simeon was Informed by the Holy Spirit that he would see the promise of God. (Luke 2:25-26)

King David's relationship with the Lord of Host was both spiritual and a heart- felt love relationship. (2 Samuel 7:21-22) Yahweh, by the power of the Holy Spirit, had a personal relationship with the prophets of Israel, and several like Elijah were given special powers and specific task. (1 Kings 18:1 - 21:29)

Yahweh's Spirit descended upon Jesus, and interacted with Jesus, and empowered Jesus. (Mathew. 3:16-17)

The prophet John offered prophecy concerning the blessing of the Holy Spirit. (Luke 3:16) The purpose of the Holy Spirit is to give comfort and strength.

We who are believers have been baptized with the Spirit of God. (John 14:13-18)

This baptism of the Holy Spirit gives the believer a special relationship of friendship with the God of Love. (1 John 4:2-3) The evidence of the Spirit of Christ is not speaking in tongues, performing miracles, or accomplishing moral or religious task; the evidence of the Spirit is love for others. (Matthew 25:40-45)

In the beginning, at the time of creation, the presence of the Holy Spirit was evident by the amazing beauty and order of all that was created. Today, the invisible presence of the Holy Spirit is seen in the presence of Love. (1 John 4:7-8)

# 73
## Transcendent

Yahweh is the most-high God. He is the Almighty transcendent One. He is unequalled, unique, unparalleled, unrivaled, supreme, and amazing.

Transcendent is defined as that which cannot be described, explained, or articulated. Ultimate, unequalled, unique, unparalleled, unrivaled, supreme, surpassing, and amazing are adjective descriptions of transcendent.

Although the word transcendent may be easily defined, the concept is difficult to explain. Basically, that which is transcendent exists in the realm of the unknown, or incomprehensible. Evidently, Yahweh exists apart from and is not subject to any limitations of the universe. As well, he is not simply the answer for unknowable questions; he is the explanation of existence and of the unknown.

Although Yahweh exist beyond the realm of normal human experience, the transcendent one is not unknowable. Yahweh has chosen to reveal his presence or existence in various ways. His existence can be seen in the natural world that he created. He has made himself known through angels and prophets and visible light. He has revealed the kingdom of heaven through his Son and his Holy Spirit.

The word, law, and truth are descriptive expressions of the revelation of Yahweh through his son Jesus the Christ. All revelations are testimonies of the will of the One true God of heaven and earth. Jesus is the fulfillment of the law. Jesus is the word of Jehovah. Jesus is the truth of his righteousness and of his amazing gift of grace.

Several accounts of scripture describe a transcendent act of revelation, of a being referred to as the angel of the Lord. In the book of Judges, the angel of the Lord came to tell the Israelites that although God had led then into the land of Canaan and the covenant made with them would never be broken, God was not pleased that several of his instructions had not been followed. (Judges 2:1)

Years later, when the children of Israel committed acts of evil in the sight of the Lord, God allowed the Midianites to rule over them for seven years. Finally, God sent the angel of the Lord to deliver them from their enemies. (Judges 6:11-12)

When Gideon realized that the angel of the Lord was standing before him, he exclaimed, "Alas, O Lord God, for I have seen the angel of the Lord face to face." Gideon was obviously afraid that his life would be taken. And the Lord said to Gideon, "Peace be with you, do not fear, for you shall not die." (Judges 6:22-23) A specific description or explanation of the angel of the Lord was not offered. An explanation of how or why the angelic being spoke directly for Yahweh is not available.

Jesus offered several lessons about a new kingdom, a kingdom of Heaven on earth, that is called the kingdom of God or the kingdom of Heaven. The apostle Paul offered a brief description of life in the new kingdom. Paul said that what we shall be cannot yet be seen; however, when Jesus appears we will be like him, for we will see him as he is. (1 John 3:2)

Hebrew scholars and many of the people used reference words instead of the unspoken YHWH, to speak of God as an act of respect for the holiness of Yahweh. One such word was the simple word of heaven; therefore, when the presence of God was recognized by saying, "the kingdom of Heaven is present" the children of Abraham would have understood the meaning that "YHWH himself is present." When Jesus said, "the kingdom of heaven is present" he was referring to a new state of reality, a spiritual reality of which he, as the Messiah, is a central part. He was declaring that I AM is in your presence. He was also saying that I am Emmanuel, God with us, and I am establishing the transcendent kingdom of heaven on earth. On the cross, Jesus cried out, "It is finished," and declared that the kingdom of Yahweh was firmly established.

This unequaled and unique act of revelation was an amazing event. This act was the completion of God's amazing gift of grace, the final the act of salvation, which is the theme of the entire Bible. This was the completion of the long-awaited promises of prophecy offered to the children of king David.

Jesus admonished the Israelites in parables because their hearts were closed, and he blessed the disciples because they were able to understand. He also said that many prophets and righteous men had desired to see what the disciples were allowed to see and to hear, which was the gift of love and grace that was present in Jesus Christ. (Matthew 13:16-17)

Jesus explained what the transcendent presence of Yahweh on earth meant, and what this kingdom of heaven would be like. The words of the kingdom would be sown, but many would not understand; and the deceiver, Satan, would try to destroy the fruit of love that would be produced. The devil would sow weeds among the seeds; but the seed would survive. The kingdom of eternal life would be established by the seed of Abraham and would be like the mustard seed, the smallest of seeds, that would grow into a garden plant. The seed of the kingdom would be like leaven that a woman put in bread. After the leaven has started, it will spread to the entire loaf to become the bread of life. (Matthew 13:18:36)

Because the disciples did not understand the parables, they asked for an explanation. They wanted to know the meaning of the parable of the tares of the field. (Matthew 13:36) The words Jesus offered to the disciples is a clear explanation of an ultimate, unequalled, unique, unparalleled, unrivaled, supreme, surpassing, and amazing revelation. (Matthew 13:37-52) This kingdom of heaven will exist because Yahweh has come down from his Heaven to be with us on to earth. No wonder prophets and righteous men wanted to see and hear about this unparalleled transcendent event. This unique presence of the living transcendent God is indeed an amazing kingdom of love and life.

At a certain time, the Pharisees demanded that Jesus should tell them when the kingdom of God would come. Jesus answered, "The kingdom of God will not come with observation. Neither shall it be said, Lo here it is, or Lo there it is. For the kingdom of God is in your midst." (Luke 17:20-21)

The Son of man came to establish the kingdom of God, and he also offered words of prophecy concerning the coming of the Kingdom of Heaven. These words deserve to be read and understood. (Luke 17:22-37)

## 74
## Truth

Truth is a word used in scripture to describe beauty, honor, righteousness, and that which is enduring and everlasting. (Psalm 100:5)

Truth is that which is accurate, correct, right, valid, factual, or authentic. Truth is unaltered or unchanged correctness.

The words of Jesus that were given to the apostle Thomas are words of truth. His words are everlasting words of eternal life. Jesus said, "I am the way, the truth, and the life. No man comes unto the Father, but by me." (John 14:6)

The God of Abraham, Isaac and Jacob is truth, in the same way that he is love. Truth is the essence of his very nature, just as honor is his nature. As well, Yehoshua is the way, the truth, and the life!

Truth is accurate and verifiable. As well, truth remains a truth even when not verified or not considered to be verifiable, or accurate or acceptable. Truth exists in the absence of proof.

Truth requires completeness. Truth cannot be a half-truth, or incomplete truth. Any alteration or distortion of an image, statement or situation will eliminate the actual truth; therefore, a slight alteration of truth can be as destructive as complete distortion.

For the numerical number one to exist, the number must be complete and whole, absolute, and unaltered. The complete number one may be referred to as an absolute number one. If any portion of one is incomplete or missing an absolute number cannot exist. Spiritual truth, like an absolute numerical number one, must be complete or whole. Truth must be accurate, absolute, and unaltered.

Any variation from a state of absoluteness would create a state of untruthfulness. An untruth is a lie or false statement. It is impossible for God to lie or to be untruthful. (Hebrews 6:18) Yahweh is a complete One of truth. The Father, the Son and the Holy Spirit are a complete One. Yehoshua is the truth, the whole complete truth that exist.

The Pharisees took counsel, debated and devised a scheme, concerning how they might entangle Jesus in a theological discussion. First the teachers complimented Jesus with words of truth, and then presented a question which they think that he would be a able to answer. They wanted to know, according to the laws of Moses, if the Jews were allowed to pay taxes to Caesar. This was a theological problem, for many of the Jews considered paying taxes an act of worship to Caesar. (Matthew 22:15-17) In this situation, the Pharisees spoke words of truth but were untruthful deceivers. Truth is truth regardless of the origin or source of the statement. However, a truth cannot remain as a truth when used out of context or when offered as part of an intended false or exaggerated statement.

Truth, especially the truth that is Jesus, is required as a defense against evil. Without truth, chaos and confusion, doubt and mistrust may be established. With truth, evil can be eliminated.

Love requires truth. Untruth creates separation and disunity. With truth, the existence of peace and joy and prosperity is possible. Shalom is a greeting of unity and love.

Truth provides trust and assurance. Untruth creates despair. Truth is a gift from God. Untruthfulness is a curse from the deceiver.

Truth is to be shared openly and honestly. There is no need for truth to be hidden.

The sharing of disinformation, altered truth or false statements, is dishonest, deceitful, and harmful. The truth of Yahweh is never hidden or guarded. All that Jesus did, all the words that he spoke and the deeds that he did were done openly; nothing has been hidden. Everything that God has done and all that he has said has been recorded in Scripture; nothing remains hidden. The gospel has been shared truthfully and openly. In Rome, Paul was in his rented house "preaching the kingdom of God, and teaching concerning the Lord Jesus the Christ, with confidence and without restrictions." (Acts 28:30-31) The Apostle Paul, the bondservant of Christ Jesus, was sharing the truth of the gospel.

To believe the words of Jesus is to know the Truth. To know the Truth is to know Yahweh. The one who denies that Jesus is the Messiah is one who denies that God is Love. The one who denies Truth does not understand the miracle of existence. (1 John 1:20-23)

The words of scripture are truth. Scripture is the word of God. Every word of God is tested and true. (Hebrews 6:18) We must be careful to rightly interpret the words of scripture, for the truth of scripture must be presented without distortion or lack of clarity. (Proverbs 30:5-6)

According to the words of the psalmist, God heals the broken in heart and binds up their wounds. He counts the stars and calls them all by their names. He is great in power, and his understanding is infinite. (Psalm 147:3-5) The most amazing truth about God is that He is love. He is One who has chosen to offer loving kindness to mankind, to those who accept his love and keep his commandments. (Exodus 20:1-6) (Exodus 20:20)

When Christ Jesus was brought before Pontus Pilot, Jesus truthfully stated that he is the Messiah, the heavenly King of Israel. Pontus Pilot then asked, "What is truth?" Just as God is Love, Christ is Truth, for he and the Father are One. Jesus is the truth of Love. (1 John 5:9-13)

The existence and presence of Yahweh is a truth that must be accepted as an act of faith. However, although one may not understand, lack of understanding or scientific proof does not eliminate the truth that Yahweh does exist, and that Jesus is the Son of God. The evidence of the presence of Truth is available.

The evidence and proof of the presence of Deity is the existence of love and evil. In the scientific studies of biological life and evolution, an adequate explanation for the existence of the non-physical presence of love or evil has not been identified or explained. Logically speaking, in a world of non-created existence, love and the presence of evil should not exist.

The apostle James has clearly stated that every good gift, and every perfect gift, is from God. The gift of love and truth and everything else of value is given from the Father of lights, with whom or in whom there is no untruth or indecisiveness. (James 1:17) Jesus is the Truth and the Word of God, and everything that he has said is the simple absolute truth, the whole truth and nothing but the truth. When he spoke to the religious leaders of Israel, Jesus was painfully truthful. He scornfully accused them of hypocrisy. Jesus said, "You do not enter the kingdom of God yourselves, and you are a restriction to others that are trying to come in." (Luke 11:52)

An understanding of spiritual truth is of extreme importance. (Luke 11:23-28)

God is Love, and God is Truth; for Jesus is the Truth; and the Son and the Father are One. Those who worship God must worship him in spirit and truth, for Yahweh is One with the Holy Spirit. (John 4:24)

Jesus said to Nicodemus, "If I have told you earthly things and you believe not, how shall you believe if I tell you of heavenly things?" (John 3:12)

Yahweh is the God of truth. Truth is freedom. Truth is life. God has said that if we wish to have eternal life, we must know the truth, for the truth will set us free. We will be free indeed. (John 8:32)

We can praise the Lord with joyful songs of praise and celebration, for Truth endures forever. (Psalm 117:1-2)

# 75
## Unchangeable

According to the inspired words of scripture, it would be easier for heaven and earth to pass away than for one stroke of a letter of the Law to fail. (Luke 16:17)

To be unchangeable is to be stable, permanent, immovable, changeless and always the same, whether in the past, present, and future. To be unchangeable is to be valuable, dependable, and worthy.

The formation and preservation of visible existence is governed by laws of order that cannot be seen. For example, the fate of our physical existence depends upon the stability of matter and energy in the universe. Too much energy with less matter, or the reverse, would create universal instability. Therefore, the basic unchangeable nature of the universe, the stability of matter and energy, provides for the existence of life, at least for life on our planet, at this time of stable natural existence. The unchangeable nature of the universe is of great value.

The probability that the design, order, and unchangeable laws of the universe were established by a cosmic unknowable happening is more than one trillion to one. In other words, our universe is an incredibly well-designed and ordered existence that cannot be theoretically explained by a theory of spontaneous origin.

The inherent value of a diamond is the durable state of the crystal; however, a diamond can be shattered and reduced to worthless fragments. In contrast, Yahweh is completely unchangeable in every possible way. YHWH is absolute and unchangeable.

As well, the unchangeable law of God, the Word of God, will never fail and will never pass away. The word of God, like a precious jewel, is valuable and worthy. The Word is everlasting, and forever unchangeable.

Yahweh is a God of unity and stability. He is unchangeable. He is the same yesterday, today and forever. As well, most of his decisions or actions are never changed. The unchangeable nature of the words of God was stated somewhat differently by the apostle Matthew. Matthew stated that until heaven and earth pass away, the smallest letter or stroke shall not pass away from the Law, until all is accomplished. (Matthew 5:18)

Although the nation of Israel was unable to keep the laws of the Mosaic covenant, Yahweh did not reject the nation of Israel or change the law. All the prophets of Israel expressed confidence in the firm promises offered by the Father of Israel. The prophet Malachi spoke directly for Yahweh to say, "For I the Lord have not and will not change; for this reason, you O sons of Israel, have not been destroyed." (Malachi 3:6)

The apostle Paul offered praise to God for his unchangeable nature, for we have a strong assurance of the promises made to us who have faith in Jesus Christ. The unchangeable purpose of God has been confirmed with an oath, and we have a hope of eternal life that is dependent upon the steadfast promises of God. (Hebrews 8:17-20) Our hope of the promise of eternal life by faith in Jesus Christ has been confirmed by the unchangeableness of God and by the unchangeable faithfulness of the love of Christ.

The promise of assurance was given to Israel; and in the words of the New Testament this promise was shared with us. For Jesus Christ is the same yesterday and today, and forever. (Hebrews 13:8) The gifts and promises of God are unchangeable and every good thing that has been bestowed and every perfect gift is from our Father of Heaven. (Romans 11:29) (James 1:17) We have a strong assurance of the promise of eternal life, because it is impossible for God to lie. (Hebrews 6:16-18)

The amazing unchangeable nature of Yahweh is described as a fortress of solid rock. (Psalm 18:2) We are citizens in the house of God, the temple of God, where God will reside by the presence of the Holy Spirit. (Ephesians 2:20)

His plan for mankind has not been altered or changed and his requirement for honor, one to another, has not changed. (Matthew 5:22) As well, his requirement for love has not been altered. The first commandment is the same, yesterday, today, and tomorrow. Our commitment to God must also be unchangeable. We are to love the Lord our God, with all our heart and soul and our neighbor as ourselves.

We must remember that love bears all things, believes all things, hopes all things, endures all things, and never fails, for love is unchangeable; and God is steadfast Love. (1 Corinthians 13:7-8)

# 76
# Unity

According to the words of truth and wisdom, the rich and the poor have a common bond; the Lord is the maker of them all. (Proverbs 22:1)

Unity is a state of being united as a complete whole.

The concept of unity is easily illustrated by three basic symbols ...the circle, square and triangle. The mathematical concept of unity is expressed by the number one. The number one may be used to represent an abstract concept of any object, substance or thought that may be visible, invisible, or yet to be determined or described. One can be one whole, or one of a combination of agreeable, or even of misaligned parts; however, oneness is union in agreement in harmony and not in disarray. Oneness requires order, structure, and purpose or identity, and perhaps even time.

One object, whether of a single matter or of several different substances, is still a single unity. The earth, in many parts and many elements or substances, is one world. As previously stated, one is a simple and complex word that is difficult to define; therefore, the unity of one may also be difficult to describe. Although there is much about unity that cannot be explained; unity is of extreme importance to almighty YHWH.

Yahweh is a Deity of unity, a unity of One. (I Corinthians 8:4-6) (John 14:9) (Ephesians 4:4-6)

The Father, the Son, and the Holy Spirit reside together in the unity of Love. (John 7:16) No one knows and understands the Son except the Father in Heaven. No one knows and understands the Father in Heaven except the son of God and anyone to whom the Son reveals Him. (Luke 10:22) The Lord our God is One Lord. (Deuteronomy 6:4-5) Even the demons or devils believe in the unity of Deity. (James 2:19)

There is only one Deity. He is the God of existence, the Father of creation. He is the I AM, and we exist in Him. He is the One who is Love. We are saints in the house of the Lord and in the body of Christ. Our Lord is Jesus Christ, by whom are all things, and we exist through Him. (1 Corinthians 8:4-6) He is the one who has said, "I and my father are One." (John 10:30) He is the one and only mediator between God and mankind. (1Timothy 2:5) He is the only one who can offer eternal life. (1 John 2:23)

The unity of Deity has been clearly explained in scripture. There are three in heaven ...the Father, the Word, and the Holy Spirit. These three are One. (1 John 5:7)

The scribes, Pharisees, and the Sadducees often challenged Jesus. Their primary goal was to identify anyone who falsely claimed to be the promised Messiah. They were confident that they would be able to discredit this uneducated teacher by challenging his understanding or practice of the Mosaic law.

When questioned about eternal life, Jesus countered their argument by reminding the scribes that according to the words of scripture, "God is the Father of the living and not of the dead." One of the scribes, having recognized that Jesus had given a wise answer, asked Jesus, "What is the first, the greatest commandment of all?" Without hesitation, Jesus answered by offering the words of Shema Yisrael. Jesus said, "The first of the commandments is: Hear, O Israel; The Lord our God is One Lord. You shall love the Lord your God with all your heart, and with all your soul, and with all you mind, and with all your strength. This is the greatest commandment. The second commandment, that must be included with the first, is: You shall love your neighbor as yourself. There is no other commandment greater than these." (Mark 12:29-31) By including the second commandment, Jesus stressed the importance and necessity of unity.

The noted lawyer complimented Jesus for his accurate statements and then added his own personal agreement. Having determined that the lawyer understood the requirements of love and honor, Jesus responded, "You are not far from the kingdom of God." And no one, after that, asked any more questions. (Mark 12:32-34)

Jesus clearly declared unity with the Father. At trial, before the chief priest, and the elders of the people, Jesus was asked, "Are you then the Christ, the Son of God?" Jesus answered, "You say that I am." (Luke 22:70) Perhaps Jesus was speaking to the Pharisees who believed, but were afraid to follow him, when he loudly declared, "He that believes on me, believes not on me, but on him that sent me. And he that sees me sees him that sent me. I have come as a light unto the world, that whosoever believes on me should not abide in darkness." (John 12:42-46)

Jesus also proved his divinity, by the power that had been given to him. On a certain day, when Jesus was teaching and healing, a man who was paralyzed was brought before him. Having recognized the faith of the man and his friends Jesus said, "Your sins have been forgiven." (Luke 5:18-20) The scribes and Pharisees immediately asked among themselves, "Who is this; for he speaks blasphemies; who can forgive sins, but God alone?" (Luke 5:20-24)

Jesus testified to the religious leaders of Israel concerning unity with the Father by saying, "As the Father knows me, even so I know the Father." (John 10:15) However, the Pharisees were not able to understand. Jesus told them that if God were their Father, they would love him. Then Jesus plainly said, "Truly, I say to you, before Abraham was born, I AM." Jesus explained his unity with the Father; and admonished the religious leaders for failure to understand. Jesus said, "Your father Abraham rejoiced to see my day; and he saw it and was glad." (John 8:42-59)

With words of prophecy and statements of truth, Jesus continued to explain his unity with the Father. (John 10:1-42) The recorded words of Jesus should be read and studied. When Jesus said, "I and my Father are One," the Jews picked up stones, and intended to execute him. (John 10:30-31)

The unity of the Father and Son is an amazing oneness that cannot be adequately explained. Obviously, Yahweh and Yehoshua are the same in character and purpose; however, their exact personal relationship has not been specifically explained. Perhaps lack of understanding is directly related to failure to understand that unity does not require uniformity. Although Jesus may say that the Father is greater, he is one with the Father. As well, although Jesus became flesh, and resided among us, he is Deity. Although Jesus existed with God as Deity, he emptied himself and took the form of a bondservant, made in the likeness of mankind. (Philippians 2:6-8)

Awareness, knowledge, or revelation of the Father is through the Son or by the Holy Spirit. The Son is the revelation of the Father. Jesus said that all things concerning salvation have been delivered unto him by his Father. The only way to know Jesus is through the revelation offered by the Father. As well, we cannot fully know God until the Son explains or reveals the Father to us. (Matthew 11:27)

This understanding or revelation of God basically remains as an act of faith. We must believe the miracles and teachings of Jesus. We must believe and accept the truth that Yahweh is with Jesus, and that Jesus is in the Father. The Father and the Son of God are One. (John 11:37-38)

The most Important aspect of the oneness of deity is that the son, who is the Christ, has been highly exalted by Yahweh, who is the Father of heaven and earth. (Philippians 2:9-10)

Yahweh, as an act of grace has established the unity of his children in heaven and earth. The apostle Paul has clearly stated that there is neither Jew nor Greek, bond nor free, male nor female; for you are all one in Christ Jesus. (John 3:16) (Galatians 3:28)

We are expected to honor this principal of unity. (Philippians 2:1-8) We are required, by love and appreciation, to maintain the unity that has been offered by the power of the Holy Spirit. We are required to honor the lessons of love and unity that Jesus demonstrated to his disciples. (John 13:15) We are required to live a life of meekness and charity, so that the least among us will be honored. (Luke 9:48) (Titus 3:1-11) As well, our teachers and leaders, deacons and elders, must be servants of all. (Mark 10:44) We are commanded to love one another, for the primary requirement of spiritual unity is love. (John 15:17)

Spiritual unity is often neglected because we do not comprehend the blessings of unity. This truth has been clearly stated by the apostle Paul, "Fulfill my joy, that you are like-minded, having the same love, being of one accord, and of one mind." (Philippians 2:2-3)

The apostle also said, "With all humility and meekness, with long-suffering and love, endeavor to keep the unity of the Spirit in the bond of peace; for there is one body, and one Spirit. There is one Lord, one faith, one baptism, one Deity and Father of all, who is above all and through all and in us all." (Ephesians 4:1-6)

## 77
## Useful/Practical

The apostle Paul said, "All scripture is profitable for doctrine, for reproof, for correction and for instruction in righteousness." (2 Timothy 3:16) All scripture is useful and practical.

To be useful is to be functional, practical, and adequate for a required task or service. A direct requirement of usefulness is to be available. A requirement of being beneficial may or may not be expected.

The word of God is functional, practical, adequate for correction and practical instruction, and for obtaining eternal life.

Yahweh created the heavens and earth. All that he has created is functional, beneficial, useful, and natural. God said, "Let there be light; and there was light." God saw that the light was good. The light was functional and adequate for the required task or service. The light was also good and acceptable and beneficial. The light was useful. And all that Yahweh created was practical and useful. (Genesis 1:1-31) In an organized practical manner, the heavens and the earth were created. (Genesis 2:1)

Yahweh created the earth and universe with natural order and purpose. God was pleased with all that had been created. (Genesis 2:3)

Yahweh does not approve of anything that proves to be non-useful or non-beneficial. As a Father, Yahweh expected the children of Abraham to appreciate usefulness, and to protect the natural state of creation. Yahweh gave a blessing to Israel. He expected this gift to be appreciated. Jesus told a parable about a certain man who planted a vineyard to teach this lesson of appreciation. (Luke 20:9-16)

The disciples of Jesus are also required to be available to accomplish a practical task of sharing the love of Christ. (Matthew 11:28-30) This statement of truth deserves a complete explanation.

The gift of the indwelling of the Holy Spirit has been given to every believer. (1 Corinthians 12:13) The Holy Spirit, the gift of unity has been given to us; however, differing spiritual gifts are given for specific purposes. (1 Corinthians 12:27-31) The gifts of wisdom, knowledge, faith, healing, prophesy, miracles, and love are given to maintain the oneness of the body of Christ. These worthy gifts are given to those who are in the kingdom of God; however, the greatest gift is the gift of faith and love, which is referred to as charity. (1 Corinthians 12:31)

Therefore, every believer has the gift of charity, for without the Holy Spirit one cannot truly say or believe that "Jesus is Lord." (1 Corinthians 13:13 & 12:3)

The requirement for care and protection of the gift of charity is emphasized by the parable of talents. The wicked and unfaithful servant, that hid his talent, offered a defense for his actions. Yahweh is not a hard deity who reaps where he has not sown. (Matthew 25:14-30) Yahweh is a loving Father who expects his gift of love to be appreciated and enjoyed and used in a natural way. Every gift that is given by God is good and perfect. (James 1:17) He expects his gift of love to be shared with others. (Matthew 25:34-40)

After his death, burial, and resurrection, Jesus appeared before the disciples at the sea of Tiberias. Jesus shared a meal with the disciples, and then he asked Peter, "Son of Jonas, do you love me?" His instructions for Peter were practical and useful. Jesus said to Peter, "Feed my sheep. Follow me." (John 21:1-24) Jesus did not tell Peter to build temples or houses of worship. He did not tell Peter to study to be moral and religious. He did not give Peter a religious duty, or a requirement to practice being like Jesus. He did not say to Peter, "Follow me and learn to love me." He did not say, "Follow me, and prove that you are worthy of being my disciple." He told Peter to "to love others in the name of Jesus."

According to the commands of our Father in Heaven, we are to be available to be used to offer charity and love to others. Our task is practical and useful. (Revelation 3:15-16) Our task is practical and simple. (Matthew 11:28-30) To accomplish our task of following Jesus, we should have practical and useful thoughts and plans. (Philippians 4:8)

We are to be useful, functional servants of love.

# 78
# Vengeance

Vengeance is an act of judgment and justice. Yahweh is the only One who is allowed to judge, for only Yahweh can offer justice.

Vengeance involves retribution or judgment for an injury or wrong committed.

The book of Nahum, who was a minor prophet of Israel, was written as a prophecy for the destruction of Ninevah. Nahum described the judgment of God with harsh words; however, Nahum also declared that God is slow to anger. Nahum said that Jehovah would take vengeance on his adversaries, that the wicked would not be acquitted, but Nahum did not identify Yahweh as a God of vengeance. (Nahum 1:2-3)

Many of the Old Testament psalmists and prophets like Nahum called for vengeance or justice. Quite often the retribution requested is severe. (Psalm. 109:6-13) (Psalm 137:7-9) Considering the harsh judgments of the psalmist, and the critical attitudes often expressed by some who have professed faith in Jesus, we may clearly understand why God has reserved vengeance for himself.

Yahweh is not a God of vengeance. (Ezekiel 18:23)

Yahweh is a God of justice. This statement is a fact that should be reinforced and clearly understood. Vengeance is not a preferred action by a God of love. Vengeance is given only because of the requirements of justice. Because Yahweh is righteous and pure and holy, justice will be required.

For this reason, the proper emphasis for the believers is love, not vengeance.

We have been clearly instructed to bless anyone that persecutes us. We are required to bless our enemies and not curse them. We are not to repay or return evil for evil. We are to live in peace with all men. Retribution or judgment for evil will be given only by God. (Hebrews 10:26-31) When our enemies need charity, loving kindness must be given. In so doing, we will overcome evil with good. (Romans 12:14-21)

Vengeance is required for the sake of justice, and protection or defense against injustice. (Luke 18:1-9) However, although vengeance is required for the sake of justice, God is full of compassion and empathy. He is righteous and pure and holy.

Our obligation concerning righteousness, and the judgment of sin is to have faith in the son of man, so that when he returns, he will find faith on the earth. (Luke 18:7-8)

# 79
# Victory

To live is to be a Christ-one, and to die is victory. (Philippians 1:21)

Victory is success, triumph, conquest, mastery or supremacy in a struggle against any adversity or any acknowledged adversary. Victory is an act of defeating an enemy or opponent in competition or battle; however, victory can also be a simple successful personal accomplishment.

For Yahweh, victory is not success, triumph, conquest, mastery, or supremacy in a struggle. Yahweh does not have a personal conflict or need to defeat an enemy or opponent in competition or battle. For Yahweh, victory is a natural consequence of supremacy.

To imply that Yahweh is a God of victory does not mean that he has intentionally established a contest or has designed a plan of destruction so that he might declare victory. The Almighty has no need of triumph, ascendance, or dominion. He is and will always be the Supreme existence. He has no need to prove or to affirm his position of deity or authority. He has the right and authority to say, 'I am that I am. I will always be as I am; and there is no other as this One!'

Simply stated, Yahweh is a God of victory because triumph over evil is a natural consequence of truth and love.

For mankind, winning a battle or contest offers relief, peace, joy, and celebration. However, for contests or struggles among mankind, even in times of war, victory is not possible. Victory can only be achieved when war or conflict is eliminated. The only true enemy of mankind is evil. Victory will only be achieved when evil has been destroyed or eliminated. The judgement for evil is death; and victory over death is eternal life. (1 Corinthians 15:55)

Our advisory is the enemy of love. (Ephesians 6:12) We are not of ourselves able to have victory over evil or death. Our defense is truth, which is Jesus Christ, the word of life. We are to remain humble, without pride, to appreciate the victory of Christ. Our names are written into the book of life. Victory! (Luke 10:20)

God is Love; and God is life. Because he is life, he will never be defeated by evil or death. He exists in eternity. He is the almighty supreme being of life and existence and love. He is the essence of success, mastery, or supremacy. (Romans 8:35-39) This is the reason that the apostle Paul said, "In all things we are more than conquerors through him that loved us." (Romans 8:37)

Our adversary is death. Resurrection is victory over our enemy. Our adversary is doubt. Hope is our victory. We have no need to be apprehensive. We have no need to fear. We have the assurance of scriptural prophecy. We have foreknowledge of victory. Eternal life is victory. (2 Timothy 1:8-10)

Eternal life is a mystery. In the Kingdom of Heaven, we will be changed to a state of incorruption and immortality. Death will be eliminated by eternal life. Victory has been given through our Lord Jesus Christ. (1 Corinthians 15:49-57) (1 Thessalonians 4:13-18)

We will shout, "Hosanna in the highest heaven. Make way for the Messiah! Freedom!" (Matthew 21:9)

# 80
# Wisdom

The treasures of wisdom and knowledge, understanding of existence and love, can be found in Jesus Christ. (Colossians 2:2-9)

Wisdom is the quality of having knowledge, insight, experience, and sound judgment. The value of wisdom is fully and abundantly explained in scripture.

Yahweh is a God of wisdom. Wisdom may be simple or impressive, common or profound. (Ecclesiastes 9:13-16) (Job 28:12-13) According to the words of scripture, "The fear of the Lord is wisdom; to depart from evil is understanding. (Job 28:23-28)

Supreme knowledge and understanding, was in the beginning with God, before creation. (Proverbs 8:22-30) The wisdom of God is pure, gentle, and beneficial. (James 3:17) The wisdom of Deity is beyond comparison and understanding. The infinite wisdom of Yahweh is pure and perfect truth. (Proverbs 3:19-20) (1 Corinthians 3:18-21)

The wisdom of Yahweh is illustrated in the story of temptation. Jesus, when tested by Satan, answered with words of wisdom. (Luke 4:1-12) His response was pure, peaceable, gentle, reasonable, full of mercy, unwavering and without hypocrisy.

The wisdom of Yahweh is supreme knowledge and understanding. As well, the wisdom of Yahweh is expressed as power and strength and control. (Daniel 2:20-23)

(Proverbs 8:12-14) (Ecclesiastes 8:17)

God gives wisdom, knowledge, and understanding to those who are worthy of receiving his instructions. (Proverbs 2:6-7) Those who reject the teachings of wisdom that are offered by God are not wise. (Proverbs 1:7) (Psalm 36:1-4)

Although the wisdom of Yahweh will not be completely understood or appreciated, wisdom has been offered as a blessing to anyone who will listen to the words of Yahweh. (Matthew 11:15) As well, the teachings of wisdom, offered in the book of Proverbs are available for all to read. (Proverbs 3:6-17)

In the book of Proverbs, a collection of teachings of wisdom, the writer declares that the one who reads, understands, and accepts the teachings will be blessed. These words of wisdom should be placed into one's mind and heart and soul; for the word of God is life. (Proverbs 8:11 & 24:13-14) (Colossians 2:2)

Wisdom is also a gift of blessings and joy. A joyful heart makes a cheerful countenance, but when the heart is sad, the spirit is broken. The teachings of Proverbs are often practical common sense. "A dish of vegetables served with love is better than a fattened ox served with hatred." (Proverbs 15:13, 17)

Wisdom may be expressed in thoughts or actions and in compassion and understanding. (Matthew 15:22-29) Jesus clearly stated that he had been sent only to the house of Israel, and not to the gentiles. However, the Greek woman in this account was rewarded for understanding that Yahweh is always willing to offer loving kindness. When she returned home, she found her daughter well. (Mark 7:24-30)

The true wisdom of Yahweh, the wisdom of life "that was with him in the beginning, that was the mystery hidden from the eyes of all the living, that was His daily delight" is found in his only son Jesus Christ. Jesus is the one in whom all the treasures of wisdom and knowledge of God are hidden. (Colossians 2:2-3, 9)

The wisdom of Yahweh is expressed in the teachings of Jesus and in his responses to those who wanted to know who he was. (Mark 12:13) The wisdom is found in the words of the One who is the way, the truth, and the life. His words are the words of eternal life, that bring joy, peace, and the unity of love. (James 3:17) His wisdom is offered as a blessing of eternal life. (John 3:10-21)

Although the gift of wisdom is a blessing, the apostle Paul offered a stern warning concerning use of knowledge and wisdom. (1Timothy 6:3-5) The apostle stated that the gospel should be presented "without wisdom of words, lest the cross of Christ should be made of no effect." (1 Corinthians 1:17-19)

The gift of wisdom has been freely offered, in Jesus Christ, as a gift of love from Yahweh. If we do not have wisdom, we can ask God to give us the knowledge and understanding, for he is willing to freely give wisdom to anyone. (James 1:5)

# 81
# Wonderful

Yahweh is worthy of praise and honor for all his works are wonderful. (Psalm 98:1) (Psalm 40:5)

The meaning of wonderful is to be marvelous, magnificent, superb, glorious, fantastic, astonishing, enjoyable, or inspiring. To be wonderful is to be magnificent.

Majesty and splendor are descriptive words used to describe the presence of the brilliant light, and the honor and love of Deity. The word beautiful is used to describes the glory of God. The word wonderful is used to describe that which can be seen and experienced but is difficult to explain.

Many of the psalms are also words of praise for the magnificent deeds of Yahweh. The proper response is to stand in awe and rejoice in the Lord. We should praise him with songs of praise, for the earth is full of the goodness of the Lord. We should praise him for all the wonderful works that he has done. (Psalm 33:1-22)

Emotional responses are often difficult to verbally explain. What words could be used to describe the emotions that a scientist might feel after having discovered the answer to an unknown, to see or to understand a mystery of science that no one has ever seen or has experienced before. How would we describe the feeling of being the first human to observe the entire earth, drifting in space beneath us. How do we describe the wonder of hearing a child say, "I love you." How will we feel when we stand in the presence of God to hear him say, "Well done, thou faithful servant, enter into the joy of your creator."

ONE

How would we have felt if we had been present when I Am that I Am said, "Let there be light!" What would we have felt if we had been standing among the shepherds to hear the angels of heaven singing, "Glory to God in the Heavens!" What will we experience when we stand in the very presence of Yahweh and his Son, the Christ of love.

God is wonderful. Everything about him is wonderful. He is the very essence of wonder and majesty and supreme beauty. He is the inspiration of wonder. He is marvelous, magnificent; and every aspect of his character and nature is wonderful. He is wonderful in love and compassion and empathy and protection and in giving, and in every possible good that exist or might exist. Yahweh is marvelous, magnificent, superb, glorious, amazing, fantastic, and inspiring.

Amazingly, being wonderful or magnificent is not an aspect of Yahweh's character that exist for a purpose, such as recognition or praise. Yahweh has not expressed any self-center nature or purpose for his existence. His love is not offered so that he may be wonderful or magnificent. Love is present because Yahweh is love; and love is freely given to mankind as a gift. Simply stated, holiness or being wonderful is a natural characteristic of Deity, without design, purpose, or intent.

We may study scripture and be able to list the characteristics of Almighty YHWH, but the words to adequately explain the wonder of his existence or to describe the radiant beauty of the light that surrounds him will not be found. In the same way, the words necessary to completely describe the amazing wonder of his love and grace will not be discovered. The words to express appreciation for the wonder of almighty love and grace will not be found.

We live in its presence and know that it comes from above. We experience the freedom of its radiant light and feel comfort in the darkness of night. We are blessed with peace that cannot be described. We feel the wonder of it in our heart and our life. We know the joy of its embrace. We exist in the presence of glorious, fantastic, astonishing, inspiring, amazing, wonderful grace.

# 82
# Word

The gospel, which is the word of God, endures forever. (1 Peter 1:24-25)

Even a simple definition of "word" or the use of a word is difficult to formulate.

Although a theological understanding of the use of the phrase "the Word of God" is of extreme importance, and a comprehensive discussion would reveal much concerning the character, nature, and purposes of Yahweh, a complete presentation of the meaning and purpose would require extensive explanations, therefore for this topic, only brief statements without comprehensive discussions will be offered.

A proper understanding of the character or nature of Yahweh is not possible without understanding that the word of God is the word of Life. The descriptive title "The Word" is used to identify the existence of supreme Deity.

The use of the phrase "the word of Life" is an illustration of the complex nature of simplicity and complexity. For example, the fact that the Bible is the word of God requires an extremely complex explanation. In essence, ever simple statement concerning the word of God requires a comprehensive explanation.

The use of the phrase "the word of God" requires an extensive theological explanation; therefore, because this book is not intended to be teachings of theology the following is only a brief listing of separate facts or points of discussion.

A full understanding of the majesty and wonder of God's commandment of "Let there be light" is not possible. These spoken words are recorded without complete explanation. (Genesis 1:3) In the beginning, the word of God, the holy existence of Deity, was present. This is the word of Life.

A primary theological understanding concerning the Word, is that the description may be singular or plural. A word or words spoken by Yahweh reveal both his character and purposes. The words of God are expressions of his love.

The word of God is a phrase that is applied in various ways and in different situations. The phrase often refers to the written word, which is the scripture of the Testaments. At other times the phrase is used to mean the living word, which is Jesus Christ. The phrase was also used by the prophets of Israel as a means of describing the prophetic messages that were given to them by the Spirit of God. For example, the prophet Ezekiel said, "And the word of the Lord came unto me, saying, Son of man, prophesy against the shepherds of Israel." (Ezekiel 34:1-2)

Although the word of God may be expressed in differing ways, the words are the words spoken by Yahweh. Yahweh has spoken. And a voice came out of the cloud saying, "This is my beloved Son; hear him." (Luke 9:35) Yahweh is One who speaks with power and authority. What has been spoken are the words spoken by God. The words of God are Truth. The Word is the living word, which is Jesus Christ the Messiah. Jesus said, "I am the way, the truth, and life." (John 14:6) The word is the gospel, the good news. (Luke 1:2)

The word is an expression of God's authority and power. The word is also an expression of his majesty and holiness. The words spoken by Yahweh are expressions of his character and of his acts of grace. "Thy word is a lamp to my feet, and a light to my path." (Psalm 119:105)

In the Old Testament the fact that God spoke to Abraham, Moses, Joshua, and to other prophets and citizens of Israel, has been abundantly recorded. All the words of Yahweh that were spoken to the children of Israel are of extreme importance.

The word of life, the word of grace and truth, is written within or into the law of Moses. These are words that declare the precepts of Yahweh, that express the character and wishes of an almighty Deity.

Credit should be expressed to Hebrew scholars for understanding that the written word of God was a blessing from Jehovah. After Nehemiah and Ezra had reconstructed the walls of Jerusalem, the citizens gathered in the square in front of the Water Gate. Those who had gathered asked Ezra to bring the book of the law to be read. The book was read from early morning until midday, while Ezra the priest stood above the crowd on a wooden podium.

The priest read from the law of God, and translation was provided so that the people understood the reading. Because the people were weeping as the priest read the words of the law, Nehemiah said, "This day is holy to the Lord your God; do not mourn or weep. Go, eat of the fat, drink of the sweet, and share with those who have nothing prepared. This day is holy to our Lord. Do not be grieved, for the joy of the Lord is your strength." (Nehemiah 8:6-12)

Several of the psalms express a deep appreciation of the power and majesty of the written word. (Psalm 29:1-11)

The Israelites clearly understood that the precepts of God are the words of life. However, the Israelites often acted arrogantly and did not listen to God's commandments. (Nehemiah 9:29) (Romans 10:4)

The children of Abraham also understood the blessing to those who live in the law of the Lord. The commandment to love God was understood. The commandment to love others was often neglected. (Psalm 119:1-11)

The living word contains the mystery that was hidden or unexplained. The living word is the word that was in the beginning, that was manifested, that became flesh.

The promise of the gospel, the word of God, has clearly been described in the words of scripture, offered by the apostle John, "And the Word was made flesh, and dwelt among us, and we beheld his glory, the glory as of the only begotten of the Father, full of grace and truth. For the law was given by Moses, but grace and truth came by Jesus Christ." (John 1:14-17)

The word of God is the gospel, which is also a spoken word of "let there be light." The gospel is the good news of Jesus Christ. (Luke 8:11) This word was offered with an amazing prophecy of joy and peace by the prophet Isaiah. Isaiah said that "the mountains and the hills shall break forth before you into singing and all the trees of the field shall clap their hands." (Isaiah 55:11-12)

Jesus Christ is the "word of God" who has brought salvation, or eternal life, to mankind. We who have accepted the word of truth are "born again, not of corruptible seed, but by the word of God, who lives and abides forever." (1 Peter 1:23)

The living word of life is the amazing presence of the Holy Spirit. The presence of the Holy Spirit has been offered as a guide or interpreter for those who wish to understand the living word, that is Jesus Christ. (1 John 1:1-4)

We will not truly know or understand God without reading and knowing and understanding both the written word and the living Word of God, which is Jesus Christ. We will not understand unless we hear the words that Jesus spoke. We will not truly know God unless we experience the words spoken by the Holy Spirit. The inspired words of God have been written, "that ye might believe that Jesus is the Christ, the Son of God; and that believing ye might have life through his name." (John 20:31)

The living and abiding Word is the evidence of the deity of Jesus Christ. For mankind, the living word is life. Speaking of himself, Jesus said, "Man shall not live by bread alone, but by every word that proceeds out of the mouth of God." (Matthew 4:4) In the words of the Lord's Prayer we pray for this blessing, "Give us this day, our daily bread." (Matthew 6:11)

Jesus shared the Father's words of wisdom with his disciples, and to all who would listen. (Luke 12:13-59) Concerning practical wisdom and conduct, the truth is that what one considers to be a treasure will be a priority of life. (Luke 12:34) These words of life of the New Testament should be read with an open mind and heart; for these words offer the gift of eternal life.

The word of God, which is Jesus Christ, also includes the sovereign power and authority of Deity. (Hebrews 4:12-13) The living word is the living and abiding Word of God that abides forever. (1 Peter 1:23)

The words of God, spoken by Jesus Christ, offer meaning and understanding of life, existence, truth, freedom, and liberty. (John 8:31-32) This statement is a fulfillment of the Old Testament scripture, "Thy word is a lamp unto my feet, and a light unto my path. I have sworn; and I will perform it, that I will keep thy righteous judgments." (Psalm 119:105-106)

In one scriptural account, the Holy Spirit was directly involved in explaining the Gospel. The complete story describes how Jesus used the words of scripture, beginning with the words of Moses and all the prophets, to explain the prophecies concerning the word of life. (Luke 24:1-53) The response of the two disciples is a testimony of the power of scripture. Scripture is more easily understood when the Holy Spirit, the living word of God that has been given as a gift to every believer, is allowed to be involved in the process of interpretation and understanding.

The apostle James taught that our words should be influenced by the word of God so that they might be full of wisdom, for the fruit of righteousness is sown in peace by those who are peaceful. (James 3:16-18) The apostle James used scriptural words of wisdom to admonish the believers who were striving among themselves. (James 3:9-10)

The word of God was in the beginning. And Yahweh said, "Let there be light." And there was light. (Genesis 1:4) As well, the word is with us today. (Matthew 28:20) (John 1:1-5)

If we do not understand that the word was God, we shall be unable to understand that in the beginning the word of God existed. As well, we shall not be able to understand the meaning of the fact that Jehovah spoke directly to Joshua. (Joshua 4:14-15)

As stated, the primary emphasis concerning the phrase, the word, is to understand that Yahweh is the One who has spoken, he is the One who speaks. The words recorded in scripture are the words of God. The meaning of the statement that the Bible is the inspired word of God is the same as saying, "This is what God has written or has spoken or has prophesied."

Descriptive accounts of biblical events can easily take attention away from the fact that the words of scripture are the words of God, describing what Yahweh has accomplished. For example, while reading the story of David and Goliath, we must understand that Yahweh is present, overseeing the event, providing power and might.

At times only a few spoken words are used to express a multitude of meaning, for brief statements may speak louder than words. For example, the account of the creation of mankind was delivered with only a few words, "Let us make man, in our own image." (Genesis 1:26) An explanation of this choice has not been provided. Only a brief description of the event, has been offered in the written word of Life.

At times the presence of Yahweh is evident, but words or thoughts are not recorded. Yahweh is silent. However, in every biblical account, Yahweh is present. When an account is brief, the emphasis may be on the presence of Yahweh. For example, in the account of the birth of Jesus, the shepherds found their way to Mary and Joseph, and the baby, as he lay in the manger. (Luke 2:16) Without a description of the presence of Yahweh, we are only able to visualize the Father of Heaven and Earth, present, in silence, to say, "this is my Son in whom I am well pleased." (Matthew 3:17)

When we read the words, "It is finished," we may hear the silence presence of Yahweh as he turns his face away. (John 19:30) When we read, "Do you know what I have done for you?" we may hear the Spirit of truth speaking. (John 16:12-13) When we hear the words, "Behold, I stand at the door and knock," we hear God say, "For I so loved the world...." (Revelation 3:20) (John 3:16) When we understand the good news, we hear a heavenly Father say, "I love you."

The witness and testimony of the word of life has been given by the apostle and disciples of Jesus Christ. (John 3:11)

# 83
# Work

On the seventh day, the work of creation of the heavens and the earth was completed, and on that day, God rested. (Genesis 2:1-2)

Work is activity involving physical or mental effort done for the purpose of accomplishing a task.

Yahweh is not a God of work or labor.

The common synonym for the word work is the word labor. The synonyms of the word labor are related to torture, affliction, persecution, or travail. This implies that work is a task that is accomplished with difficulty or struggle. Nothing that Yahweh has accomplished has been accomplished with difficulty or struggle; therefore, his deeds of creation are not acts of work or labor.

Daily activity or common chores should not be called labor. Labor is defined as activity that is accomplished due to compulsion or reward. The work of creation that Yahweh accomplished before the seventh day is entirely different than working to accomplish a task. The biblical statement is that Yahweh completed his deeds, not that he ended his labor. His deeds, the creation of the heavens and earth, were completed. The seventh day was sanctified as a rest, a time for peace and hope and love. The seventh day was a time of fulfillment. Yahweh was not resting because he was exhausted from acts of labor. As well, although Yahweh ended his work, this does not mean that Yahweh places emphasis upon the accomplishment of a task. The celebration was not rejoicing for the work or labor performed, but for the fulfillment of the deeds which were acts of creation.

Yahweh is omnipotent; he has no need to boast about any works that he has done. Nevertheless, he has accomplished many deeds of love, for the work of God is love.

The requirement of the Sabbath, that no work was to be done except for service to the Lord of Hosts, was given to Israel for several specific reasons.

The day of rest was a way for the Hebrew people to remember and honor the original day of rest that was ordained by Yahweh after the completion of the amazing work of creation. Yahweh blessed the seventh day and sanctified the day, or made the day holy, for "that in it he had rested from all his work which he created and made." (Genesis 2:3) This was not a special acknowledgement of a completed task. This was a celebration of existence and life. The Seventh Day is a recognition of existence and love. This is a thanksgiving of the creation of a new and amazing existence.

The Sabbath was also intended to reinforce the fact that Yahweh alone is worthy of service, honor, and worship because all things have been created by him and for him.

The Sabbath was to be a unique acknowledgement for the children of Abraham. They were to be known as the children of YHWH, for their king was Jehovah, the King of kings and Lord of lords. This was a covenant relationship. (Exodus 31:12-17)

The Sabbath day was a gift of peace, given from God to the Hebrew people. The Sabbath was to remind Israel that they were no longer slaves and that labor as service to others was no longer required. The Sabbath was to remind the people that Yahweh never intended for his children to be in slavery. Yahweh's plan for the nation was not for work but for liberty, and joy and peace. (Exodus 20:8-11)

The Sabbath was a prophesy of a future time of peace and freedom, that would be offered as a gift of grace. The time of rest offered by faith in Jesus Christ was to be a gift of eternal life that could not be earned by work or labor. Yahweh had decided to offer eternal life as a gift of love and grace. The requirement of eternal life would be faith in Jesus Christ the One who would be the creator of the kingdom of Heaven. (1 Peter 1:3-9)

Just as the creation of the existence of our earth required actions, deeds, or works, the gift of eternal life required works of creation. (Genesis 2:1-2) This work of creation of eternal life for mankind was completed by Jesus. (John 19:28-30)

Jesus said, "I must work the works of Him that sent me, while it is day; the night cometh, when no man can work." (John 9:4) Jesus had deeds or works to accomplish. He completed his task of love and shouted, "It is finished!" The days of work had ended. No other act or deeds were required for creating the Kingdom of Heaven and the gift of eternal life. No other works can or will be accomplished.

The work of salvation was to be accomplished by the power of the Holy Spirit. As well, for the Holy Spirit to accomplish the work of salvation, holy vessels would be required for the indwelling of the Holy Spirit. New wine skins would be required for this new life or kingdom. (Luke 5:38)

This situation of "entering into his Sabbath" has been explicitly explained in scripture. We have been chosen by the will of God. (1 Peter 1:2-3) We have been crucified, and reborn. (Romans 6:6) We are consecrated and made holy through the sanctifying work or deeds of the Holy Spirit. (Hebrews 10:14) (1 Thessalonians 4:3) We are cleansed from sin and made perfect and holy, by the blood of Christ. (Hebrews 9:14) We are washed clean, justified and forgiven, and prepared as a worthy vessel, a new wine skin, for the indwelling of the Holy Spirit. (1 Corinthians 6:11) (1 John 1:9) (2 Timothy 2:21)

This has not been accomplished by any works of man. This is the sanctifying work of the Holy Spirit. (John 19:30) (1 Corinthians 6:11) We are sanctified by truth. (John 17:19) This is a work or deed of the Holy Spirit, a work which will not and cannot be incomplete. (Philippians 1:6)

As believers, we are alive in the "time of rest" given through faith in Jesus Christ. Although proof of faith is required, for faith without good deeds of love is dead or worthless, we will not be judged by a law of works. (James 2:14, 17) We live in a Sabbath, a time of rest from all works. We live in Jesus who is our Sabbath. (Hebrews 4:3-9) The only deeds or works to be accomplished are works of love, for the work of God, is to believe Jesus. (John 6:29)

Yahweh is a God of liberty and freedom. We are to speak and act as those who are judged by the law of liberty. (James 2:12) When we look intently at the perfect law, the law of liberty, and abide by it, we will be blessed in all our deeds of love. (James 1:25) We who have professed faith in Christ have received the sanctifying gift of the Holy Spirit. We are servants, followers, and friends of Christ. We are worthy of being called saints because we have been sanctified by the Holy Spirit. (1 Corinthians 1:2) (Philippians 4:21) Believers are chosen ones who have deeds of love that must be accomplish. (John 14:12) The required works are not works to earn the gift of salvation, or to gain rewards or favor with God. These works of love are requirements of faith.

Jesus Christ is our Sabbath, a gift of eternal life of freedom and peace. (Matthew 11:28-29) Our gift of freedom must not be used to live a life of selfish purpose. Our deeds are to be works of giving, not self-centered acts of religious service. Our purpose is to accomplish the deeds of Christ. (2 Corinthians 5:20)

Yahweh never intended for the children of Abraham to be in captivity in Egypt, and a day of rest and peace was given to remind them to rest in the freedom of his love and protection. As well, we live in sabbath so that we may "rest in the love of Christ." In our Sabbath, our life in Christ, we are to remember the time of creation of existence, life, and love in the kingdom of Heaven. We are to rest in the knowledge that we have eternal life, that we have been made holy, and to remember that we have been given a covenant of eternal life, for God never intended for mankind to be slaves to sin.

The primary rule or thought concerning works is the statement that salvation cannot be obtained by righteous deeds, lest any man should boast. (Ephesians 2:9) This statement reveals an interesting truth concerning religious practices.

Unless our works are offered as gifts of love, our works are of no lasting value. (1 Corinthians 13:2) Love is to be offered, not for our benefit, and not as proof of our faith, and not as an assigned task, but as a direct result of faith. Deeds of love and honor, loving our neighbor as we love ourselves, should be a natural consequence of having received the Holy Spirit. (Matthew 22:38) A simple truth is that if one is alive, one should be breathing. If we are spiritually alive, outward actions should be a direct result of the spirit within. We are to consider the example of Abraham who was justified by faith and not by his deeds. In the same way we are justified by works of love, and not by faith only. (James 2:20-24) For as our body without the spirit is dead, so faith without deeds of love in the name of Jesus is also dead. (James 2:26)

We are required to love as Jesus loved. We are to forgive as Jesus offered forgiveness. We are expected to be Christ-ones. (1 John 2:6) (1 John 2:6-11) We are to do the good and acceptable will of God. (Romans 12:1-2) Acceptable acts of worship or religious activity are to be deeds of charity and faithful acts of obedience to the Holy Spirit. (James 1:27) We must remember that personal profit or honor has not been offered, even for works or deeds that prove our faith. Worthy deeds of love are a result of faith and love, not the reverse. The apostle James offered a logical truth concerning religious acts, "What does it profit, my brethren, though a man may say that he has faith and does not have deeds of love, can such faith save him?" (James 2:14)

Interestingly, the requirement of doing good deeds has been, for many Christians, a path into the false teachings of performance theology. The joy or satisfaction received by doing good deeds may create an awareness of having accomplished something that is pleasing to God. This awareness may create a desire to continue to be pleasing to God, by doing more good works. The result is a false sense of religious accomplishment, or a feeling of goodness. (Luke 18:11) This situation is often called spiritualism. The problem remains that goodness, or even the deeds of faith, are not of oneself, but of God. The feelings of pride, satisfaction, or boasting about religious works are unjustified.

The words of the Lord's prayer include the words "lead us not into temptation but deliver us from evil." The words, "bless us for our religious service and good deeds," are not found in this amazing prayer. The honor of being a disciples of Christ must be accepted with humility and absence of pride. (Philippians 1:21)

The task of love that we have been given is simple, and the yoke that we share with Jesus, is easy to wear. (Matthew 11:28-30) Yahweh is a God of liberty. He is not a God of works. He has chosen to set us free from the law of works to give us rest in Jesus, our Sabbath. (Romans 8:1-18) (Hebrews 4:9-11)

When we know the Truth, which is Jesus Christ, we are free to love others. Loving God or loving others is not an act of labor. Loving others is accomplished for the joy set before us. We know the truth and we are free indeed. (James 1:18-23)

# 84
# Worthy of Worship

God alone is worthy of worship. No man is worthy of adoration or supreme praise. (Isaiah 2:22) The things of this world are not worthy of praise, and only God is worthy of our service. (Luke 4:8)

To be worthy is to deserve respect, praise, and adoration.

Although Yahweh is worthy of praise and worship he should not be characterized as a deity of worship. (Luke 4:8) Yahweh does not require religious acts of devotion. Love and honor to God should be offered as a natural response to his love. (Matthew 22:37) This simple relationship of faith and love can be expressed as joyful celebration in his presence. (Nehemiah 8:6-12)

His commandment and requirement for the children of Abraham was that they must not worship any god but the Lord. (Exodus 22:20) A secondary condition of honor and devotion was established by the introduction of the commandment to remember the Sabbath and keep it holy. (Exodus 20:8) The Sabbath is a holy day; however, the words and to worship are not included in the commandment. The "day of rest" was given for man, not to God. (Mark 2:27) Praise, devotion, or honor for Yahweh has not been restricted to a holy day or place of worship. Our sabbath is not a special day that is designated for worship or as a time for "spiritual practices." Jesus is our Sabbath, our freedom and rest in grace. (Matthew 12:8) (Hebrews 4:1-9)

The lesson concerning worship that Jesus offered to the woman of Samaria should be carefully considered. Jesus said, "Believe me, a time will come when the Father will not be worshipped in this mountain or in Jerusalem. God is Spirit. He must be worshipped in spirit and in truth." (John 4:21-24)

Considering the requirement to love with mind and spirit, and as well the need to worship in spirit and truth, we must conclude that true worship must be within the heart with love. The essence of worship in spirit and in truth, of having faith in Jesus who is Truth, is to bear fruit of love in the name of Jesus. (John 15:16)

A lesson concerning the forgiveness of sin, taught by Jesus to the Pharisees, also included a lesson about worship. Jesus did not come to save us so that we might offer sacrifices or to be righteous worshippers. He did not come to offer mercy and grace to the righteous. He came to the unrighteous, who need to repent. Jesus said, "I will have mercy (loving kindness) for others, and not sacrifice (worship) for I did not come to call the righteous (religious worshipers) but sinners (who can be used to offer love to others)." (Matthew 9:10-13) We are to be "living stones, in a spiritual house, a holy priesthood, to offer spiritual sacrifices acceptable to God by Jesus Christ." (1 Peter 2:5-9)

When Jesus returned to visit his disciples, he did not require a gathering for worship. Instead, he served a meal and sat down for fellowship with the small group of believers, that he called his friends. (John 15:15) He did not travel with the disciples to the synagogue in Jerusalem to worship in the temple. (John 21:1-13) As well, Jesus did not teach a lesson about worship; he taught a lesson about love and obedience. (John 21:15-25) Yahweh does not require a particular place of prayer or a specific order of worship. (John 4:21) His only requirement is that he must be worshiped in spirit and in truth. (John 4:21-24)

Although any specific person may be worthy of praise, God is the only One who is worthy of adoration and worship. (Philippians 2:10-11)

This passage is a lesson of humility, offered by Jesus, for all who are his disciples. Jesus taught that titles of praise or recognition, such as Rabbi, teacher, or Master are basically unnecessary or unacceptable. The rule of unity is that "the one that is greatest among you shall be your servant; and whosoever shall exalt himself shall be abased; and the one that shall humble himself shall be exalted." (Matthew 23:8-12)

This passage of scripture should not be used to legalistically restrict the use of the titles of master, or teacher or father; however, placing any believer in an elevated status or position is restricted. This restriction is not a rule of religious order; this is a requirement of unity and love. All believers are of equal status. All believers are saints. No Christian is worthy of excessive honor, for all power and goodness is a gift from the Holy Spirit. No one should be elevated above a level of mutual respect. No woman or man is worthy of adoration or praise. Yahweh is the only One that is worthy because he is of great value and eminent worth. He alone possesses righteousness and honor. No man can meet this standard; for no man can claim to be good, or worthy of praise. (Romans 3:10)

Yahweh the Father is worthy of worship; and Jesus, who is One with God, is worthy of honor and worship. (1 Chronicles 16:23-34) (Revelation 5:13)

Jesus is worthy of praise, devotion, and service. We are free to worship him with acts of love to others, for or deeds of love are gifts of worship to our Heavenly Father. (Hebrews 13:15) (Ephesians 4:1) (1 Thessalonians 2:11-12)

Jesus is worthy of a new song. He is coming to reign. (Psalm 96:1-3) (Psalm 98:1) (Psalm 98:8-9)

Yahweh and Jesus are worthy of worship, for we have been given eternal life and spiritual freedom. We are free to worship and to praise his holy name, in any place, at any time. We are free to honor God with tradition and religious service (Luke 22:15-20) or to worship in spirit and truth. (John 14:17) We are free to praise Yahweh, without judging how others praise or worship. (Matthew 7:1-2)

Let all of us that hath breath praise the Lord. (Psalm 150:6) (Psalm 145:1-4)

# 85
# Wrath

The wrath of Yahweh has not been completely explained, but the furry that has been described is awesome. (Nahum 1:6-8)

Wrath and anger are comparable, yet completely different in force. Anger can be the result of displeasure, disappointment, resentment, frustration, or annoyance but rarely reaches the intensity of fury or wrath. An emotional or physical retribution caused by an extreme state of anger is referred to as wrath. Wrath is like a raging storm or devastating disaster, with dire consequences.

Teachings about the wrath of God have been included in the prophetic words of the prophet Nahum. The wrath of God is never undisclosed or excused. The wrath of God is openly presented in scripture. However, although the wicked will not be acquitted, Yahweh is slow to anger. He is a God of love and forgiveness. (Nahum 1:2-3)

Because the necessity of judgment is not fully understood, the wrath of God is also difficult to understand. We are thankful that his love is supreme, and that his wrath is withheld from those who trust him. We stand in awe of his wrath, and we honor him for his gift of grace. (John 3:16)

Yahweh is not a God of wrath; he is a God of grace. Although the wrath of God is like a raging storm, wrath is not offered as retribution. We can be thankful that God is a God of loving kindness, and that support is offered in times of trouble. (Nahum 1:7)

Many of the kings of Israel and Judah proved to be unworthy of the honor that was entrusted to them. Several were guilty of acts of evil in the sight of the Lord. Yahweh was not pleased. His anger was withheld for an extended time, but eventually a righteous response was required.

God allowed the Chaldeans to ransack the city of Jerusalem. The Chaldeans took the vessels of the temple, and the treasures of the king to Babylon. This was done to fulfill the prophetic words of the prophet Jeremiah. The Israelites would remain in captivity until the land of Judah and Israel had "enjoyed her Sabbaths." Israel was to remain desolate for seventy years. (2 Chronicles 36:9-21) The wrath of God was poured out against the house of Israel for having failed to keep a covenant of love with their Almighty God. The wrath of the Father was given as correction and discipline, but not as retribution.

The prophet Malachi shows a striking contrast between blessings and wrath. The wrath of Yahweh that is brought against the arrogant and evildoers is severe. However, for those who fear his name, "the sun of righteousness will rise with healing in its wings." (Malachi 4:2)

As stated, the wrath of God is difficult to comprehend. When the children of Israel dishonored the precious things that God had given, and chose to worship before idols, the Father of Israel became righteously troubled. (Ezekiel 16:19-22)

Although wrath may be expressed, the primary characteristic of God is love, not anger. Yahweh is not a God of judgment or condemnation. Yahweh is a God of grace. As Jesus said, the Father of Israel has always desired to offer love and forgiveness to his children. (Luke 13:34) As prophesied, the wrath of God will be turned away from Israel. According to the prophet Ezekiel, Yahweh will be calmed and angry no longer. (Ezekiel

16:42) He will remember his covenant with Israel that was made with Abraham, Moses, and king David. And He will establish an everlasting covenant, a time of peace when wrath is no longer necessary. (Ezekiel 16:60)

John the Baptist understood the necessity of the wrath of God. He understood that judgment would be necessary for those who would fail to honor God. (Matthew 3:1-8)

This special Prophet also understood that Yahweh is holy and righteous and justly entitled to offer judgment against evil and unrighteousness. However, according to the words of Jesus, the love and grace of God is never restricted. (Matthew 23:39)

Jesus Christ has been offered as a gift of grace to take away the wrath of the Father; however, his coming also reveals the judgment that stands against those who will reject his precious gift of eternal life. (Matthew 13:37-51) (John 3:36)

Jesus was not reluctant to reveal the predetermined wrath and judgment of God. (Matthew 25:41&46) (Mark 9:48) Without excuse or explanation, Jesus said, "I have come to send fire upon the earth; and what will I, if it is already kindled?" (Luke 12:49) The rejection of the gift of life and liberty is a direct rejection of love. The rejection of love is separation from Yahweh.

Any justification for mankind to expression anger or wrath does not exist. God is the only One worthy of wrath. Anger would be an act of self-righteousness. The wrath of man can never work the righteousness of God. If we are to be reflections of his righteousness, we should maintain an attitude of meekness, lack of anger or disagreement, in our social interaction with others. (James 1:19-20) Because we are to love as he loves, his desire is that we should put away anger. (Ephesians 4:26-27

We are free from the need to be angry. We have been set free from the condemnation of judgment and wrath. (Romans 8:1) (Philippians 4:4) We have been rescued from the wrath of God through Christ Jesus. (1 Thessalonians 1:10) (Romans 5:9) We should consider the words of the apostle Paul and praise him for his mercy and grace. (Romans 5:8-12)

CHAPTER FIVE

# I AM THAT I AM IS LOVE

## Personal Perspective

The statement, God is Love, is the sentence of life. This single sentence is an explanation of existence and of the presence of faith, hope and love. This sentence declares the existence of God and also offers a promise of eternal life.

Instructions or interpretations concerning the teachings of scripture should be offered with caution. The apostle James recommended that only a few should be allowed to become teachers. A teacher will receive a stricter judgment. (James 3:1-2)

The words of the Apostle Paul should also be considered. A teacher is required to have wisdom and knowledge of the gospel. (Ephesians 1:17-23) The apostle Paul also said that the purpose of teaching is for edification, exhortation, and comfort. (1 Corinthians 14:3)

I have evaluated passages of scripture concerning the character and the will of our Heavenly Father. Anyone who reads what has been written has the privilege of evaluation. (1 Corinthians 14:29)

A choice of life has been offered, that demands a response. (John 3:14-16)

Perhaps you are thinking, as king Agrippa said, "Almost thou hast persuaded me to be a Christian." I would respond with the words of the apostle Paul, "I would to God, that not only you King Agrippa, but also all who hear the witness for the good news, might become a disciple of Christ Jesus." (Acts 26:23-29)

The good news is that God loves you. The truth is that because Yahweh is a God of compassion, the words of Jesus could be interpreted as a personal statement. For our Father of heaven and earth, loved you so much, He gave his only son, that if you believe, you will have eternal life. For Yahweh did not send his son to condemn you. He sent his son that you might receive his precious gift of salvation, of eternal life and freedom.

My prayer is that you will read what has been recorded in the Bible concerning existence and love. My prayer is that you will be able to believe that Yahweh does exist and will be able to say within your heart, "I have decided to have faith in Christ Jesus; for me to live is Christ and to die is eternal life." (Philippians 1:21)

As you consider your relationship to the Lord of lords and King of kings, you should consider the words that the apostle John offered to his disciples, "The Father loves the son and has given all things into his hand. The one that believes on the son has everlasting life." (John 3:35-36)

Jesus, the Lord of lords, has clearly testified, saying, "I AM." Jesus is Yehoshua of Bethlehem, the Messiah, the Son of the Living YHWH. We share the testimony of the apostles and disciples of Jesus, for we have come to know that Jesus is Lord, the Holy One of God. We believe in the miracles of existence, love, and eternal life. We know that the Father of Heaven, the One to whom we pray, is the Father of Israel, the Lord of the Universe.

I had originally intended to include a topic of Assurance, for assurance from God has been clearly offered in the words of scripture. However, after reading passages that are illustrations or examples of assurance, I realized that assurance is more of an action instead of a characteristic. An assurance, a promise of peace, liberty, and life has been abundantly offered. The Word of God is a gift of assurance. Jesus has said, "For God so loved …" (John 3:16-17) Jesus also said, "I am 'Yahweh with you,' and I will always be with you, to give freedom, love, and life." (Matthew 28:20) The gift of assurance is also offered by the Apostle Paul and the authors of Scripture. Their words of encouragement and assurance are abundantly offered in the inspired words offered by God. (Ephesians 1:1-23)

When we need assurance, all we need to do is to read the words of Jesus and the words of the Apostles. The story and the purpose of God's gift of love has already been recorded – for us.

My prayer is that you will read what has been written for you.

"Rejoice in the Lord always; and again, I say, Rejoice." (Philippians 4:4-9)

Our Father, creator of heaven and earth, hallowed be thy name. Thy kingdom come and thy will, not our will, be done on earth as it is in Heaven. Give us this day, life in the love of Jesus Christ and forgive us of our debts as we offer love and forgiveness to others. Lead us not into temptation or separation from your will and deliver us from all that is not love. For thine is the kingdom and the power and the glory forever and ever. Amen. (Matthew 6:8-13)

Gary W. Parnell
Southwestern Baptist Theological Seminary - MDiv. 1983
Anacortes, Washington

# ABOUT THE AUTHOR

Gary W. Parnell

Birth: Loraine, Texas November 1, 1941

Loraine ISD 1948 -1960

Tarleton State University Bachelor of Arts 1965 Master of Education 1973

Texas National Guard & Army Reserve 1st Lieutenant 1966-1973

Southwestern Baptist Theological Seminary Master of Divinity 1983

Church Planter Apprentice, SBC Home Missions 1983-1987

Mission Pastor Southern Baptist Convention Anacortes, Washington

The essence of wisdom is to understand God. An understanding of God is better than strength or power because eternal life is available to anyone who wishes to know the Deity known as YHWH. This book has been written for the one who wishes to know God and enjoy life.

Gary W. Parnell
Southwestern Baptist Theological Seminary -MDiv. 1983
Anacortes, Washington

Printed in the United States
by Baker & Taylor Publisher Services